NARCO-CULTS

Understanding the
Use of Afro-Caribbean and
Mexican Religious Cultures
in the Drug Wars

NARCO-CULTS

Understanding the Use of Afro-Caribbean and Mexican Religious Cultures in the Drug Wars

Tony M. Kail

CRC Press
Taylor & Francis Group
Boca Raton London New York

CRC Press is an imprint of the
Taylor & Francis Group, an **informa** business

CRC Press
Taylor & Francis Group
6000 Broken Sound Parkway NW, Suite 300
Boca Raton, FL 33487-2742

© 2015 by Taylor & Francis Group, LLC
CRC Press is an imprint of Taylor & Francis Group, an Informa business

No claim to original U.S. Government works

Printed on acid-free paper
Version Date: 20150319

International Standard Book Number-13: 978-1-4665-9545-3 (Paperback)

Visit the Taylor & Francis Web site at
http://www.taylorandfrancis.com

and the CRC Press Web site at
http://www.crcpress.com

Dedication

This book is dedicated to the men and women of law enforcement. Thank you for being the thin blue line. Thank you to every wife, husband, and child who stands behind an officer.

In memory of the victims of the drug war.

Contents

Foreword

It's very easy to make certain assumptions about drug traffickers. After all, most of what Americans know about kingpins and street dealers comes from the movies and overly dramatic television shows. Cartel members are usually depicted as cold, heartless, and cruel killers who only care about power and money and fear nothing. Sometimes this is true, but more often than not, drug traffickers and *sicarios*, or hitmen, employed by cartels fear plenty—for there is plenty to fear.

Therefore, it seems counterintuitive that one example of an entity so many traffickers—and oddly enough, police officers—rely on for protection immediately inspires fear at first glance. The image of a cloaked skeleton often bearing a menacing grimace and holding a scythe isn't something most God-fearing folk would expect to see holding court in a shrine. However, Santa Muerte, the "Saint of Death," is a largely misunderstood and widely worshipped religious figure that plays a very prominent role in the drug wars of the 21st century. Many people who have nothing to do with the criminal underworld also pray to her, which is one of the more commonly held misconceptions related to Santa Muerte and other folk saints worshipped by narcos.

While most people who know something about how spirituality plays into the world of drug smuggling have heard of Santa Muerte or maybe Jesus Malverde or Santería, the details of more obscure African religions and Latin American folk saints and cults remain a mystery. This is usually esoteric fare reserved for academic study in most instances, but knowledge about narco-cults and spirituality related to the drug trade can be incredibly useful to narcotics officers and even the average street cop.

I've been training state and local law enforcement officers on Mexico's drug war for five years, and I find one thing to be consistent: if officers aren't knowledgeable about a subject—through no fault of their own—they can't be in a position to ask the right questions to help them connect the dots. For example, if officers aren't familiar with how certain Mexican cartels transport drugs between certain U.S. cities or what gangs they cooperate with for street distribution, they can't ask questions after an arrest that might lead to a cartel connection. The same goes for religious or spiritual signs or artifacts officers might come across at a crime scene. The more an officer knows about the various cults and entities related to the drug trade, the deeper an officer can dig into a suspect's background and motives.

I have been researching and writing about drug trafficking organizations and narcoterrorism for more than eleven years, and specifically about Mexico's drug war and border security issues for more than eight years. Most of what I know about narco-cults and saint worship in the world of kingpins and killers comes from Tony Kail's work. I have yet to come across anyone with more knowledge about and insight into this topic, and this book isn't his first rodeo. He has been researching and writing about this topic for more than two decades, and you won't find a better repository for information about narco-cults and how that knowledge can benefit law enforcement officers than in his books.

But all the expertise in the world about what most would call a niche subject is useless to the layman without context. It's not of much use to be thrown immediately into heavy narrative about rituals and violent practices when starting to read a book about these issues. You have to learn more about the world around narco saints, cults, and drug traffickers' religious practices before you can draw any conclusions about their significance and the often nuanced roles they play. This involves a survey of the drug war landscape as it existed in the past and operates now, identifying the major players, knowing the dangers traffickers and their pursuers face, and knowing the basics of cults and their standard practices.

You will find all of that in the pages to come. This book isn't written like an encyclopedia, although it's an indispensable reference. Interspersed between the histories and terms officers need to know are numerous true stories and chilling anecdotes that bring the material to life. You will be educated, surprised, and sometimes shocked. It's a journey into a world few people really know about, yet is an intrinsic part of a violent conflict almost everyone in the western hemisphere has heard or read about. It's not a world for the faint of heart, but neither is police work. Any officer with the potential to be involved in drug investigations will be well served by soaking in the information on the pages that follow.

Sylvia M. Longmire, MA and Owner of Longmire Consulting
Author of *Cartel and Border Insecurity*
Contributing Editor for *Homeland Security Today* and *Breitbart Texas*
Tucson, Arizona

Preface

Readers who are unfamiliar with many of the religions described in this book may be tempted to view them as foreign or exotic or even bizarre. As a former law enforcement officer, I can attest to how some practices may even appear deviant or criminal to the untrained eye. As a student of cultural anthropology, I can attest that the majority of these religions are highly misunderstood by the general public.

It is imperative that you, as the reader, understand that the vast majority of these religions are practiced by law-abiding citizens who do not have any connections with the drug trade. All of these religions have a moral code that also includes a belief in a moral code among their deities. The majority of practitioners that I have encountered hate the thought of criminals misusing their sacred religious paths. In fact, most clergy that I have encountered do not want these types of cases to be representations of their religion.

The information in this text may be misinterpreted as putting a "black eye" on a specific religious culture. The truth is that drug traffickers have already put a black eye on these religions by misappropriating them with their illegal activities. Members of these religious faiths should be outraged that their faiths are being corrupted by these criminal organizations. In my opinion, outrage should transform into action where religious specialists and clergy take a stand against those who misuse their faiths for selfish means. This text seeks to provide officers with a clear understanding of how these religions may be practiced by normative practitioners. The text also looks at how criminals prostitute these cultures for their own selfish means.

The last thing that this text is meant to encourage is bias or prejudice against any of the African- or Latin-based religious traditions. It should be clearly understood that the religious cultures mentioned in this text in themselves are not narco-cults. It is important not to "criminalize

entire populations believed to have a common culture" (Schneider, 2005*).
As with terrorism, any religion from Buddhism to Christianity can be
maligned by criminal and psychotic individuals.

Officers may find that many in the normative religious communities
of these cultures can be very cooperative in assisting law enforcement.
Some clergy in these communities have been approached by those in
drug trafficking organizations for their assistance in providing spiritual
services. Some of these members of clergy have become reliable informants in areas where traditional undercover operations may not have
been successful.

It is my hope that this text will serve to build cultural competency
among agencies, provide insight into the criminal elements that bastard-
ize various forms of spirituality, and encourage officers to understand the
tremendous value of culture and how it affects mankind.

Tony Kail

* Schneider, Jane, and Peter. *Mafia, antimafia and the struggle for Palermo.*
Berkeley, CA: University of California Press, 2005.

Acknowledgments

I want to personally thank each individual and agency that helped in the creation of this book. Cultural information, criminal cases, testimony, and articles have all served as valuable pieces to this puzzle. Thank you to Robert Bunker, Strategic Studies Institute, Chivis, Borderland Beat; Sylvia Longmire, Longmire Consulting, Tucson, Arizona; Office Special Enforcement Unit, Butte County Sheriff's Department, Butte County, Califonia; Rafael Martinez, Miami, Florida; Edwin Santana, New Jersey Gang Investigators Association; U.S. Drug Enforcement Agency; the girl with the dragon tattoo; Sgt. Rolando Garcia, San Juan Police Department, San Juan, Texas; Webb County Sheriff's Department, Laredo, Texas; Michael Vincent, Orange County Sheriff's Department, Orlando, Florida; Southern Institute of Forensic Science; Donna Fontana, Forensic Anthropology Services, New Jersey; St. Lucie County Sheriff's Department, Fort Pierce, Florida; Dawn Perlmutter, Symbol Intelligence, Yardley, Pennsylvania; Orange County Sheriff's Department, Santa Ana, California; Sgt. Phillip Edwards, St. Helens Police, St. Helens, Oregon; Lt. Doug Gregg, Washington County Sheriff's Department, Johnson City, Tennessee; U.S. Customs and Border Patrol; Leigh Thelmadatter; Dongringo; Polk County Sheriff's Department, Lakeland, Florida; Rosendo Perez, New Jersey Gang Investigators Association; Chester County District Attorney's Office, Chester County, Pennsylvania; Sgt. John Boese and Investigator Chris Lo, Metro Nashville Specialized Investigations Division, Nashville Metropolitan Police Department, Nashville, Tennessee; John Garza, Texas Narcotics Officers' Association; Photographer Ignacio Carvajal García; U.S. Marshal Robert Almonte; Chief Bradley Taylor, De Valls Bluff Police Department, Arkansas; Richard Couto, Animal Recovery Mission; Lisa Barker, LB Photography, Humboldt, Tennessee.

About the Author

Tony M. Kail serves as a trainer and subject matter expert in the area of esoteric religions and security threat groups for a number of agencies, including the National Gang Academy in Orlando, Florida, and the Symbol Intelligence Group. Kail has spent 25 years researching and training on the subject of religious groups and criminality. He has conducted ethnographic fieldwork among a number of esoteric religious communities throughout the United States and Africa.

As a former law enforcement officer, Kail has provided training for state and federal agencies, including the U.S. Army, U.S. Capitol Police, Federal Bureau of Investigation, and several state gang investigator associations. Kail is the author of a number of books, including *A Cop's Guide to Occult Investigations* (Paladin Press, 2003) and *Magico-Religious Groups and Ritualistic Activities: A Guide for First-Responders* (CRC Press, 2008). His books appear on the 2011 FBI suggested readings list on Mexican narco-cults. He is a member of the International Law Enforcement Educators and Trainers Association.

chapter one

Mexican drug trafficking organizations (DTOs)

Mexican drug trafficking organizations (DTOs), also known as cartels, are responsible for the majority of drug trafficking into the United States. These networks are involved in the production, transportation, and wholesale distribution of illegal drugs. Ninety percent of the cocaine entering the United States comes through Mexico. This mass movement increased after many of the prominent Colombian cartels, such as the Cali and Medellín cartels, were destroyed in the 1990s by the Colombian and U.S. military. Mexican cartels have an advantage over traditional street and motorcycle gangs, as they have control over smuggling routes into the United States through the southwest border. These same cartels also have the ability to manufacture, transport, and distribute illegal drugs through sophisticated networks. Drugs are transported in small quantities across the border by foot and in noncommercial vehicles. Large quantities of narcotics are trafficked in commercial and noncommercial vehicles, planes, and boats.

Because the cartels operate heavily along the U.S. southwest border, they pose a major threat to the security of American military, law enforcement, and civilians. The U.S. Drug Enforcement Administration reports that Mexican drug syndicates operating along the U.S. southwest border are far more sophisticated and dangerous than any of the other organized criminal groups in America's law enforcement history.

The war on drugs in Mexico

The phenomenon known as the drug war in Mexico rages as a result of Mexican DTOs battling over geographic territories and, more specifically, drug distribution routes. The cartels not only battle each other over these territories, but also battle against the Mexican law enforcement authorities. While Mexican authorities have always struggled with drug smugglers, the cartel-based networks are a sophisticated breed of criminal enterprise. The growth of the cartel networks and their expansion throughout the world also produced extreme acts of violence in a campaign to spread drug distribution routes. Mexican law enforcement authorities have become active targets of these groups. In Nuevo Laredo, Mexico, in 2005, a police chief who had only been sworn in for six hours was shot more than 50 times after he announced a crackdown on the cartels. Numerous law enforcement officers have been murdered by cartels in an effort to demonstrate the cartels' power and influence throughout Mexico.

Since 2006, more than 60,000 people have been killed in cartel-related violence and more than 26,000 have gone missing (Morris, 2013). The spread of cartel-related violence has brought this once hidden underground of drug dealers and violence into the cities and counties of the Mexican and American public. Acts of violence, including public hangings, beheadings, and torture, have become trademarks of the cartel culture. Cartels publicly claim ownership of communities by flying "narco banners" (*narcomantas*) or signs that display the cartel's name and challenges to rivals in the area. Internet postings, including videos of beheadings and shootings, are used to intimidate communities and rivals. Bodies of victims are displayed as warnings to rivals and threats to local communities. There are increasing acts of violence toward innocent civilians as well as journalists covering the drug war.

Acts of cartel violence are rising, as many cartels have attained and are using military-grade weaponry and technology. Once small-time drug trafficking rings, many of these groups have evolved into international terrorist groups. Acts of violence are no longer limited to interpersonal struggles with rival cartels. The U.S. State Department has issued warnings to American citizens traveling in Mexico due to numerous kidnappings, car jackings, and robberies of U.S. citizens. Residents of many Mexican communities have become all too familiar with these acts of violence. Embedded reporters in the country release news stories and photos via the Internet to the rest of the world to bring awareness of these acts of violence.

Mexico's drug war

In 2000, Mexican President Vincent Fox sent troops into Nuevo Laredo, Mexico, to fight the cartels. More than 100 people died in a fight between members of the Sinaloa and Gulf cartels. In the six years to follow, the Mexican government arrested more than 300 cartel "enforcers," known as *sicarios* (Spanish for "assassin"), for committing acts of violence. These enforcers were responsible for intimidating Mexican citizens and public officials on behalf of the cartels.

In 2006, newly elected Mexican President Felipe Calderón launched a government-sponsored campaign against drug cartels throughout Mexico.

At the time there were four dominant cartels that were responsible for drug sales and drug-related violence: the Tijuana/Arellano Félix cartel, the Sinaloa Federation, the Juárez/Vincente Carrillo Fuentes cartel,

Figure 1.1 Cartel. The threat of transnational criminal organizations is posing a threat to international security of all nations. Drug cartels are no longer bound by specific geographic borders but have infiltrated countries around the world.

and the Gulf cartel. The U.S. Drug Enforcement Administration (DEA) would later report the growth of seven deadly cartels that included the Sinaloa Federation, Los Zetas, the Tijuana cartel, the Betrán-Leyva organization (BLO), the Gulf cartel, La Familia Michoacana (LFM), and the Juárez cartel. Analysts have reported that these seven cartels have splintered into several organizations, spreading an epidemic of violence and crime throughout Mexico.

On December 11, 2006, President Calderón sent more than 6,000 federal troops to his home state of Michoacán to begin the fight against the cartels. In January 2007, Calderón donned a military uniform as he began to review the progress of the campaign in Michoacán. This image became a public symbol of the militarization of the drug war. By 2011, Calderón called Mexico's Congress to approve changes to the law enforcement and military structure. Calderón sent in more than 20,000 soldiers to engage in the fight with the cartels. The strategy to fight the cartels focused on arresting or killing high-ranking members of the cartels, assuming that without leadership, the cartels would fold. Unfortunately, the cartels continued to flourish.

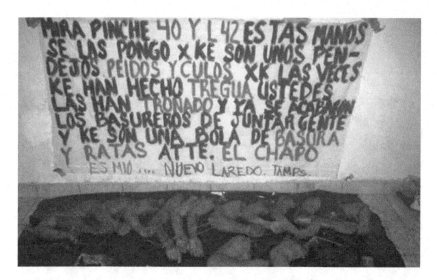

Figure 1.2 Victims of cartel violence. The drug war has raised the degree of violence perpetrated by trafficking organizations. Beheadings, dismemberments, and mutilations have become the modus operandi of many contemporary cartels.

In 2013, the violence of the cartels spilled over into the United States. Incidents involving such atrocities as beheadings of cartel rivals in rural communities, kidnappings along southwest border towns, and targeting of law enforcement officials have ramped up, along with the growth of the cartels. Cartels are now enlisting the aid of U.S. street gangs, prison

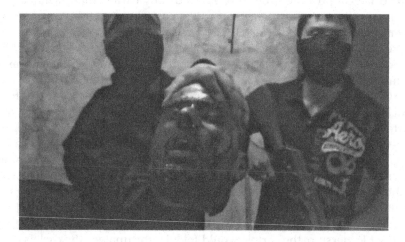

Figure 1.3 Photo of beheading.

Figure 1.4 Members of the Sinaloa cartel displaying the massive amount of fire-power used against rival cartels and law enforcement.

Figure 1.5 Photo of guns.

Figure 1.6 Photo of gun and bags of ammunition.

gangs, and security threat groups. Transnational gangs like MS-13, Barrio Azteca, Mexican Mafia, and the Texas Syndicate provide street and prison support for the cartels in the United States and Mexico. Cartels have a vested interest in the U.S.–Mexican border region around Texas and Mexico. This region is 1,000 plus miles long and includes 18 ports of entry, making it an accessible route into the United States for drug traffickers. As a result, Arizona, California, and New Mexico serve as major distribution points for narcotics distribution. In 2010, law enforcement agencies seized more than 2,535,003 pounds of cocaine, methamphetamine, heroin, and marijuana along the southwest border. Cartels have also become very active in human and weapons trafficking into the United States.

Acts of crime and violence from the cartels have not been limited to the border regions of the United States. American cities small and large have been affected by the cartels. The following are just a few of the incidents as a result of the spreading of the cartels.

Alabama: A father and son in Leighton, Alabama, were arrested as part of an investigation into a drug trafficking organization that was responsible for trafficking drugs into Alabama and Chicago. Both father and son were found to be members of the deadly Juarez cartel.

Figure 1.7 Los Zetas. Los Zetas began as a paramilitary arm of the Gulf cartel. The organization broke off and became one of the most violent and aggressive cartels in the drug war.

Figure 1.8 Los Zetas cartel throwing a "Z sign" with hands.

Figures 1.9 and 1.10 Examples of Los Zetas violence. Los Zetas combine military-based tactics with ritualistic forms of murder that focus on beheadings and dismemberments.

Arizona: Police in Tempe, arrest 20 members of a drug trafficking cell for the Sinaloa cartel. The cell was responsible for moving 3 tons of marijuana, 20 pounds of methamphetamine, and $2.4 million of cash throughout the state. Officers seized an airplane and 10 vehicles used to transport drugs from Arizona to Alabama, California, and New York.

Figure 1.11 El Chapo. Joaquin Guzman Loera became a folk hero to some Mexican communities that viewed his rise to fame as a billionaire drug czar as an example of success to emulate.

Arkansas: Sixteen members of the Gulf cartel were responsible for moving over 100 kilograms of cocaine into Arkansas from Mexico. An inmate in the Federal Correctional Complex in Forrest City, Arkansas, was responsible for recruiting dealers for the cartel that upon their release would work for the organization. The leader of the operation, known as Idalia Ramos Rangel (aka Big Momma), not only directed the Arkansas traffickers, but also directed a drug trafficking organization in Matamoros, Mexico.

California: A state task force arrested members of the La Familia Michoacana cartel in Fontana, California, during an investigation that netted 107 pounds of methamphetamine, 5 kilograms of cocaine, and half a pound of heroin.

Colorado: Twenty-three people linked to the Los Zetas cartel were found responsible for smuggling over $36 million in marijuana in tour buses into Commerce City, Colorado. Over 45,000 pounds of marijuana bricks were brought from Durango, Mexico, to El Paso, Texas, and into Colorado for distribution. Police also discovered 53 grams of methamphetamine, 2 kilograms of cocaine, and an AK-47 among members of the organization.

Delaware: A former enforcer for the Arellano Feliz cartel who claimed to have strangled three victims to show his faithfulness to the cartel was discovered plotting to kill the District of Delaware

Figures 1.12 and 1.13 Traitors: There is a constant threat that those who dare speak out against the cartels will become victims of violence. Many reporters who are embedded in Mexico reporting on the drug war must remain anonymous for fear of death. (Courtesy of Borderland Beat.)

Figures 1.14 and 1.15 Execution videos: The marriage between cartel violence and technology has created a public forum for cartels to use to demonstrate their capability for violence in order to maintain power by creating fear in rivals and communities.

Figures 1.16 and 1.17 Grow operations in Mexico under control of cartels are heavily guarded and maintained by specialists.

Figures 1.18 and 1.19 American grow operations. Drug traffickers set up these types of operations in rural areas where they can grow contraband without fear of discovery. (Courtesy of Butte County Sheriff's Office Special Enforcement Unit.)

Figure 1.20 Armed guard. This Mexican national was discovered guarding a grow operation for a drug trafficking organization through surveillance cameras that local law enforcement had embedded in the landscape. (Courtesy of Butte County Sheriff's Office Special Enforcement Unit.)

prosecution team that was responsible for putting him in federal prison.

Florida: Members of the Central Florida High Intensity Drug Area Task Force made several undercover buys of methamphetamine from a local drug trafficking organization that is tied to the Gulf cartel.

Georgia: Rodney Benson, special agent in charge for the Atlanta field office of the U.S. Drug Enforcement Administration says that Atlanta, is a strategic operations center for Mexican organized crime. Forty-five members of La Familia Michoacana were discovered operating a $2.4 million drug ring throughout the region.

Illinois: Five members of the Los Zetas cartel were discovered to be involved with moving 550 pounds of cocaine and over $2 million worth of drug profits between Chicago and Mexico.

Figure 1.21 Cartel Jalisco New Generation. Also known as CJNG, this group operates as a group of enforcers for the cartels.

New Mexico: Former Columbus, New Mexico, Police Chief Angelo Vega collected more than $2,000 a month from the Juarez cartel in exchange for protection and help smuggling drugs and guns into his city. Police cruisers were used for cartel operations, and background checks and license plates were run by the chief for members of the cartel. Vega was also responsible for pulling over three Bureau of Alcohol, Tobacco and Firearms agents under orders of the cartel.

Ohio: Police arrested Edgar Campos-Barraza (aka El Cholo), an assassin for the Sinaloa cartel in Sandusky. Barraza had been living in Ohio for a decade before Mexican and American federal authorities discovered his whereabouts.

Oklahoma: A three-year investigation led by the Federal Bureau of Investigation discovered that an Oklahoma farm was being used to train race horses for Jose Trevino Morales, the brother of two leaders of the Los Zetas drug cartel. Investigators discovered that the cartel had funneled over $22 million back to the cartel in Mexico in laundered money.

Texas: Twenty-two-year-old former U.S. Army Private First Class Michael Apodaca was paid $5,000 to murder a member of the Juarez cartel

Figure 1.22 and 1.23 Body messaging. Murdered victims serve as billboards for the cartels. Messages that include threats and challenges serve to strike fear in the hearts of the community.

Figure 1.24 La Familia Michoacana. Also known as LFM, cartel leadership appropriates elements of Judeo-Christian ideology and a messianic mythology to spiritualize cartel activities. Murders committed by the cartel are known as divine justice.

and informant for the U.S. Immigration and Customs Enforcement Agency. Apodaca killed Jose Daniel Gonzalez-Galena outside of his home in an upscale El Paso neighborhood by firing eight shots into Galena and then jumped into a getaway car driven by an accomplice.

Washington: U.S. Immigration and Custom's Enforcement Division, Bureau of Alcohol, Tobacco and Firearms, and Department of Homeland Security conducted Operation Black Ice, which resulted in 34 indictments and the seizure of 20 pounds of heroin, 30 pounds of methamphetamine, $2 million, and 31 firearms. The drug trafficking ring was discovered to be tied to the Beltran-Leyva cartel in Mexico.

A haunting banner appeared in 2008 in Tamaulipas, Mexico, seeking new recruits for the vicious Gulf cartel that read:

> Soldiers of Merida and Federal Preventive Police, stop living in misery, come and work for the Gulf cartel. We offer salaries in dollars, loans, life insurance, money to send your children to school and housing for your family. Do not allow yourself to jump onto that truck, stop living on the sidelines. Instead, pick your own new year model car or

Figure 1.25 Los Caballeros Templarios. This cartel uses imagery and mythology taken from a fraternal order of knights that was responsible for providing protection to pilgrims traveling to the Holy Land.

Figure 1.26 Narcoterrorism. The growth of narcoterrorist groups combines the crime and violence associated with the drug trade and the threat of traditional terrorist behaviors to influence society.

Figures 1.27 and 1.28 The displaying of victims of cartel violence has become more frequent in Mexico. The motivation is to create fear and remind communities that the cartels are in power. The letter Z on the foreheads of the victims in Figure 1.27 indicates they were members of the Loc Zetas cartel. (Courtesy of Borderland Beat.)

Figures 1.29 and 1.30 Acts of extreme violence. The growing trend among drug trafficking organizations is to match the level of violence that rival cartels use. Cartels like Los Zetas are providing training for new recruits in beheading and disemboweling.

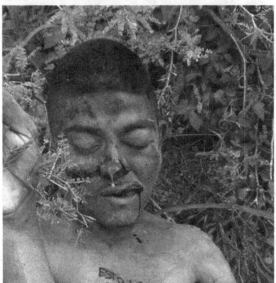

Figures 1.31 and 1.32 The barbarism of the drug cartels is creating an epidemic of emotional trauma among many Mexican communities. Children and adults alike are becoming physical and emotional victims to cartel violence. The growing trend among drug trafficking organizations is to match the level of violence that rival cartels use. Cartels like Los Zetas are providing training for new recruits in beheading and disemboweling.

Figure 1.33 Cartel life. A cartel member poses with his pet African lion. (Courtesy of Borderland Beat.)

truck. What more could you want? We offer work in Tamaulipas, Mexico, the United States and around the world. This is the land of the Gulf cartel.

These are just a few of the incidents documented by law enforcement throughout the United States. American intelligence agencies continue to release warnings and potential threats of cartel violence toward U.S. citizens and law enforcement officers.

The cartels

Much like street gangs, the names, leaders, and hierarchies of cartels are ever changing. Alliances and rivals change as well. The following are some of the key players in the contemporary cartel culture.

Figure 1.34 Narco corrido CD cover.

Los Zetas

One of the most organized and sophisticated cartels in Mexico is the Los Zetas organization. The name *Los Zetas* comes from the organization's first commander, Arturo Guzmán Decena, who was known as Z1, a name given to high-ranking officers in the Federal Judicial Police and used in radio transmissions. The Spanish letter Z, pronounced "zeta," became the nickname used to refer to this violent criminal enterprise.

Los Zetas began when the leadership of the violent Mexican Gulf cartel recruited ex-members of the Mexican military to fight for the cartel. One of the most prominent figures was Decena, who served as a lieutenant in the Mexican Army. Decena brought along 31 members of the Mexican army's Grupo Aeromóvil de Fuerzas Especiales, or "Special Air Mobile Forces Group," as well as several others. Many members of this elite unit had extensive training in combat and brought this to the drug wars. Members were trained in combat, surveillance, technology, and numerous special skills. The group's mostly military background has given them the ability to perform aerial assaults and to train new members in marksmanship and covert communications. The group currently operates several military-style training camps in Mexico.

The group soon began to lure the talents of many corrupt law enforcement officers from local and federal levels. The organization even boasts

Figure 1.35

Figure 1.36

Figures 1.35, 1.36 and 1.37 Examples of narco fashions. The shirt represents the Gulf cartel, while the hats and jewelry contain images of popular narco saints. (*continued*)

Figure 1.37

Figures 1.35, 1.36 and 1.37 (*continued*) Examples of narco fashions. The shirt
represents the Gulf cartel, while the hats and jewelry contain images of popular
narco saints.

members of the Guatemalan military special forces known as Kaibiles.
The organization continues to recruit new members throughout the
world, extending into Southeast Asia and South America. Members of Los
Zetas became known for their ability to use large-scale weapons, including bazookas, ground-to-air missiles, helicopters, and grenade launchers.
In 2008, the Mexican military discovered a Gulf cartel safe house that held
Zetas weapons, including over 500 firearms, such as .50 caliber Barrett
sniper rifles, rocket and grenade launchers, assault rifles, and over a half
million rounds of ammunition.

Zetas activity would become legendary, as kidnappings, assassinations, and savage mutilations would become hallmarks of the organization. Los Zetas would eventually become involved in a number of criminal enterprises internationally, including facilitating human trafficking. The violence of Los Zetas crossed into the United States in 2008 when members dressed as Phoenix, Arizona, police officers entered a residence and killed a drug dealer. Members of the Zetas are known for their brutality. Zetas have been documented placing rivals in oil drums and dousing them with gasoline and setting them on fire. This practice popularly became known as *el guiso*, or "stew." Zetas are known for beheading rivals and skinning some of their enemies.

Los Zetas membership began to grow and outnumbered the membership of the Gulf cartel. A split eventually occurred between the Los Zetas and the Gulf cartel. Intelligence sources reported that infighting between the two groups, including disagreements over leadership, eventually led to this splintering. Los Zetas members began to act on their own without orders from the Gulf cartel. Today the Zetas are very active, with reports from the FBI claiming that Los Zetas has become very active in human trafficking into the United States. Los Zetas has been documented recruiting American teenagers in Texas. Teenage recruits known as Zetillas, or "Baby Zetas," have been transported to Mexico, where they have been trained in the group's training camps to become assassins for the cartel. In 2005, Los Zetas was discovered as being connected to at least three murders in the city of Dallas, Texas. Law enforcement agencies have discovered disturbing trends of juveniles being used by Los Zetas to traffic narcotics into the United States ("Teen Drug Smuggling Arrests Jump," *El Paso Times*, 2009).

Sinaloa Federation

The Sinaloa Federation is also known as Cartel de Sinaloa (CDS). It is also known by the names Guzmán-Loera organization and Pacific cartel. They are originally based out of the city of Culiacán in Sinaloa state. In the late 1980s, the cartel was considered to be the largest drug trade organization in Mexico. The federation was born after the 1989 splintering of the Mexican-based Guadalajara cartel. After the arrest of Guadalajara leader Miguel Ángel Félix Gallardo, the cartel split into four very powerful drug cartels: the Juarez, Tijuana, Gulf, and Sinaloa cartels.

The federation was originally led by Joaquin Guzmán Loera, known as El Chapo, and Hector Luis Palma Salazar, known as El Guero, both lieutenants in the Guadalajara cartel. The cartel was originally known as Alianza de Sangre, Spanish for "Blood Alliance." After the arrest of Salazar, "El Chapo" Gúzman took over as leader of the cartel.

Gúzman became financially wealthy from the exploits of the cartel. *Forbes* magazine listed him as one of the world's top billionaires. Gúzman has become a folkloric figure among Mexican communities, demonstrating that a local can rise to such an unprecedented status.

In April 2012, Gúzman and his men left the dismembered bodies of 14 members of the Los Zetas cartel in Nuevo Laredo with a narco banner signed with his name. Gúzman helped in establishing a billion dollar network with the Hell's Angels motorcycle gang and the Canadian Mafia to funnel marijuana into New York.

The Sinaloa cartel is typically associated with a region known as the Golden Triangle. The Mexican states of Sinaloa, Durango, and Chihuahua are known for the massive amounts of poppy and marijuana produced in the region. The Sinaloa cartel operates in 17 states throughout Mexico and also maintains distribution cells in U.S. states like Arizona, California, and Texas. In 2009, U.S. officials arrested 750 members of the Sinaloa cartel throughout the United States in Operation Xcellerator.

The organization is involved in the transportation and sales of cocaine, marijuana, and heroin. The cartel has become infamous throughout Mexico for its use of aggressive tactics. The group is responsible for kidnapping a number of famous television reporters in Mexico and demanding that news stations air stories about the relationship between the Los Zetas cartel and Mexican law enforcement.

In response to the Los Zetas, the federation created a group of enforcers known as Los Negros and Los Pelones. Los Negros were headed by Edgar "La Barbie" Valdez Villarreal from the Beltrán-Levya organization while still aligned with the federation. The group of enforcers split off in 2008, and La Barbie took Los Negros with him. Federation members have been discovered obtaining grenades from the Mexican navy along with ammunition from the Mexican army.

Beltrán-Levya cartel

Also known as Beltrán-Levya organization (BLO), this cartel was formed by four brothers from Sinaloa, including Marcos Arturo, known as El Jefe de Jefes, Carlos Alfredo, and Héctor Beltrán-Levya, known as El H. The brothers became involved in the drug trade at an early age and worked with Joaquin "El Chapo" Gúzman Loera in drug smuggling operations. Both families are believed to have served in the now defunct Guadaljara cartel. The brothers served in the deadly federation, performing assassinations and violent acts of intimidation against rival cartels.

The Beltrán-Levya brothers became related to Gúzman when a cousin married into the Gúzman family. This alliance between the two drug dealing families became known as Alianza de Sangre, or the "Blood Alliance."

The group has become known for infiltrating various government agencies and obtaining information on antidrug operations. In 2005 a report from a Mexican intelligence agency nicknamed the cartel Los Tres Caballeros, or "The Three Horsemen." A Mexican reporter began to write articles about the cartel using the intelligence report as his source, including details regarding the organization's ties to the government. The reporter had uncovered several details about the cartel's activities, including the use of government officials in moving large amounts of cocaine. The cartel was also mentioned for its use of aircraft in moving drugs across the U.S. border into Arizona. Once across the border, the group would set up stash houses to store drugs until distribution. The reporter went missing not long after the publication of these articles.

In 2008, Alfredo Beltrán-Levya, known as El Mochomo, was arrested. This disrupted the activities of the Federation, as he was an important conductor of business for the organization. Arturo Beltrán-Levya put out a hit on the commissioner of the Mexican federal police as a result of his brother's arrest. The Beltrán-Levya brothers believed that Joaquin "El Chapo" Gúzman Loera was responsible for their brother's arrest and ordered a hit on El Chapo's son. Cartel hitmen murdered Chapo's son in a shopping center parking lot.

The arrest of Alfredo Beltrán-Levya created a massive split between key players in the cartels. The Beltrán-Levya family began to associate with members of the Juarez cartel and Los Zetas. In 2010, violence erupted in the city of Reynosa, Tamaulipas, when members of the BLO and Los Zetas battled against members of the Gulf cartel, the federation, and LFM.

As of 2013, the Beltrán-Levya brothers have lost Alfredo and Carlos, as they were arrested, while brother Arturo was killed by Mexico's marines in 2009. Hector has formed a cartel known as Cartel de Pacifico Sur, or "South Pacific cartel." One of the most famous personalities among the Beltrán-Levya cartel is Edgar Valdez Villareal, known as La Barbie. Villareal is a Mexican American who served as a leader in the enforcement group Los Negros and later struggled to become leader of the BLO after the death of Arturo Beltrán-Levya. La Barbie became known for his use of torture and decapitation to his enemies. He was arrested in Mexico City in 2010.

"El Chapo" Gúzman Loera was arrested by Mexican and American authorities in Sinaloa state in February 2014.

Gulf cartel

Also known as Cartel del Golfo, the Gulf cartel is based out of Matamoros in Tamaulipas state. The cartel is active in several regions of Mexico, including northeast Tamaulipas and the Monterrey area of Nueve León. The cartel is responsible for trafficking cocaine, marijuana, methamphetamine, and heroin into the United States from Mexico.

The Gulf cartel is a very violent organization that has been documented as imposing taxes on anyone trying to sell drugs through Gulf cartel territory. The group is known for kidnappings and extortion.

The origins of the Gulf cartel can be found in the early days of bootlegging. In the 1930s a Mexican bootlegger named Juan Nepomuceno Guerra was active in transporting whiskey into the United States from Mexico. Some 40 years later, Guerra became involved in the drug trade and began to transport drugs such as marijuana and heroin into the United States. Guerra's nephew Garcia Ábrego joined his uncle in the trade and eventually took over several operations of the organization. During the 1980s, the organization became involved in the cocaine trade, and in 1995 Ábrego became the first drug trafficker in U.S. history to be placed on the FBI's Ten Most Wanted Fugitives list. Ábrego was captured in 1996 and currently is imprisoned in the United States.

After the arrest of Ábrego, the fight for leadership in the cartel has a bloody history. One of the first leaders, Sergio "El Checko" Gomez, was assassinated by Salvador "Chava" Gomez for the leadership position. Salvador was later assassinated by Osiel Cárdenas Guillén who wanted the throne as cartel leader. In 1999, Guillén was notified that an informant against the Gulf cartel was being transported by the DEA and FBI through Matamoros, Mexico. Members of the cartel discovered the route and surrounded the vehicle carrying the informant. A standoff took place between members of U.S. law enforcement and the Gulf cartel. Because Guillén threatened members of the American law enforcement community, pressure was put on Mexican officials to locate and arrest the leader. Guillén was arrested in 2003 and imprisoned.

Since the arrest of Guillén, fellow cartel members Antonio Ezequiel Cárdenas Guillén and Jorge Eduardo Costilla took over as leaders in the cartel. Los Zetas were initially used by the Gulf cartel as enforcers, but have since turned against the cartel and established new allies in the drug war. In 2008, 175 members of the Gulf cartel were arrested throughout Italy and the United States.

Tijuana cartel

Also known as Cartel de Tijuana or Arellano Félix Organization (AFO) or Fernando Sánchez Organization, the Tijuana cartel is based from Tijuana in Baja California state. The cartel is responsible for trafficking cocaine, marijuana, methamphetamine, and heroin into the United States from Mexico.

Miguel Ángel Félix Gallardo, the founder of the legendary Guadalajara cartel, was imprisoned in 1989 for the infamous murder of DEA agent Enrique "Kiki" Camarena.

The cartel is extremely violent and has been documented as infiltrating ranks of the Mexican judicial system. The organization has employed mercenaries to conduct countersurveillance on law enforcement authorities. Intelligence agencies report that the cartel obtained sophisticated electronic countersurveillance equipment as well as automated weapons. The cartel controls Tijuana Plaza and territory outside of Mexicali.

Juárez cartel

Also known as Cartel de Juárez and the Vicente Carrillo Fuentes Organization, the cartel is based in Ciudad Juárez, Chihuahua, Mexico, across the border from El Paso, Texas. The Juárez cartel has control of one of the main trading routes for transporting drugs into the United States.

The cartel began in the 1970s under the leadership of Rafael Aguilar Guajardo. Cartel leadership was handed over to Guajardo's nephew Amado Carrillo Fuentes in 1993. Amado's family joined the organization and aided in distributing drugs for the cartel. Amado died in 1997 due to complications during plastic surgery. His surving brother Vincente Carrillo Fuentes then took the reins as cartel leader.

By 2005 authorities named the Juárez cartel the dominant cartel that controlled the cocaine trade from Mexico into the United States. The organization had monopolized trafficking routes into Texas and built a reputation among other cartels for being brutally violent. The group frequently beheads rival cartel members and leaves their corpses and heads in public areas to instill fear in rivals and communities. In 2010 the cartel planted a car bomb to murder federal police officers. The group is known to employ kidnapping and extortion. On July 27, 2011, members of the cartel placed narcomantas (banners) in Chihuahua City and Juarez, threatening DEA and U.S. Consulate employees with death or dismemberment if they did not stop meddling in the affairs of the cartel.

The cartel uses two enforcer groups in the United States and Mexico to enforce its power. In Mexico the cartel uses a group of former and current law enforcement officers known as La Linea, while in the United States the organization uses the street gang known as Barrio Azteca. La Linea is currently going by the name New Juárez cartel. The group made its first appearance on September 26, 2011, in an Internet YouTube video. The video featured members of the cartel dressed in black paramilitary uniforms interrogating a captured prison guard believed to be working for the Sinaloa Federation.

La Familia Michoacana (LFM)

Also known as La Familia, or "The Family," this organization is based out of Michoacán state. The group is largely involved in shipping methamphetamines, cocaine, and marijuana into the United States from Mexico. The group has also been involved in human smuggling. The group exerts heavy intimidation over public officials in Michoacán, including claims that the group selects the chiefs of police and local officials of government.

The organization started back in the 1980s as a form of protection for the people of Michoacán. The group was made up of vigilante citizens who sought to protect their community from drug dealers and kidnappers. As the group grew, the focus of the organization changed drastically. In the 1990s the organization became an ally to the notorious Gulf cartel to protect Michoacán from rival drug gangs.

The group is known for its use of violence and intimidation. One of the famous incidents of violence took place in 2006, when members of La Familia beheaded five victims and threw the victims' heads into a night club along with the message "The Family doesn't kill for money. It's doesn't kill women. It doesn't kill innocent people, only those who deserve to die. Know that this is divine justice."

In July 2009 the group attacked Federal Police headquarters in Morelia. In the same year the group offered to disband if the Mexican government would commit to safeguard the security of the state of Michoacán. The president of Mexico refused to negotiate with cartel members and rejected any dealings with the group.

Los Caballeros Templarios

The core group that remained faithful to the leadership of Nazario Moreno changed its name to the Knights Templar, while La Familia Michoacana splintered away from its original organization. The cartel, which is stationed out of Michoacán, is involved in trafficking methamphetamine, marijuana, cocaine, and heroin. A spokesperson for the U.S. Drug Enforcement Administration office claims that the cartel is the biggest distributor of methamphetamine into the United States from Mexico. The group has been documented receiving chemicals for drug manufacturing from Chinese companies in exchange for iron ore that is traded in the port city of Lazaro Cardenas, which is allegedly controlled by the cartel.

The organization has crept into the United States, as was revealed in December 2012 when the Drug Enforcement Administration revealed a 21-month operation known as Operation Knight Stalker. The operation focused on members of the Knights Templar cartel in California and Mexico. The investigation discovered over 1,000 pounds of methamphetamine, 200 pounds of cocaine, 28 pounds of heroin, and 320 pounds of marijuana being trafficked by the cartel. Sixteen people with ties to the cartel were arrested in San Diego, California. In June 2013, law enforcement authorities in Austin, Texas, completed an investigation into an operation that brought together members of the Tango Blast street gang and members of the Caballeros Templarios. Thirty-seven suspects were eventually indicted for distributing heroin and methamphetamine. The group also was involved in a large-scale money laundering operation.

More information is available in the chapter on Judeo-Christian narco-cults.

Street gangs

There are a number of street gangs in the United States and throughout Latin America that affiliate and work alongside many of the cartels. A 2011 intelligence bulletin from the FBI San Antonio field office advises that Los Zetas have sought associates in numerous American street gangs. Intelligence showed that an alliance was made between the cartel and the prison gang Texas Mexican Mafia to collect drug debts, carry out hits, and traffic drugs in and out of Laredo, Texas. Intelligence also showed that Los Zetas were buying AK-47 semiautomatic assault rifles from members of the Houston-based Tango Blast street gang. Agencies have also documented relationships between members of Mara-Salvatrucha (MS-13) and the Los Zetas cartel.

In April 2014 three enforcers from MS-13 were sent by the Sinaloa cartel to Minneapolis, Minnesota, to recover stolen drugs for the cartel. Enforcers kidnapped two individuals who were believed to have stolen 30 pounds of methamphetamine and $200,000 from a stash house from the cartel. The pair were tortured for hours and threatened, and their families threatened, if they did not return the drugs.

Narcoterrorism

The proliferation of drug cartels and the level of violence targeting combatants and noncombatants in the drug war has resulted in a new typology of these terrorist organizations. The U.S. Drug Enforcement Administration (DEA) defines narcoterrorists as "an organized group that is complicit in the activities of drug trafficking in order to further, or fund premeditated, politically-motivated violence perpetrated against noncombatant targets with the intention to influence."

The concept of narcoterrorism is credited to have been coined by a former president of Peru, Belaunde Terry. The term was used to describe terrorist-type attacks against the Peruvian drug enforcement police from the violent communist group Sendero Luminoso, or "Shining Path." The blending of narcotics trafficking and terrorist activities could be seen in the 1985 attack on the Supreme Court of Bogotá, Colombia. Members of the Medellin drug cartel joined forces with the M-19 terrorist organization and attacked the supreme court in order to prevent the extradition of several cocaine dealers to the United States. Eleven judges were killed in the attack.

In the late 1980s narcoterrorism was used to describe much of the activity between the Soviet Union and the drug trade. Recent use of the concept has been applied to terrorist groups that utilize drug sales as a means of funding terrorist activities. The violent actions against noncombatants that cocaine czar Pablo Escobar used are examples of narcoterrorism. Terrorist organizations such as the Taliban and Colombia's Fuerzas Armadas Revolucionarias de Colombia (FARC) flourish from the profits received by drug sales.

Whereas terrorism is commonly performed to implement policies or ideas about an organization or cause, narcoterrorism may be carried out strictly for the furtherance of the drug business. In some cases, terrorist acts are performed more for religious or political motivation and less for furthering the drug business.

The International Institute for Security and Cooperation lists five distinct categories of narcoterrorism:

1. Narcotics traffickers use terrorist tactics to further the organization's criminal enterprise. They avoid prosecution and hinder or prevent enforcement activity through intimidation of judges, prosecutors, police, and the public. Examples include Colombian and Mexican drug cartels.
2. Terrorist organizations provide protection for narcotic traffickers or allow shipments to travel through regions without interference for money, but are not involved in narcotics trafficking. Examples include Al Qaeda and Auto Defensas Unidas de Colombia (AUC).
3. The organization is actively involved in narcotics trafficking and using proceeds to fund terrorist activities. Examples include FARC and Sendero Luminoso (Shining Path).
4. Drug trafficking organizations share their smuggling routes, money laundering capabilities, and other criminal enterprises with terrorist organizations in exchange for money and weapons. Examples include FARC.
5. Government and terrorist organizations allegedly flood their enemy with narcotics aimed at the destabilization of the target government and the undermining of its society. Examples include the Taliban and various Asian, Cuban, and Colombian organizations.

Narco violence

The level of violence associated with contemporary drug cartels is unprecedented. While acts of violence associated with the drug trade are nothing new, the current wave of violence associated with Mexican-based drug cartels has become increasingly more brutal. Cartels are recruiting assassins with military and police backgrounds in order to have effective manpower in their ranks. Consider the following Internet ad that was discovered among ads for kitchenware on a website:

> Services offered by ex-military. Trained to kill. Work is professional and discreet. Guaranteed completion within 10 days or less. I have previous work experience through jobs I have done in Spain. Asking price for job is $6,000. Serious inquiries only.

Ritualized violence in the form of beheadings, hangings, and dismemberments is becoming commonplace among the cartels. Photos and videos of acts of violence are shared across the Internet to frighten rivals and communities. Psychology professor Clark McCauley states, "These gangs have to keep escalating because they want the shock value, but the shock value wears off. Now, to get a headline you have to get more heads, or more bodies, or do something more horrific." At one time beheadings were enough to bring attention to the messages that cartels were trying to communicate through this "theater of violence" (Juergensmeyer, 2000). Today beheading acts have become even more dramatic as cartels distribute videos of cartel members using chainsaws to dismember rival cartel members and filleting and skinning rivals before displaying their bodies in the streets.

Narcocultura

Much like the world of American gangster rap culture, the drug war has acquired it's own form of popular culture. Commonly known as *narcocultura*, or "narco culture," an entire industry has been built upon the aesthetics, personalities, and history of the drug war.

Journalist Alma Guillermoprieto defines narco culture as

> The production of symbols, rituals and artifacts that allow people involved in the drug trade to recognize themselves as part of a community, to establish a hierarchy in which the acts they are required to perform acquire positive value and to absorb the terror inherent in their line of work.

The symbols, rituals, and artifacts that are common to narco culture celebrate the lives of cartel leaders, drug trafficking groups, and group violence. Historically the outlaw has been a popular symbol in Mexico. During the mid-19th century, the outlaw Joaquín Murrieta became very popular among Mexican pop culture. Murrieta was known as the Robin Hood of Mexico. During the California Gold Rush Murrieta was known as a bandit who would steal from the rich and give to the poor. Legend stated that Murrieta was whipped by white Americans with a horse whip. Murrieta's wife was raped and his half-brother lynched. Murrieta became a bandit who set out to steal horses and help the impoverished. Murrieta became a symbol of hope and is believed to be the inspiration for the popular fictional character Zorro. His struggle against Anglos represented the struggle that many Mexicans felt was their own. Mexican culture has a number of high-profile rebels who became popular legendary icons, including Emiliano Zapata Salazar, an important leader in the Mexican revolution, and Pancho Villa, a general in the Mexican revolution. Today spiritual figures such as Jesus Malverde and Santa Muerte have become popular outlaw images in Mexican culture.

Clothing, jewelry, music, and cinema bring the world of the Mexican drug trafficker into the limelight, celebrating the lives of these individuals much like comic book heroes in the West. Journalists have noted that much of the cartel lifestyle is becoming very popular among disenchanted youth and young adults in Mexico. Cartel leaders are viewed as examples of how someone can rise above the poverty and hardships found in poorer communities of Mexico. Drug dealers, murderers, and terrorists are seen as celebrities that youth can seek to aspire to be. Many of the cartels flaunt the lifestyle in front of children in hopes of recruiting them as they get older. Gulf cartel leader Osiel Cardenas Guillen threw a party in 2006 at the Adolfo Lopez Mateos baseball field in Reynosa, Tamaulipas. Over 18,000 kids attended and were treated to gifts, food, and prizes. The cartel leader delivered inspiring cards to the youth at the event:

> Perseverance, discipline and hard work are the basis of success. Continue your studies and be a role model. My best wishes to the future leaders of tomorrow. Happy Children's Day, your friend Osiel Cardenas Guillen.

A 2013 survey of 1,400 junior high school students in eight Mexican states found that more than 26 percent of the students aspire to become narcos or sicarios for the cartels. This has also created a fertile breeding ground for young cartel members known in the drug world as narco juniors.

Juniors are often prized by the cartels, as youth are not usually suspected to be cartel members. Juniors also stand a chance of not serving prison time if arrested because of their age. Adding to this influence, there are a growing number of children of cartel leaders that are appearing in social media glamorizing the cartel lifestyle. Teenage daughters of the leadership of the Los Templarios Caballeros cartel are featured in Facebook and Instagram networks performing music and wearing symbols of the cartel. The son of cartel leader Chapo Guzman has been featured in social networking photos glamorizing the narco lifestyle by posing in photographs with African lions and automatic weapons.

Narco culture has become such a huge phenomenon that a university in Sinaloa has dedicated an entire department to the study of narco culture. Dr. Robert Bunker of the Strategic Studies Institute identifies six distinct attributes found in narco culture:

1. An element of antiauthoritarianism. This demonstrates a rejection of the state, the legal system, and the formal economy.
2. Criminality with an emphasis on narcotics trafficking and drug use.
3. An attitude of machismo. This can be seen in the popular images of males with guns, money, cars, and extravagant homes, as well as having beautiful women.
4. Heroic tales surrounding the rise of underdogs. There is a constant theme of local poor guy becomes rich in the drug trade. This provides a role model to aspiring narcos.
5. Acts of violence that include beheadings, torture, and early death.
6. A disfranchisement among women. Family roles and distorted sex are part of this disfranchisment.

Narco terminology

The culture of the drug war has its own language laden with terms describing the trade, violence, and social norms of the war.

Ajuste de cuentas: To take revenge or settle a score.
Antrax: Also known as anthrax, a term used to denote a group of enforcers for the Sinaloa cartel.
CDG: Gulf drug cartel.
Chapos or chapparines: Troops from Joaquin Guzman Loera's Sinaloa cartel. Taken from Guzman's nickname El Chapo.
Charoliar: Someone who pretends to belong to a cartel and may have inside knowledge regarding the organization.

Chicarra: A term used to describe torture by burning parts of the body with electrical wires.

CJNG: Cartel Jalisco New Generation. An enforcer group also known as GN or GNX.

Cuerno de Chivo: "Horn of the Goat." Refers to the AK-47, the weapon of choice for many cartels. The name comes from the description of the curved magazine on the weapon.

DTO: Drug trafficking organization.

Encajuelados: Victims found in the trunks of cars.

Encintados: Victims found bound and blindfolded with duct tape.

Encobijado: Manner in which hitmen wrap a victim in a blanket and duct tape.

Estaca: A group of three or more armed men patrolling a specific area.

Familia: Also known as LFM or La Familia, refers to the La Familia Michoacana cartel.

Foco: Crystal meth.

GATE/GAFO/GOES: Acronyms of Mexican state police agencies.

Gente Nueva: Hitmen (sicarios) of Chapo Guzman.

Guiso: The disposal of a body in a barrel of acid. Also known as "stew."

Halcons: Lookouts and street informants for the cartels. The term is also used to refer to a group of Mexican commandos with a history of civil rights abuses.

Jefe de jefes: The name that is applied to most prominent drug lords in Mexico. Also known as capo de capos. Frequently used to refer to Miguel Angel Felix Gallardo, a Mexican drug lord who formed the Guadalajara cartel and at one point controlled most of the drug flow from Mexico to the United States.

La Linea: Hitmen of the Juarez cartel.

Levanton: Used in northwest Mexico to refer to a forced abduction.

Los Linces: A unit of hitmen employed by "El Viceroy" Vincete Carrilo-Fuentes and the Juarez cartel. The group is comprised of former military soldiers and uses military-style uniforms, vehicles, and ordinances.

Matazetas: A group that is responsible for executing members of the Zetas cartel. Speculation exists that this could be a rival cartel or an independent group of killers.

Mota: Marijuana.

Narco: A general term for a drug trafficker.

Narcobloqueo: A blockade of hijacked cars used to block police or military vehicles to scenes.

Narcofosa: A dumping ground for victims of drug violence. Also known as a narco cemetery.

Narcomanta: A banner or poster placed in public to deliver a message from or to cartels.

Perico: Cocaine.

Pez gordo: A "big boss."

Plaza: A territory or turf.

Polizetas: Police in service to the narcos.

Pozolero: The person within a cartel with knowledge of chemistry and specializing in disposing bodies.

Rematar: "Rekilling" a victim. The term is used to describe an especially brutal execution.

Sicario: Hitman or assassins.

Straw purchasers: Surrogate purchasers of guns.

Tiendita: The location where drugs will be sold.

Narco corridos

One of the most popular aspects of narco culture is the musical style known as narco corrido. The narco corrido style of music takes its form from the early epic narrative songs from the Middle Ages, which told stories of heroes and quests and historical events. Early forms of the music featured guitars and singers until the influence of Germans in Texas brought the use of the accordion to the corridos, giving them a polka sound. Early corridos were melodious ballads about notable Mexican figures like Pancho Villa.

The contemporary narco corrido takes the stories and legends of drug cartels and personalities in the drug war and sets them to music. Today some researchers have called narco corridos gangster rap with accordions. One of the first popular groups to play narco corridos was Los Tigres del Norte. The group's songs glorified the drug trade by crooning stories of marijuana dealers escaping police and evading their enemies.

Today there are hundreds of narco corrido groups. Songs glorify the use of AK-47s, beheadings, and assassinations. Narco corrido musicians have performed songs singing the praises of drug dealers and, in some cases, disrespecting leaders of rival cartels. In 2006 singer Valetin Elizadle was shot after a concert where he performed a song that apparently insulted members of Los Zetas. In the next two years following Elizadle's death, over 14 narco corrido musicians were murdered in drug trafficker-related violence.

Many of the narco corrido groups are hired to perform concerts for members of drug trade organizations. The Arellano Felix family of the Tijuana cartel supported the popular music group Los Tucanes by buying the members of the group outfits and instruments in exchange for the group writing and performing songs that glorified the cartel. In Tijuana, Mexico, narco corridos are played by cartels across police radio frequencies when there has been an execution of a cartel member.

In May 2011, lawmakers in Chihuahua and Sinaloa issued a ban on narco corridos. The music has moved across the border into the United States, as many narco corrido artists now perform concerts throughout the United States. Narco corrido music is available in many American media outlets, such as music stores and on Internet websites. Some cite the popularity of narco corrido music in the United States as outgrowing the popularity of the music in Mexico.

There are new styles of the corridos being produced by young artists. Movimiento Alterado, or "Altered Movement," is a style of corrido that combines Mexico's norteno music and lyrics focusing on the drug war and cartels. The genre originated in Culiacan, capitol of Sinaloa. Promoters of the music in the United States have recorded over 5 million downloads of music videos in the style dedicated to singing the praises of cartel bosses and assassins. Jose Manual Valenzuela, an expert on narco corridos from Mexico's College of the Northern Border, claims that this trend of promoting corridos through the Internet and social media is a reflection that music about drug traffickers is becoming more socially acceptable.

Narco corridos are now being performed by members of the narco rap industry. The genre of narco rap appears to be growing in the United States and Mexico, as members of the genre are now joining with mainstream American hip-hop artists. A number of American rap artists have started bringing elements of the Mexican narco culture into American music. Rapper Gucci Mane dedicated his first album to Joaquin "El Chapo" Guzman, the main capo of the Sinaloa cartel. Rapper Tony Yayo of the East Coast rap group G-Unit (which includes famous rap artist 50 Cent) dedicated an album to Guzman and featured a photo of the drug lord on the cover of his CD.

Narco entertainment

Television shows known as *tele novelas* are very popular in Latin America. These shows are limited-run dramas that feature soap opera-type stories. There is a growing trend of *narco novelas* that feature stories dramatizing the lives of drug dealers and those involved in the drug war. In 2010 Panamanian President Ricardo Martinelli criticized the growing popularity of narco novelas streaming out of Colombia. Martinelli suggested that the shows were inflicting damage to the moral fiber of Panama.

Narco cinema is a genre of movies focusing on the life and trials of the drug trafficker. As early as 1976, Mexican-made movies about drug dealers and their adventures have been portrayed in cinematic form. Many of the films are financed by cartels, and some even star members and leaders of the various organizations.

Narco fashion

There is a growing fashion industry built upon the narco lifestyle. The style of fashions known as narco moda is an entire industry built around the drug cartel trade. Shirts and belt buckles decorated with marijuana leaves and regional names such as Sinaloa can be found among narco culture. The stereotypical image of the narco for many years has been a cowboy-type image complete with a cowboy hat, boots made from exotic hide, and silky shirts with gold jewelry. Some variations of this image include a large sombrero, tacky belt buckles, and long elongated boots. Many of these images are meant to mimic the image of the prosperous cattle ranchers or *rancheros* in Mexico. Drug war analysts have noticed a notable change in the style and dress of many of the high-profile drug cartel leaders. Some of the current narco chic styles of fashion among younger leaders include polo-style athletic shirts, fashionable boutique brand shirts like Ed Hardy, Nike brand tennis shoes, and clothing decorated with narco culture terminology.

References

Agren, David, Mexico's baby gangsters, *Maclean's*, February 4, 2013, Vol. 126, Issue 4, p. 1.

Associated Press, Killings grow more gruesome as Mexican drug-cartels try to out shock, October 10, 2011.

Beith, Malcom, *The last narco: Inside the hunt for El Chapo, the world's most wanted drug lord*, New York: Grover Press, 2011.

Bunker, Robert J., Narcocultura and spirituality: Narco saints, Santa Muerte and other entities, *Journal for the Study of Radicalism*, in progress.

Fiegel, Brenda, *The recruitment of assassins by Mexican drug cartels*, Foreign Military Studies Office Joint Intelligence Center, February 3, 2009.

El paso TIMES, Teen Drug smuggling Arrests Jump, March 30, 2009.

Finnegan, William, Silver or lead? *The New Yorker*, May 31, 2010.

Grayson, George W., *La Familia drug cartel: Implications for U.S.-Mexican security*, Strategic Studies Institute, December 2010.

Hartelius, Jonas, Narcoterrorism, Swedish Carnegie Institute, February 2008, http://www.ewi.info/pdf/Narcoterrorism%20FINAL13FEB.pdf

Jurgensmeyer, Mark. *Terror in the Mind of God: The Global Rise of Religious Violence*, University of California Press, 2003.

Longmire, Sylvia M., and John P. Longmire, Redefining terrorism: Why Mexican drug trafficking is more than just organized crime, *Journal of Strategic Strategy*, November 2008, Vol. 1, No. 1.

Mexico's deadly homage: The country must awaken to narcos' grip on its pop culture, *San Diego Union-Tribune*, March 31, 2009.

Mier, Manuel Suárez, The impact of narco communications on Mexican society, *Guera de Comunicacion*, December 19, 2012.

Morris, Evelyn Krache, Think again: Mexican drug cartels, *Foreign Policy*, November/December 2013, Issue 203, pp. 30–33.

Naval Postgraduate School, *Violent Mexican transnational criminal organizations in Texas: Political discourse and an argument for reality.*

Palafox, Galia Garcia, Sinaloa cartel approves Movimiento Alterado's drug ballads, *Huffington Post*, December 21, 2011.

Peikov, Rodolfo, Narcoterrorism, International Institute for Security and Cooperation, December 9, 2009.

Rockwell, Natalia Mendoza, Boots, belt buckles and sombreros: Narco culture in the Altar desert, NACLA Report on the Americas, May/June 2011, Vol. 44, Issue 3, pp. 27–30.

Rush, Matthew, *Violent Mexican Transnational Criminal Organizations in Texas: Political discourse and an argument for reality.* Naval Postgraduate School, Monterey, CA: Pennyhill Press, 2012.

Salmani, Barak A., and Paula Holmes-Eber, *Operational culture for the war-fighter*, Marine Corps University Press: Quantico, VA, 2009.

chapter two

Narco-cults

In 2009, Mexican Federal Police Commissioner Facundo Rosas warned the Mexican press of the danger of an explosive mixture of religion and criminal activity. Likewise, American military analysts have recently noted a growth of movements known as spiritual insurgencies. Spiritual insurgencies refer to revolutionary movements that are motivated by spiritual agendas. New religious movements that exhibit violence also fall under this label. Historically, many rebellions that have appeared to be strictly grievances against authorities have also contained elements of spirituality. Rebels that see violence as a holy struggle between the forces of good and evil have a sacred form of motivation. This motivation can affect the how, when, and where of attacks or criminal activity among those with a spiritual agenda.

Some of the cartels, such as La Familia Michoacana and Los Caballeros Templarios, that combine spiritual goals with the desire to make money from the drug trade could be considered forms of spiritual insurgencies.

In his testimony before the House Foreign Affairs Subcommittee on the Western Hemisphere in 2011, Dr. Robert Bunker spoke about the growth of a spiritual insurgency among the Mexican drug cartels. Bunker shares that there is a cultural shift into narco culture that results in a spirituality that includes a belief in spiritual protection and a higher morality by members of the narcotics trade. This cultural shift creates a spiritual insurgency that promotes not only criminal activity and lawlessness, but also a twisted form of ethics. Bunker went on to explain that the growth of this combination of spiritual beliefs and cartel agenda could eventually result in true believers who commit acts of martyrdom for God and cartel, much like Al Qaeda terrorists.

The U.S. military has taken notice of the importance of recognizing religion as a factor in war. Lt. Col. Prisco Hernandez of the U.S. Army writes that religion can be used as a powerful weapon in times of war. Hernandez lists two conditions that are necessary for religion to be used as a weapon. The first is to have a community of believers who are willing to take action based on a shared belief. The second condition is that this same community of believers must view their belief as a liberating force from oppression. In the hands of drug traffickers, religion has and will continue to be a growing weapon in the war on drugs. Sociologist

Mark Juergensmeyer concludes that "religion gives moral justification for killing and provides images of cosmic war that allow activists to believe they are waging spiritual scenarios" (Juergensmeyer, 2003).

Defining narco-cults

Just as there has been an entire narco culture built around the cartels, there have been a number of spiritual movements that have originated within the cartel subculture. These spiritual movements fulfill a number of spiritual and psychological needs among cartel members. In many cases, the culture of world religions and spiritual traditions has been "hijacked" by members of the drug trade.

The use of the word *cult* presents an issue when dealing with religious groups. The term itself has several different meanings according to the worldview of the beholder. In many instances, the term is viewed as a criticism or slanderous description of an unfamiliar religious group.

However, this text will use the term *cult* to refer to an institution as described by American anthropologist Anthony F.C. Wallace. Wallace describes the cult institution as "a set of rituals all having the same general goal, all explicitly rationalized by a set of similar or related beliefs and all supported by the same social group." Wallace goes on to describe four types of cult institutions:

Individualistic cults: As the most simplistic form of cult, the individualistic cult operates without any specific type of religious specialists. Individuals are able to interact with the supernatural world and with supernatural forces without any assistance of a spiritual leader. Rituals are performed by the individual when necessary. Examples of this can be seen in the use of folk saint worship of Santa Muerte and Jesus Malverde on an individual basis by smugglers needing spiritual protection.

Shamanistic cults: Shamanistic cults are characterized by the organization recognizing a religious specialist who is born with abilities to interact with supernatural forces. The religious specialist has the ability to perform rituals that include healing, divination, and spell casting. In the shamanistic cult there is a distinction between the religious specialist and the layman. Typically the shaman works in a part-time capacity and may charge for his spiritual services. This can be seen in the use of *curanderos* and *santeros* by individuals and groups as spiritual advisors to narco groups and individuals.

Communal cults: Communal cults have more elaborate beliefs and practices than the shamanistic cults. Communal cults are operated by laymen who are responsible for various rituals according to a

Figure 2.1 Narco-cult symbols. Religious cultures are being hijacked by members of drug trafficking organizations to provide spiritual and psychological empowerment.

religious calendar or as an occasional event. Various social groups are recognized according to age, gender, or kin. Some members may belong to secret societies operating within the cult. Some Santería-based houses can be considered communal cults, as they have established seasonal rituals and specific ritual specialists and elders have specific roles in the temple.

Ecclesiastical cults: Ecclesiastical cults are the most complex forms of cult institutions. The groups recognize the office of a full-time clergy and professional religious specialists. Leadership members of ecclesiastical cults do not act as private entrepreneurs such as shamans, but are formally elected or appointed. Members of the clergy are responsible for performing rituals and ceremonies for individuals, groups, and the whole community. There is a clear distinction between clergy and laymen in these groups. La Familia

Figure 2.2 Witchcraft. This example of a magical working illustrates the use of witchcraft as a means of controlling. The plate contains the names of individuals submerged in urine. This is believed to exert control over those listed on the paper.

> Michoacana is an example of a narco-cult that observes various offices of spiritual leadership that serve the organization on a full-time basis.

Using Wallace's anthropological model of cults as a basis, I propose defining *narco-cult* as follows:

> An individualistic, shamanistic, communal or ecclesiastical cult that functions as a source of spiritual or psychological empowerment for individuals or organizations connected to drug production or trafficking.

The function of the narco-cult

The narco-cult provides several functions for drug trafficking organizations. Participation in the cult provides psychological, social, and spiritual functions for the trafficker. The glamor of the drug subculture focuses on a life of materialism that puts monetary gain above the basic fundamental needs of human life. Psychologist Tim Kasser states in his *High Price of Materialism* that "research shows that materialism—the pursuit of money and possessions, of a life-style based on the consumption of market goods

Figure 2.3 Protection. This ritual vessel, known as the *nganga* in the religion of Palo Mayombe, was appropriated by a drug trafficker to protect his cocaine trade.

and services—seems to breed not happiness but dissatisfaction, depression, anxiety, anger, isolation, and alienation."

Spirituality brings about a therapy for stresses related to the pursuit of materialism and the life of violence that many cartel members experience. It also provides meaning for those who are searching for identity and purpose.

Order

Some practices utilized by members of narco-cults may be characterized by local societies as witchcraft. These practices are not to be confused with the contemporary practices of neo-pagan witchcraft or Wicca. In the African and Latin American cultural context, witchcraft is a form of power that can be bought and used by any level of society.

Figures 2.4 and 2.5 Protection from the law. The top image is of a Santa Muerte shrine used to protect the operation of a brothel. The bottom image is a shrine to Saint Judas used to protect a member of the narcotics trade.

Figure 2.6 Protection for the law. This image of a Mexican federal police officer shows the officer wearing an amulet of Santa Muerte. While there are many narco traffickers who worship the death saint, there are many who are law-abiding citizens who seek protection from her as well.

The belief in witchcraft serves a number of psychological and social functions. It is particularly powerful in the atmosphere of social disorder. In the world of violence, drugs, and crisis, witchcraft can provide a means of reducing fears. Witchcraft provides a spiritual empowerment. Rituals may also reduce the anxiety of those involved in the daily stresses of the drug war. Witchcraft provides the ability to manipulate the supernatural against enemies.

Witchcraft can also provide a means of alleviating suffering caused by financial hardships or social conflict. Rituals that promise financial success from the spiritual realm can be performed by clergy or laymen.

Figures 2.7 and 2.8 Matamoros. One of the first documented narco-cults was discovered by American and Mexican law enforcement in 1989. Members of a drug
trafficking organization appropriated elements of Afro-Caribbean and Latin religious cultures to protect their drug trade. Rivals and innocent bystanders were
murdered and placed inside ritual vessels to propitiate the spirits.

One traditional Mexican healer shared that many Mexican citizens are
seeking spiritual assistance from healers and ritual experts because they fear
threats and extortion. Witchcraft may provide assistance to those involved in
the drug trade as well as those seeking shelter from the drug trade.

Ethics

Some narco-cults have their own code of ethics. La Familia Michoacana (LFM) has a written set of rules based on the teachings of the group's founder. Violations of the group's code of ethics results in discipline by group leadership. The first violation of the code results in a severe beating. The second violation of the code brings about a more severe beating and isolation. The third violation is punished by execution.

Protection

Consider the following story: A Cuban Santería priest speaks into a two-way radio as three Hispanic men cross over the border into Arizona. One of the men, who is transporting drugs under his clothes, wears several multicolored Santería necklaces (*elekes*). The man responds to the priest on the radio as a U.S. Border Patrol agent begins to follow him. As the "coyotes" begin to run from the agent, the agent draws his weapon and aims it at the smugglers. As the priest whispers an incantation into the radio, the agent mysteriously disappears into thin air. The men jump into the agent's truck and drive away as the priest kneels before the image of Elegua, a Santería deity who is believed to be the owner of fate and the crossroads. Images of drug smugglers bowing in front of statues of saints and figures like Santa Muerte are seen as music begins to play away in the background.

This is a scene from a popular narco music video called La Clika Del Elegua from Mexican musician El Pelon Avile. The video is a perfect depiction of how spiritual traditions are used by modern-day drug smugglers for protection in the drug war.

As Mexico is ground zero in the drug war, the reliance on spirituality and religion is cherished in Mexican culture. Parallel to those seeking refuge in traditional world religions, there is a segment of the population that finds solace in the realm of the metaphysical. Some Mexican politicians have demonstrated their beliefs in the power of metaphysical religions.

Elba Esther, also known as La Maestra, the leader of Mexico's powerful teacher's union Sindicato Nacional de Trabajadores de la Educacion (SANTE), became infamous as Mexico's most hated woman. Esther was made union boss by President Carols Salinas de Gortari. Her reputation for spending frivolous amounts of money on her family and friends, as well as her tenacious attitude, earned her much dislike from the Mexican public. As President Ernesto Zedillo came into office, Esther learned that she would be removed from her position by the newly elected president. Esther is alleged to have sought spiritual assistance from African religious specialists in Morocco and Nigeria.

Esther was alleged to have been bathed in the blood of a lion that was slowly tortured and sacrificed in order to give her spiritual protection from the newly elected president.

The heavy scent of spirituality among the cartels is so prevalent that some members of law enforcement have sought shelter in magical religions for protection. Members of the Mexican police have been documented in the media as undergoing various rituals for protection from the cartels. Some officers have even had tattoos of sacred religious symbols placed on their bodies to give them magical protection. One officer in Tijuana shared that his tattoos gave him protection from bullets that killed his comrades during a gunfight.

Consider this story from Reuters:

> Police running scared from drug gangs in one of Mexico's deadliest cities are using bizarre rituals involving animal sacrifice and spirit tattoos to seek protection from raging violence on the U.S. border.
>
> In secret meetings that draw on elements of Haitian Voodoo, Cuban Santeria and Mexican witchcraft, priests are slaughtering chickens on full moon nights on beaches, smearing police with the blood and using prayers to evoke spirits to guard them as drug cartels battle over smuggling routes into California.
>
> Other police in the city of Tijuana, across the border from San Diego, tattoo their bodies with Voodoo symbols, believing they can repel bullets. "Sometimes a man needs another type of faith," said former Tijuana policeman Marcos, who left the city force a year ago after surviving a drug gang attack. "I was saved when they killed two of my mates. I know why I didn't die."
>
> Violence has exploded along the U.S. border since President Felipe Calderon set the army on drug cartels in late 2006. Turf wars have killed 19,000 people across Mexico over three years.
>
> Badly paid Mexican police have long prayed to Christian saints before going out on patrol in Mexico, the world's second-most populous Roman Catholic country after Brazil.
>
> Cops are part of a messy war between rival trafficking gangs and the army as cartels infiltrate police forces, offering officers cash to work and even

murder for them or a bullet if they say no. More than 150 police are among those killed in Tijuana and the surrounding Baja California state since 2007.

Army raids on homes of police working for cartels have found ornately adorned Santeria-type altars covered with statues and skulls stuffed with money paying homage to gods and spirits.

"We all know that guns and body armor are useless against the cartels because they are well-armed and can attack any time. But this is something we can believe in, that really works," said a Tijuana-based policeman called Daniel.

Black Magic

A battle between top drug lord fugitive Joaquin "Shorty" Guzman and the local Arellano Felix drug clan has wrecked tourism in Tijuana and shuttered manufacturing businesses.

Small groups of police in the city started turning to strange rituals about 18 months ago, a practice spotted when municipal cleaners found a trail of dead chickens on beaches.

Priests and police say the animal sacrifices release life to rejuvenate spirits that will shield officers against hitmen. They believe the effects are intensified on full moon nights.

Many police see a need to shield themselves from witchcraft used by drug gangs who mix Caribbean black magic and occultism from southern Mexico using things like human bones, dead bats and snake fangs to curse enemies and unleash evil spirits.

Others worship the Mexican cult of "Saint Death", a skeletal grim reaper draped in white and carrying a scythe.

The rituals are carried out by sometimes shadowy Mexicans who have menial day jobs and are priests by night. They claim to be trained in Voodoo, Santeria and other religions from time spent in the Caribbean and in Mexican towns like Catemaco, a center for witchcraft on the Gulf of Mexico.

Police have the quiet support of their superiors.

> "We know some agents use charms, saints
> and other methods for their protection," said Baja
> California federal police chief Elias Alvarez. "They
> look for something to believe in."
> Mexico's often poorly armed police are intimi-
> dated by hitmen with automatic rifles, grenades
> and rocket launchers and despite low wages of
> around $300 a month some pay up to $160 for a tat-
> too of a Voodoo spirit like the three-horned Bosou
> Koblamin who protects his followers when they
> travel at night.

Some members of cartels attach themselves to belief systems and
symbols that are considered evil and dangerous by many in mainstream Mexican society. The term *narcosatánicos* was frequently used in
the 1980s to refer to members of the drug trade who allegedly worship
Satan. Mexican authorities who have sought spiritual protection claim
that the cartels have aligned themselves with these malevolent powers. Some police officers claim that the spiritual protection they have
received has given them the ability to locate criminals and drugs as well
as provided protection from violence. Some of the officers even wear
magical amulets for personal protection while on duty. For example,
while the image of Santa Muerte is favored by many criminals seeking protection from the spirit of death, the image is also worn by many
police officers in Mexico, as death is a constant guest to both the police
and criminal.

The business of protecting drug traffickers

There are an increasing number of cases in which religious specialists are
being used to provide spiritual services for drug traffickers. Some cases
involve the consulting of clergy that typically make their services available to the public through spiritual supply stores, and in some cases clergy
strictly dedicated to one organization are utilized.

In some cases, ritual specialists have become victims of violence and extortion at the hands of the cartels. *New York Times* reporter Karla Zabludovsky
reported that self-proclaimed warlock John Joseph said that he has received
calls from members of cartels such as Los Zetas demanding money from
magic practitioners who perform readings and spiritual services.

Some documented cases in which specialists were used include
the following.

In August 2002, authorities in Nuevo Laredo, Mexico, arrested
Enrique Sánchez Rodriguez for the murder of Patricia Elizabeth Sánchez.

Rodriguez claims that he murdered the woman because he needed to free a drug trafficker from prison. Rodriguez told authorities, "My soul belongs to the devil and I am in the service to the Mafia." Rodriguez went on to say that he had to commit the sacrifice at the time that he did because "this year was the largest moon in history and lasted seven days. The new moon is ending and required me to present offerings or sacrifices." He later admitted to sacrficing cats and dogs. Rodriguez claimed to be a Nagual, a pre-Colombian term for someone who can turn into an animal. In contemporary Mexico, the term is synonamous for *brujo*, or "witch."

Self-proclaimed sorcerer Jose Alberto Vera Cisneros shares a story in which a person claiming to be a member of a drug trafficking organization was imprisoned in Mazanillo, Mexico. The prisoner called and asked Cisneros to perform a ritual to get him released from prison. Cisneros performed a ritual calling on the spiritual to set the man free. After being released from the prison, the drug dealer gave Cisneros a car as a reward for his magical services.

The 2013 trial of Mexican cartel member Jose Trevino Morales in Austin, Texas, revealed a slight look into the use of Santería by members of the Los Zetas cartel. Morales was on trial for charges of money laundering involving the use of a racehorse operation in Lexington, Oklahoma. Funds were being fed into the operation from Mexico on behalf of the Los Zetas cartel. Morales was arrested in 2012 by the FBI and found guilty of money laundering in May 2013. During the trial it was revealed that a witness in the case had received a shipment of cigars from defendant and cartel member Colorado Cessa. The witness was questioned about the shipment of cigars and revealed "He (Cessa) sent me cigars because of my faith. Santeria is based on the Lucumi beliefs of the Yoruba in Africa then it came to Cuba with slaves. I sent people to do a cleaning on the part of Colorado."

LFM leader Gomez Martinez, known as La Tuta, was believed to have sought the services of Juan "El Brujo" Victor and Fernandez "The Witch" Castaneda as personal sorcerers to consult the spirit world in order to find out how to hide from police, what kinds of deals to make, and the names of traitors of the organization. Martinez relied so heavily on the magical services of the occultists in one case that he sent out enforcers to murder informants based upon the information provided by the occultist.

Mexico is not the only country where this practice is performed. In 2011, members of the Revolutionary Armed Forces of Colombia (FARC) organization used the services of a witch to predict military actions as well as to place a spell against the leader of the national police. The group claimed they used the clairvoyant services of the witch to predict and report police activity against the group.

Protection from law enforcement

One of the functions that narco-cult spirituality provides is protection from law enforcement. Spiritual powers are called upon to prevent detection from the police. There are a growing number of mass-produced artifacts and ritual implements that are being manufactured to aid in magical rituals seeking protection from law enforcement. Items such as the popular candles and oils labeled "Law stay away" are available in many spiritual supply shops. Some of the statues and icons used to represent folk saints, including Santa Muerte and Jesus Malverde, are kept for protection from authorities.

There are a number of rituals that are shared orally and found in written texts that are performed for protection from authorities. Many of these rituals are traditionally performed for general protection from enemies and have been customized to protect practitioners from law enforcement.

One of the most notorious examples of a narco-cult can be found in the 1989 case in Matamoros, Mexico, where Cuban-born Adolfo de Constanzo utilized practices taken from the Kongo-based Palo Mayombe religion combined with elements of Mexican brujería as a form of spiritual protection from authorities. Members of the sect murdered rival drug dealers and an American college student. Victims were tortured and dismembered, with many of their remains placed in shrines.

In May 2012, members of the Spanish Civil Guard conducted Operation Garnacha, which targeted members of a network who were responsible for trafficking hashish into Central Europe from Morocco. Members of the network consulted Santería priests for spiritual guidance. Priests would consult the spirits to identify locations for distribution and to locate ideal meeting spots for dealers and customers. When law enforcement would apprehend members of the network, Santería ritual specialists would perform rituals to remove "bad luck" from their clients.

In November 2013 a group of five men in Brownsville, Texas, pled guilty to charges of conspiring to transport over 1,000 pounds of marijuana, which was hijacked from the men. One of the men hired the services of a santero to perform rituals that would bless the 1,000-pound shipment that was destined for Houston, Texas. The following day, the priest and the five men performed a ritual to ensure the shipment would be safe. Unfortunately, the rituals did not work, as during the transporting of the marijuana in tractor trailers a group of unknown individuals stole the shipments.

Protection from rivals

Narco-cults may utilize various spiritual practices in order to seek protection from rival cartels and organizations. Rituals may be performed to stop the activities of rival gangs and to protect members of the group from rival violence. Rival organizations may wage spiritual war against each other utilizing religious practices.

Additional functions

Narco-cults may provide a number of functions for the drug trade, including providing a structured organization through which to oper-ate. Spirituality can bring additional social bonds to organizations, where members not only are financially obligated to protect each other, but also are spiritually obligated. Narco-cult organizations can provide a structure that may be used as an avenue of distribution for narcotics and illegal services. In 1993 the Bureau of Alcohol, Tobacco and Firearms (BATF) con-ducted an undercover operation in which federal agent Julie Torres infil-trated an *ile*, or "house," of Santería practitioners. The temple was used as a distribution point for selling arms.

Indoctrination

There are several forms of indoctrination that are utilized by some narco-cults. Some groups use techniques that are commonly found in coercive groups, such as religious cults and terrorist organizations. These tech-niques focus on controlling human behavior. The process of manipula-tion seeks to replace a subject's personality with that of the narco-cult personality. Techniques may include rewards and punishments used to modify behavior, the use of rules and regulations, and internalization of the group's concept of reality.

The indoctrination process into La Familia Michoacana (LFM) includes being fed information from the Bible, propaganda videos, and group literature. In some of the cartel's rehab centers designed to help those with addictions, potential members are bombarded with informa-tion for several weeks in order to teach the benefits of joining the cartel. The group, however, refrains from using the word *cartel*, as they want to be depicted as a public service organization.

Dr. George W. Grayson of the Strategic Studies Institute shares about the group's indoctrination process in his report *La Familia Drug Cartel: Implications for U.S.-Mexican Security*:

> To begin with recruits must clean up their lives by throwing off any drug or alcohol addiction they may have. Before his April 2009 arrest at a baptism, Rafael 'El Cede' Cedeño Hernández, a self-described pastor and an observer on the state's human rights commission, took charge of indoctrination. He

designed the 6- to 8-week intensive educational programs, selected the texts and videos used as part of the brainwashing, and required periodic vows of silence by the class members as if they were religious brothers and sisters. Days without talking supposedly enhanced spiritual concentration and facilitated the individual's sense of solidarity, thankfulness, altruism and complete loyalty to La Familia's leaders. Caricatures represented the three stages in the neophytes' right of passage. The first portrayed anger and deception (Así venía), the second revealed interest [in changing one's life] (Me interesé), and the third depicted total joys.

Types of narco-cults

The bases of spirituality among the narco-cults may differ among groups. Narco-cults may be formed around a number of spiritual traditions, ranging from African traditional religions to evangelical Christianity.

There appear to be three common forms of spirituality that are commonly used by narco-cults:

Afro-Caribbean religious traditions: This includes appropriation of religions such as Cuban Santería, Palo Mayombe and Bantu traditions, and Dominican and Haitian voodoo.

Mexican folk religions and practices: This includes appropriation of Aztec and Mayan religious culture, folk Catholicism, curanderismo spirituality, and brujería.

Judeo-Christian religions: This includes appropriation of Judeo-Christian aesthetics, rituals, and sacred texts.

References

Acosta, Juan Pablo Becerra M., Herramienta poco ortodoxa: Santeria contra el narco, *Milienio*, April 12, 2011.

Agren, David, Mexican officials probe drug alms to churches, *The Catholic Voice*, November 8, 2010, Vol. 48, No. 19.

Bunker, Robert J., Criminal (cartel and gang) insurgencies in Mexico and the Americas: What you need to know, not what you want to hear, testimony before the House Foreign Affairs Subcommittee on the Western Hemisphere at the Hearing "Has Merida Evolved? Part One: The Evolution of Drug Cartels and the Threat to Mexico's Governance," September 13, 2011.

Diaz, Lizbeth, *Mexican Police ask Spirits to guard them in Drug War*, Reuters, March 19, 2010.

Grayson, George W., *La Familia Drug Cartel: Implications for U.S.–Mexican Security*, Strategic Studies Institute Publications, December, 2010.

Gomez, Francisco, La tuta, bajo la guia de un brujo, *El Universal*, November 7, 2009.

Hernandez, Lt. Col. Prisco R., Dealing with absolutes: Religion, the operational environment and the art of design, *Military Review*, November-December 2010.

Juergensmeyer, Mark, *Terror in the mind of God*, University of California Press, 2003.

Kasser, Tim, *High Price of Materialism*, Bradford Books, Cambridge Mass, 2003.

León, Luis D., *La Llorona's children: Religion, life and death in the U.S. Mexican borderlands*, Oakland, CA: University of California Press.

Ramirez, Miguel, *Soy nagual, oli su sangre y la sacrifiqué*, Laredo Morning Times, No Date Available, Accessed at: http://madmax.lmtonline.com/textarchives/081602/t1.htm

Schneider, Jane, and Peter Schneider, Mafia, antimafia and the plural cultures of Sicily, *Current Anthropology*, 2005, Vol. 46, No. 4, pp. 501–520.

Wallace, Anthony F. C. *Humanity: An Introduction to Cultural anthropology*, Peoples, James and Garrick Bailey, eds., Cengage Advantages Books. Independence, Ky: Wadsworth Publishing, 2008.

chapter three

The role of religious culture in narco-cult investigation

The importance of culture

Cultural influences such as heritage, religion, languages, and folk traditions bind members of a culture to their cultural identity. Officers working cases involving members of the narco culture will find themselves dealing with a number of cultural influences that affect behavior and evidence found at crime and incident scenes. Culture can affect customs and practices that a suspect may participate in.

Culture can affect:

Suspect behavior and mindset
How a suspect may react to specific circumstances
How the suspect carries out noncriminal activities
How the suspect carries out criminal activities

Defining culture

Culture is a shared set of traditions, beliefs systems, and behaviors. Culture affects human behavior. Among social scientists in the U.S. military, culture is likened to terrain. Culture is viewed much like geographic landscape that can affect a soldier's ability to move. Culture affects the soldier's tactics and can provide insight into an enemy's mindset, as well as the culture of an ally. Without cultural awareness, the U.S. military has discovered that soldiers can increase animosity among the people they are working with and can lead to an ignorance of an enemy's cultural motivation.

Law enforcement officers can also look at the human terrain on the streets and in investigations. Culture will affect the behaviors of individuals. Street gang investigators can attest to the impact that gang culture can have on a person's dress, language, and customs. Culture dictates the material objects used by members of a culture. Narcotics officers can attest to the frequent discovery of water pipes, rolling papers, and scales among members of the drug culture. Understanding the culture can give officers insight into the meaning behind objects at scenes. Culture affects social networks and social positions. Vice investigators can attest to the networks of pimps and prostitutes that are part of the sex trade. Understanding the culture can give officers insight into the social networks of suspects.

In order for officers to understand how criminals are using culture, they must first understand the culture. The U.S. military has seen the benefit of understanding culture as found in the program known as the Human Terrain System (HTS). This program involves the use of anthropologists and social scientists to help the military understand the culture in which they are working. Soldiers are educated about the various regional cultures in their area of operation. This allows them to understand customs, behaviors, symbols, and language.

Cultural competency

A degree of cultural competency is needed in order to decode and analyze the use of culture by criminals. Cultural competency has been defined as a "set of values and principles, and demonstrative behaviors, attitude policies and structures that enable organizations to operate cross culturally." While it is not expected for officers to become religious experts, it is important that they grasp the fundamental aspects of culture in order to understand narco-cults as well as various noncriminal groups they may encounter.

Many of the cultural practices and icons used among narco-cults can appear very similar and can be confusing to investigators unfamiliar with the culture. For example, the aesthetics and practices of Cuban-based Santería may appear similar to the practices of Haitian voodoo, while the two are entirely different cultures. The discipline of cultural anthropology teaches that there are two different perspectives from which one can view culture. The *etic* perspective involves looking at a culture from the outside, while the *emic* perspective looks at culture from the inside. It is necessary for investigators to understand the emic (inside) perspective of culture in order to understand the reason why a particular ritual is performed or why a certain artifact is found at a scene.

Officers must be able to look at a culture within its cultural context. For example, an outsider can look at an officer's use of takedown lights and a pat-down as a form of disrespect while claiming the officer is infringing on his rights. The culture of police work teaches that these two techniques are used to ensure officer safety. It is only within the cultural context that these techniques can be understood.

Some basic concepts taken from the discipline of cultural anthropology can help officers identify commonalities among various cultures in order to understand their practices, symbols, and beliefs.

Figure 3.1 Culture shock. Officers who encounter unfamiliar religious scenarios may suffer from culture shock. Officers may feel a sense of disorientation or even fear. If necessary, an officer may feel the need for another officer to assist with a scene that may evoke emotions that might keep the officer from being effective at the scene.

Culture shock

Law enforcement training prepares officers for encounters with common scenarios. Most of the environments that officers will encounter are familiar territories. What happens when officers encounter a scene or evidence of a ritualistic nature that they have never encountered before?

Culture shock occurs when people encounter environments, languages, and cultures that are unfamiliar. Culture shock can cause internal stress and can affect human behavior. Officers that encounter scenes of a cultural nature may undergo stress. The unfamiliarity with these cultures combined with personal fears, beliefs, or animosity toward other cultures can affect an officer's performance. Therefore, it is important that officers familiarize themselves with cultures that they may encounter on the job. Cultural anthropology can help officers understand the cultures that they may encounter.

Supervisors and fellow officers should never underestimate the mental stresses that working scenes and cases involving these cultures can exert on officers. Officers from specific ethnic or religious backgrounds may have an aversion to these cultures. If these aspects affect the performance

Figure 3.2 Prayer and ritual. A Santería priestess consults the orishas for spiritual guidance.

of an officer's duties, supervisors may be encouraged to reassign cases to other officers.

The aesthetic appearance of some ritual scenes can be a little overwhelming for those unfamiliar with these cultures. I am reminded of a training class that I was conducting for detectives. I used a video that shows a woman performing a specific ritual that included an act of self-mutilation. As the woman began to pour her blood into a cup, a detective in the class spoke up. "We've got a man down!" he yelled. The lights came up and I could see one of the attendees lying on the floor. After emergency workers responded to the fainting officer, the detective told me, "I wasn't expecting that. It was just to much for me." While the incident was quite surprising to me, as it was to the detective who passed out, it serves as a reminder that culture shock is a very real phenomenon and can affect anyone.

Some officers that encounter scenes of a cultural nature may feel the need to seek personal spiritual protection. Officers may pray, hold personal religious objects, or just need a moment to step away from the scene. As long as this personal reflection does not affect the effectiveness of the officer or disturb the scene, it can help maintain a healthy state of mind for officers. Officers who feel personally spiritually motivated

Figure 3.3 Dark images. While some of the Afro-Caribbean religions and Latin religious cultures may have sinister-appearing images to those unfamiliar with them, they are not the same as Satanism. Although this image appears dark, it is actually used to represent a spirit in the religion of Haitian voodoo.

to destroy evidence at scenes or disturb artifacts that are not related to the crime should be encouraged to step away from the scene or leave if possible.

Family resemblances

The term *family resemblances* has been used by religious scholars and philosophers to describe common elements found in religious cultures. These family resemblances can be seen in the religions that we will be discussing in this book.

Some of the common elements that we see in religious culture include:

Belief in supernatural or superior beings: Supernatural beings may be referred to as gods, angels, demons, or spirits, or by cultural-specific names, such as the deities of Santería known as orisha or the spirits of Palo Mayombe known as the mpungu.

The significance of human life: Religion gives meaning to life. Each person is created for a reason that is dictated by the religious culture. For

Figure 3.4 Healer's table. African traditional religious specialist's table of herbs, roots, glass, and various materials used to treat clients with the aid of the ancestors.

instance, the religion of Santería teaches that man is born to serve the orishas (deities) and that each person has a guardian orisha.

A moral code: Religious beliefs surrounding a moral code seek to give guidelines for personal ethics.

An account of evil: Most religions have a form of evil or opposition. In a devotee's view, evil may be the cause of a physical illness. The practice of curanderismo teaches that the *mal de ojo,* or "evil eye," can cause sickness.

Prayer and ritual: These serve as tools for human interaction with the supernatural. Officers may encounter shrines and sites used for prayer and rituals.

Sacred objects and places: Religious objects may be used in concert with ritual and prayer to interact with the supernatural. Objects may also be worn by devotees to protect them from harm. Officers may encounter shrines where religious ceremonies take place.

Religious experience, such as awe and mysticism: Religious experiences may be personal or communal. For example, members of a Santa Muerte temple may gather on a specific day to pray to the saint of death.

Figure 3.5 This is a contemporary image of the African deity Shango. Shango is honored as a divinity among the Yoruba of Nigeria and the Fon in West African voodoo.

Institutionalized social sharing of some of these traits: The organized social sharing of a religion may be called a church or a temple. Examples of this are temples in Mexico where the members of Los Caballeros Templarios meet for rituals.

Sources of cultural intelligence

Historically law enforcement agencies have struggled to maintain a balance when dealing with religious organizations. The 1980s were labeled by social scientists as the Satanic Panic, a time marred with conspiracies that promoted theories that large-scale criminal organizations involved in Satanism were a major criminal threat to law enforcement and society. During this period, a large amount of inaccurate information regarding religious cultures was shared among many in the law enforcement community. Information from biased sources with religious agendas was promoted by some to the law enforcement community. Training for law enforcement became tainted with theological worldviews. Many of the Afro-Caribbean and Latin religious cultures were presented erroneously

Figure 3.6 Law of similarity. This doll was used by a group of Surenos gang members who hired a Santería priest (*santero*) to perform a spiritual working on members of their rival gang, the Nortenos. (Courtesy New Jersey Gang Investigator's Association.)

as forms of Satanism and as deviant practices. Religious culture should be analyzed in an objective manner that does not seek to discredit or promote a particular worldview.

Information in this text is gained from a number of sources. Investigators should also consult some of the following sources when performing research on religious cultures:

Ethnographic research: Ethnography is taken from the words *ethno*, meaning "people," and *graphy*, meaning "writing." Anthropologists and cultural researchers perform fieldwork among various cultures and document their observations in the form of ethnographies.

Figure 3.7 Law of contact. The shoes in this particular working belong to an abusive spouse. The devotee placed them in a shrine to the orishas in order for the deities to affect the abuser.

The daily life and customs of cultures are documented and compiled. These are very helpful to investigators in understanding the mechanics of culture and how a particular society may operate.

Law enforcement reports: Crimes and incidents documented by agencies can give investigators information on incidents involving individuals and organizations with ties to religious cultures.

Sacred texts: The teachings and practices of a religious culture may appear in written form as sacred texts. These may appear in the form of bibles, spiritual diaries, and manifestos. They may include narratives about important spiritual figures and myths important to religious faith. The text may contain teachings that are meant to be taken literally or metaphorically.

Scholarly literature: Academic texts that contain observations from various disciplines and sources. The texts are written for professional audiences and are usually carefully evaluated before publication.

Interviews with current and former practitioners: In order to develop accurate information about a religious culture, it is important to speak to practitioners. It is also important to get the total picture by speaking to former practitioners as well.

Figure 3.8 Tongue working. A popular spiritual working to keep someone from talking is to wrap a beef tongue shut.

Analyzing cultures

Investigators will find that there are specific cultural nuances in religious cultures that are only apparent when someone in immersed in the culture. These nuances may not be found in religious texts or from scholarly texts, but must be learned from exposure to members of the culture itself. Specific rituals and the secret (esoteric) meanings behind certain objects may only be learned by those immersed in these cultures.

Investigators may discover various interpretations of cultural elements, depending on the worldview of the subject that they encounter. For example, the Kongo-based religion of Palo Mayombe is referred to as brujería, or "witchcraft," among some members of Latin religious communities. However, this interpretation in based upon a specific cultural worldview. Devotees of the Palo Mayombe religion typically hold a different view of their religion. Officers should not make assumptions about a specific culture unless there is reliable evidence to base logical understanding on a specific worldview.

Cultural context

An officer's understanding of the context of how an element is used within a culture is very important. For example, investigators who encounter gang members using symbols of crosses in tattoos or at ritual scenes might be led to conclude that the symbols are affiliated with Catholic imagery. However, there are a number of African- and Latin-based religions that use crosses as well. Knowing the cultural importance to the suspect may provide leads to additional suspects or insights into the suspect's behavior. Culture affects the interpretation of symbols and behavior.

Anthropological terms

There are a number of anthropological terms used frequently in this text to describe elements of religious culture:

Artifacts: These are objects produced by a specific culture.

Ceremony: A formal act or set of acts established by custom as proper to a special occasion, such as a religious rite.

Cosmology: A set of knowledge and beliefs about the origins and evolution of the universe and the role and meaning of humans, life, and the world.

Deities: The gods and goddesses of a people.

Divination: The process of contacting the supernatural to find an answer to a question regarding the past, present, or future.

Folklore: The traditional beliefs, legends, sayings, and customs of a people.

Myth: A story from or about the past that is told and retold in order to express certain values.

Pantheon: A catalog of deities of a culture.

Ritual: Symbolic behavior associated with religion or magic that is repetitive, sequential, nonordinary, and believed to be powerful.

Sorcery: The use of supernatural power to inflict harm.

Symbol: An image used to express ideas too complex to explain directly.

Syncretism: The process of cultural change in which the traits and elements of one culture are given new meanings or new functions when they are adopted or adapted by another culture.

Taboo: A cultural rule of avoidance.

Worldview: How someone views the world around him or her.

Afro-Caribbean religious cultures and African traditional religions

The cultural basis for Afro-Caribbean religions is taken from the religions of traditional African societies. For example, the Yoruba religion from Central Africa serves as the basis of Afro-Caribbean religions such as Santería in Cuba, Venezuela, and the United States, Candomble and Macumba in Brazil, Shango in Trinidad, and Kele in St. Lucia. The Afro-Caribbean religions can trace their roots to African traditional religions.

African traditional religions are practiced among Sub-Saharan African peoples. Regardless of their contemporary manifestations in religions like Santería, Voodoo, and Palo Mayombe, these religions hold some very common elements. Most African traditional religions recognize a supreme deity. This is a creator being that is responsible for creating the world and human beings. In Kenya, the Kikuyu believe in a being known as Ngai, while the Yoruba of southwestern Nigeria recognize Olorun as the "owner of the heavens" and the creator of the world. The fierce Maasai warriors of Kenya follow a deity known as Enkai, the creator who gave the Maasai dominion over cattle This being can be seen among voodoo practitioners as Gran Met Bonye, among Santería practitioners as Olodumare, and among Palo Mayombe practitioners as Nsambi.

The second commonality that can be seen in African traditional religions is the reverence of ancestors. When someone dies, it is a common belief among African traditional religions that the spirit of the dead lives among the community. The ancestral spirits include the first leaders or founding ancestors of a particular group. While ranking less than the divinities of a people, these spirits are highly revered as spiritual powers. These spirits are believed to protect the tribal community from danger, bless members with fertility, and bless the people with animals and crops. The spirits of dead ancestors are revered and respected. Some groups have specific heroic figures in their tribal history that are recognized in the spiritual realm. It is believed that the dead can haunt and interfere with the lives of the living. In many African communities, shrines dedicated to ancestors are kept in homes and in villages. Food and drink may be left as offerings to ancestors, as they are believed to be extended members of a household. Ancestors may speak to members of the community through dreams or through local diviners. Ancestors are revered, as they are the keepers of tribal wisdom. Ancestors have the power to intervene in the lives of the living if the laws of the tribe are violated. Those who offend the ancestors are subject to disease, accident, and even death. This can be seen in Palo Mayombe as the Nfumbe and in Santería as the Eggun.

The third commonality that can be found among African traditional religions is the reverence of divinities. These spiritual beings are manifestations of the supreme being. The Fon people of Dahomey have spirits known as Vodun that are believed to be at work in the world. This is where we get the New World term *voodoo*. Spirits such as Mami Wata rule over natural elements in the world, such as water. The spirits known as the loa in Haitian voodoo, the orishas in Santería, and the mpungu in Palo Mayombe are all examples of these divinities.

The fourth commonality that can found among African traditional religions is the use of rites of passage and their New World manifestations as well. In African traditional religions, there are a number of rites that mark various stages of a person's life. Beginning at birth, children may be named after ancestors. In some African societies, the birth may be celebrated by rituals that include prayers, offerings, and songs. For example, among the Nandi tribe of Kenya, there are special feasts held in celebration of a child. The transition between boy and man in many African societies is marked by a rite of circumcision. In the Abaluhya tribe of Kenya, boys are placed in seclusion for a number of days after their circumcision and then painted with various substances before reentering society. A disguise is used in many African cultures to denote an expression of transition; in this case, the disguise symbolizes going from boys to men. Likewise, the use of separation, transition, and assimilation is a common pattern in African customs. In Maasai culture boys are expected to kill a lion with a spear in order to transition into manhood. There are also a number of rites performed for marriages, initiations, and funerals. These same types of rites of passage can be seen in the Afro-Caribbean religions.

The fifth commonality found among African traditional religions is the use of sacrifice. The offering of a sacrifice is a very important aspect of these religions. Sacrifices are physical offerings in exchange for spiritual work from a spiritual source. Sacrifices may be made to a supreme being, divinities, and ancestors. The Maasai of Kenya make a sacrifice of cattle known as Eunoto. The Dogon of Mali, West Africa, make sacrifices of various animals and birds six weeks before a funeral. These same sacrifices can be found in today's Afro-Caribbean religions as well.

Lastly, a commonality found among African traditional religion is the use of rituals and magic. Rituals may be performed to bring about a result, such as a good harvest, or to protect a household from spirits. The Bedik people of Senegal utilize a planting ritual to ensure a good harvest for the community. In this ritual, sacred masks are created from the bark of trees in the forest and worn by members of the community. The masked figures are believed to have the ability to chase away evil spirits and anything bringing discord to the community. There are a number of magical rituals used in the many Afro-Caribbean religions.

Magico-religious cultures

A number of narco-cults appropriate the culture and practices of magico-religious religions. The term *magico-religious* refers to a body of magical practices intended to cause a supernatural being to produce or prevent a specific result.

Magic is a set of techniques used to achieve a specific desire. Prayer, chanting, and other practices are employed to make changes in the spiritual world and in the physical world. For example, a drug trafficker faced with transporting drugs across the border may perform various magical practices in order for the shipment to go undetected. The trafficker may pray to a saint while he places an image of an American flag into a jar of honey. This is believed to magically "sweeten" the behavior of the American Customs and Border Patrol agents in hopes that they will not feel it necessary to search the vehicle for contraband.

There are a number of techniques that can be used by religious practitioners to produce magic. Magic is a personal or impersonal energy that can manipulated to produce tangible results. There are a number of varying cultural terms used to refer to magic. Mana, magick, and ache are just a few of the terms used by various cultures to describe a supernatural power or energy. Some cultures may simply refer to this power as power from God or power from various deities. Some cultures may refer to the use of magic by describing it by color. For example, magic that is performed for destructive purposes in many Latin communities is called black magic.

Occult historians speak of magic as having two forms. The first form is thaumaturgy, also known as lower magic. The word comes from the Greek words *thauma*, meaning "miracle," and *ergon*, meaning "work."

This is magic that is performed to influence everyday events such as those involving protection, love, and financial gain. For example, a practitioner might pray to the Bolivian spirit known as Ekkeko, who is known as the god of abundance. Ekkeko is believed by some practitioners to be able to bring about blessings of money and good luck.

The second form of magic, known as theurgy (aka higher magic), is performed to personally connect with a spiritual being. Devotees to a Santa Muerte temple may pray to connect with the spirit of death to feel comfort.

Spells and workings

A spell (also known as a working) is performed to send magic out to perform a specific function. The practice of performing spells is believed to work according to a religious philosophy that was founded in the sacred texts of the Hindu faith known as the Vedas.

The teaching of "as is above, so is below" is quoted in many different forms among magico-religious cultures. The philosophy teaches that whatever is done in the physical realm will affect the spiritual realm.

As a result of this popular philosophy, officers may discover various physical materials or components used in creating spells. There are two universal magical concepts that dictate how a practitioner would use these materials. The first concept is known as the law of contact, or contagious magic. This philosophy works on the principle that any item that has been in contact with someone can still affect that person. Officers may discover items such as hair, nails, or clothing placed in shrines and various sacred spaces. In one particular case, a pair of tennis shoes was found placed in a shrine in order to trap a man suspected of domestic abuse. The cultural informant shared that this would magically trap the abuser and keep him from harming his wife.

The second concept is known as the law of similarity, or sympathetic magic. The law of similarity works on the belief that any physical object that resembles a person can be used to affect the individual.

Officers may discover objects such as dolls or photographs that contain names or images that resemble the target of magic. In one particular case, members of a narcotics unit discovered that a practitioner of Mexican folk magic had created small dolls and had written the agents' names on them. While serving a search warrant, the agents discovered the dolls inside a shrine. The suspect in the case was hoping that the agents would be magically bound to keep them away from his narcotics activities.

Magical mindset

Officers may discover that the behavior patterns of subjects that hold a magic-based worldview may be affected by their perception of the supernatural. For those involved in magico-religious cultures and practices, the concept of magic is a very real phenomenon. However, this text is not an attempt to prove or disprove the reality of magic. Officers do not have to personally subscribe or dismiss a belief in magic, but should realize that the concept is very real to those who share a magical worldview.

Mental health professionals have observed that an individual's desire for control is an important motivator for superstitious behavior. This magical mindset can affect how criminal occultists view everyday life. The

Table 3.1 Afro-Caribbean Religions and their African Origins

Religion	Ethnic Origin	Regional Origin	Present Primary Location
Santeria (Regla de Ocha)	Yoruba	Southwest Nigeria	Cuba
Palo Mayombe (Las Reglas de Congo)	Bakongo (Bantu)	Congo (Central Africa)	Cuba
Voodoo	Fon	Dahomey (West Africa)	West Africa
Haitian Voodoo	Haiti	Fon	Dahomey (West Africa)
Dominican Voodoo (21 Divisions)	Fon	Dahomey (West Africa)	Dominican Republic
Ifá (Regla de Ifá)	Yoruba	Nigeria	Nigeria/Cuba
Lucumí	Yoruba	Nigeria	Cuba
Candomblé	Yoruba/Fon/ Bantu	Nigeria/West Africa/Central Africa	Brazil

magical worldview can make the devotee see a spiritual significance in issues relating to criminal acts and criminal justice. This can in turn affect how the subject deals with the spiritual.

Peter Brugger, head of neuropsychology at the University Hospital of Zurich, has discovered that individuals who participate in magical thinking have large amounts of dopamine, a neurotransmitter that the brain uses to tag experiences as magical. Individuals who perceive themselves as spiritually empowered or protected may exhibit behavior that is bold and risky.

The effect on drug traffickers

Those involved in the drug trade who subscribe to a belief in magic may see supernatural symbolism behind events and stresses. For example, a trafficker who successfully transports drugs to their destination without detection by police may feel that he or she is magically protected. A trafficker dealing with stress from the violence and chaos of the drug trade may seek magical direction from a religious specialist. Success or failure in manufacturing, transporting, and warring with rivals may be interpreted as a magical sign.

References

American Psychiatric Association, *Diagnostic and statistical manual of mental disorders*, 4th ed. (DSM-IV), APPI, Arlington, VA, 1994.

Brugger, Peter, *The 7 laws of magical thinking: How irrationality makes us Happy, Healthy, and Sane,* Hutson, Matthew, ed. London: One Wall Publishing, 2013.

Hutson, Michael, Magical thinking, *Psychology Today*, March 1, 2008.

National Center for Cultural Competence, Georgetown University Center for Child and Human Development, Washington, DC, http://www11.georgetown.edu/research/gucchd/nccc/foundations/frameworks.html

Strauss, Claude Levi, *Structural anthropology*, Basic Books, 1974.

Wittgenstein, Ludwig, *Philosophical investigations*, 3rd ed., Prentice Hall, Upper Saddle River, NJ, 1999.

Zabludovsky, Karla, Driven to cast charms against drug lords' darker forces, *New York Times*, November 1, 2011.

chapter four

Santería (Regla de Ocha)

The Afro-Caribbean religion of Santería, also known as Regla de Ocha, is practiced worldwide by millions. The religion can be found throughout the United States, Cuba, Puerto Rico, Venezuela, and Mexico. Santería first appeared in Mexico around 1950. Cuban entertainers, including actors and sports figures, introduced Mexico to the popular Cuban faith. Following the Cuban Revolution in 1959, several Cubans migrated into the United States and Mexico, bringing the religion with them.

The religion began to spread heavily in the 1960s throughout Mexico, with the establishment of public temples like the Templo Vudu Zambia Palo Monte in Mexico City. Santería became intertwined with elements from Mexican spiritism and folk Catholicism. Some researchers have found elements of Aztec, Mayan, and Olmec religions combined with the practices of Santería. The religion is also seen commonly mixed with New Age spirituality and various esoteric practices, including crystals, meditation, and tarot cards. Many adherents to the religions simply claim to follow Catholicism but practice the religion alongside traditional Catholic worship.

Today the religion is advertised in a number of Mexican print, television, and radio ads featuring priests and spiritual services for hire. Some informants have estimated that there could be close to 6,000 Santería devotees just in Mexico City.

Traffickers and the religion (case examples)

The religion of Santería has been utilized by various organizations within the drug trade. As with most of the religions used by narcos, the majority of practitioners of these faiths are law-abiding citizens. Some of the cases where the religion has been appropriated by drug traffickers include:

2011: Spanish National Police discovered the largest cocaine laboratory in European history in Madrid, Spain. A similar raid took place in the United States when members of the FBI in Miami, Florida, arrested members of Los Miami, an arm of the same drug trafficking organization. Agents discovered that the group had laundered over $26 million by buying American cars and properties in Miami. Arrested in the operation was the group's leader, Alvaro Lopez

Tardon. Tardon and other members of the network sought guidance from a Cuban-born santero known as Padrino for their criminal enterprise. The santero was paid in money and plastic surgery for his wife in exchange for performing spiritual cleansings. The priest was paid to perform a spiritual working on rival drug dealers and placed photos of them in a cauldron to keep Tardon safe. Also arrested in the operation in Madrid was the infamous "Queen of Cocaine," Ana Maria Cameno Antolin who was also known to consult Santería ritual specialists for guidance in distributing cocaine.

2012: The U.S. Drug Enforcement Administration conducted Operation Voodoo Sam, which focused on a drug running operation that brought drugs into the United States and rigged Puerto Rico's lottery system to launder money. The organization had been in operation for nine years and was responsible for distributing at least 840 kilograms of cocaine a year across Puerto Rico into New York and Connecticut using commercial airlines. The organization used Santería babalawo (high priest) Orlando Robles Ortiz to spiritually guide drug dealers. Ortiz consulted a spirit known as Samuel, kept in a small wooden shed behind his residence, about where the best drug routes were located.

2012: Members of the Spanish Civil Guard conducted Operation Garnacha, which targeted members of a network who were responsible for trafficking hashish into Central Europe from Morocco. Members of the network consulted Santería priests for spiritual guidance. Priests would consult the spirits to identify locations for distribution and to locate ideal meeting spots for dealers and customers. When law enforcement would apprehend members of the network, Santería ritual specialists would perform rituals to remove "bad luck" from their clients.

2013: The trial of Mexican cartel member Jose Trevino Morales in Austin, Texas, revealed a slight look into the use of Santería by members of the Los Zetas cartel. Morales was on trial for charges of money laundering involving the use of a racehorse operation in Lexington, Oklahoma. Funds were fed into the operation from Mexico on behalf of the Los Zetas cartel. Morales was arrested in 2012 by the FBI and found guilty of money laundering in May 2013. During the trial it was revealed that a witness in the case had sent a shipment of cigars to one the defendants, cartel member Colorado Cessa. The witness was questioned about the shipment and revealed: "He sent me cigars because of my faith. Santería is based on the Lucumi beliefs of the Yoruba in Africa then it came through Cuba with slaves. I sent people to do a cleaning on the part of Colorado."

Figure 4.1 Stash house. Members of a human smuggling ring appropriate the orishas of the Santería religion for spiritual guidance. The orishas known as *los guerreros*, or "the warriors," are traditionally kept behind doorways to protect the home. (Courtesy of Sgt. Rolando Garcia, San Juan Police Department, San Juan, Texas.)

Historical background

The Afro-Cuban religion of Santería originated with the Yoruba people of southwest Nigeria. In the mid-16th century, thousands of Yorubans were kidnapped and forced into slavery. They were then transported to British, French, Spanish, and Portuguese colonies in the Caribbean Islands to live and work on plantations as an enslaved populace. African slaves brought with them African traditional religious culture, but were eventually forced by their captors to abandon their religious obligations to the deities and to the practices of their indigenous religions.

To ensure the survival of their religion, the Yoruba slaves secretly kept their spiritual traditions alive, particularly on the island of Cuba. Meeting in houses known as cabildos, the various groups could celebrate the rituals, songs, and dances of their culture. The cabildos were identified by specific religious groups known as Regla. The Regla de Ocha was the "rule of the orishas," a phrase still used today to denote contemporary Santería. (The orishas are the Yoruba deities worshipped in Santería.) The Yoruba people found common elements in the Roman Catholic saints of

Figure 4.2 Cartel residence. After arresting members of a drug trafficking organization, officers discover a number of artifacts relating to the religion of Santería. Note: The practice of the religion does not necessarily mean that the members used the religion with cartel activities, but it is important that officers be able to identify evidence even if there is no relation to criminal activities. (Courtesy of Webb County (Texas) Sheriff's Department, Laredo, Texas.)

the slave owners' religion and the indigenous deities of Africa. A syncretism between the saints of the Catholic Church and the African deities known as orishas was formed. This allowed the Yoruba slaves to use the saints as camouflage while still observing their religion. The groups, who identified with this practice, were known as Lucumi. Today the religion is practiced in the open with the syncretism between orisha and saints being continued as a cultural tradition. Some followers have referred to the saints as the "costumes" that the orishas wear in the New World.

There is evidence that Santería moved north of the border into the United States as early as 1946, when Francisco "Pancho" Mora migrated into the States and became the first recognized babalawo (Santería priest) in America. Mora established a temple in the Upper West Side of New York City. In 1959, another significant personality in Santería history, named Walter King, traveled to Cuba to become initiated in the religion. King is noted as being the first African American to be initiated in the religion. Upon his return to the States, King changed his name to Oba Osejiman Adeummi and started the Yoruba Temple in New York City. In 1961, Mercedes Noble was ordained the first santera (priestess of Santería) in the United States. Noble, who was also known as Oban Yoko, opened a casa de santo (house of saint), which became a location for ordination rites in the States.

Figure 4.3 Operation Voodoo Sam. The arrest of *babalawo* Orlando Robles Ortiz by the DEA followed an investigation into a sophisticated network of drug traffickers who used commercial airlines to move cocaine from Puerto Rico to New York. The Santería high priest served as the network's spiritual leader. (Courtesy of U.S. Drug Enforcement Administration.)

The Mariel boatlift brought several thousand Cubans to the south Florida shores between April and October 1980. Some trepidation followed many of the Cubans as they flooded into the communities. A number of criminals had arrived on the boatlift and caused major problems for local law enforcement. About 2,000 of Cuba's most violent criminals were released by Fidel Castro in the boatlift. Many of the Mariel boat people brought with them their island culture and religious practices.

In 1992, Santería practitioners from Hialeah, Florida, protested local ordinances that banned ritual animal sacrifices by Santería practitioners. This issue was taken to the U.S. Supreme Court, where it was ruled that the city had specifically focused on Santería and should have created a generalized ordinance that did not target a specific religious culture.

Beliefs

The primary focus of Santería is to introduce humanity to the deities
known as orishas. Santería ideology teaches that humans are considered
children of these deities. It is also believed that each human being has a
personal orisha that he or she is called to serve in rituals and daily living.
The world is divided into a world that can be seen and a world that is
unseen. The world that can be seen is called Aiye and refers to the physical realm or earth. The unseen world or heaven is known as Orun. The
orishas and the dead inhabit the world of Orun.

Humans feed the orishas through sacrifices and provide earthly
instruction to guide other humans into the service of the orishas. The orishas likewise provide spiritual power to humans known as ashe. Ashe,
which is spiritual energy, can reside inside believers as well as inside ritual implements when they have been "charged" by the orishas.

(a)

Figure 4.4a Saints and orishas. During a drug-related homicide investigation,
officers discovered a shrine in the victim's bedroom. (Courtesy of Micheal Vincent,
Orange County Florida Sheriff's Department, Orlando, Florida.) *(continued)*

(b)

Figure 4.4b Former Los Zetas cartel leader Jesuś Enrique Aguilar aka 'Z7' wearing his sacred beads of protection known as *elekes* or *los collares*.

Deities of Santería

According to Santería mythology, the orishas are different manifestations of the creator deity known as Olodumare. The orishas govern all aspects of nature and human emotions. For instance, the orisha Yemaya governs the ocean waters and the human aspects of maternity, including motherhood and protecting children. Santería myths, known as patakis, are communicated orally to followers to explain the mechanics of the spiritual and physical worlds. The patakis tell of the creator Olodumare (who owns heaven) and of his son Olofi. The orishas Olodumare, Olofi, and Olorun rule over the other orishas, but are not directly worshipped.

The orishas are similar to the gods and goddesses of Greek mythology. Each deity has his or her own favorite color, number, food, drum rhythm, and tools.

Figure 4.5 Elegua is the first orisha that is addressed in ritual. He is the spirit that opens doorways. He is given offerings of toys and candy, as he is viewed as a childlike spirit in the mythology of the religion.

There are an infinite number of orishas, but typically there are a small number of them recognized by most practitioners. The following are some of the more recognized orishas in Santería.

Elegua

Consulted first before any of the orishas, Elegua is syncretized with Saint Anthony. In Yoruba he is known as Esu-Elegbara, and in Spanish he is known as Eleggua. Some houses may have Elegua represented by the Spanish statue of Nino Atocha, the Christ child or the Lonely Spirit of Purgatory. Elegua is represented by a figure made from cement with cowrie shells for the eyes, nose, and mouth. The cement figure may be purchased from a spiritual supply store (botanica). The head must be pre-pared and consecrated by a priest or priestess in order for it to function. The head is hollowed out and is filled with materials such as blood, hair, and fingernails to connect it to the initiate. Clergy must perform a cer-emony to place the spirit of Elegua into the cement head. A hole is drilled in the bottom of the icon and is filled with dirt from a marketplace, a bank, a crossroads, and a farm. Some cultural informants have spoken of the icons filled with dirt from a church or police station. It is also filled with a material known as ashe that is made from seeds and nuts from Nigeria.

Figure 4.6 Ogun and Ochosi. Examples of artifacts representing the spirit of ironworkers and the hunted.

Elegua owns the keys to the spiritual realm and is called upon at the beginning of rituals to open the doorway to the spiritual world. There is typically a small nail or blade coming out of the head. This represents the energy of this orisha. Some forms of this icon are decorated with green and yellow beads around the top of the head. This indicates that a high priest or babalawo has prepared the icon. The icon of Elegua may be found sitting on a terra-cotta plate. This indicates stability.

The image of Elegua is frequently placed near doorways. His image may be found along with a red and black beaded stick with a crook, and he may be wearing a small straw hat. His shrine may also contain toys and candy, representing his childlike nature. He may be found in other forms instead of the traditional cement, including forms made from coconuts, seashells, and large rocks.

Figure 4.7 Orishas. Examples of the various artifacts used to represent spiritual personalities in the Santería religion. Many of these artifacts are simply decorations, but in the context of the culture, they take on a whole new meaning.

Ogun

Ogun is syncretized with Saint Peter. Ogun is viewed as the divine ironworker and patron spirit of ironworkers. Among the Yoruba people in Nigeria, the name *Ogun* is found among advertising signs for shops that belong to toolmakers and carpenters. He is believed to be the spirit that helps man work with tools of iron. Ogun is represented by an iron cauldron filled with materials such as iron spikes, chains, and other implements. These items are typically covered in corojo (palm oil) butter. Green- and black-colored items will be found in his shrine as well. Ogun's patron animal is the dog. Some Ogun shrines contain stuffed animals and statues of dog images. The ceremonial knife that is used to commit animal sacrifices is often placed inside the cauldron of Ogun.

Ochosi

Also called Osoosi in Yoruba, Ochosi rules over hunting and justice. Ochosi is syncretized with Saint Norbert. He is represented by a small or large metal crossbow. Officers may see the crossbow of Ochosi hanging near the door to a home. Some shrines for Ochosi hold deer antlers and handcuffs. Ochosi artifacts may be violet in color.

Figure 4.8 *Sopera* for Obatala, the Father of Purity. The *sopera* of Obatala is always kept above other artifacts of the orishas, as he is the head of the orishas.

Oshun

Oshun is syncretized with Our Lady of La Caridad del Cobre. Also known as Osun in Yoruba, she is the goddess of love and sexuality. She also governs matters of money and rules over the river waters. Her shrines contain materials made from copper, fans, mirrors, ducks, and boats or other river-related items. Honey may be placed on the altar, as well as apple cider. Her color is yellow.

Obatala

This orisha is syncretized with Our Lady of Mercy. Obatala is the father of the orishas, and is frequently referred to as Father of the White Cloth. Obatala is said to own the heads of humans and is represented by anything white, such as cotton, doves, and eggs. He is considered the owner of wisdom and purity.

Shango

Also known in Yoruba as Sango and in Spanish as Chango, this fiery orisha is syncretized with Saint Barbara and represents fire, thunder, and lightning. Shango was an actual king in Africa who was deified after his death.

Shango's shrine contains his wooden double-bladed axe and sword. Shango's shrine will typically contain a large wooden mortar. The mortar

Figure 4.9 The orisha Oko rules over the aspect of agriculture. Shrines for Oko include images of a farmer tilling the land with his oxen.

will be used in ceremonies and was used historically among the Yoruba as the place where a child was bathed, and in death where the deceased would have his head shaved. His shrine will also contain in some instances a large wooden vessel known as the batea. The batea among the original Yoruba was used to hold the sacred stones dedicated to Shango. The vessel represents Shango's throne. Shango's sacred stones will be kept in the batea. Known as piedras de rayo, these "thunderstones" were created when lightning struck the earth. Tools known as herramientas are also kept in the batea. These tools represent various forms of powers that are associated with Chango. They include six tools (six is Chango's number) made from wood, such as a pair of axes, daggers, and arrows.

Images of Saint Barbara may be placed in homes to represent Shango. The statue may hold a sword that can be placed in an upward or downward position. It is said that the sword pointing upward represents a time of defense in the life of the statue's owner. Shango's colors are red and white.

Oya

Oya is syncretized with Our Lady of Candelaria and Saint Theresa. Oya owns the cemeteries, winds, and storms. Shrines to Oya contain masks, spears, and nine copper bracelets. Her colors are maroon and nine other colors.

Figure 4.10 Eggun. This shrine is typically built in a room that is dark and near water. Offerings of coffee and flowers are given to the dead in this shrine.

Her shrine may contain her crown with nine charms, including a hoe, pick, gourd, lightning bolt, scythe, shovel, rake, axe, and mattock (an agricultural tool).

Yemaya

Also known as Yemoja in Yoruba, this orisha is syncretized with Our Lady of Regla (Regla is a province in Cuba). This orisha is considered to be the mother over the orishas. Her name means "our mother whose children are the fish." Yemaya rules over seas and will be found in the form of seashells, mermaids, boats, and other water-based items. Yemaya's colors are white and blue.

Babalu-aye

This orisha is syncretized with Saint Lazarus. Also known as Obaluaye or Sopona in Yoruba, Babalu-aye is a title that means "father." Babalu-aye

Figure 4.11 The *boveda* is a shrine dedicated to the ancestors. There are typically nine glasses of water representing the dead, as nine is the number of Oya, the orisha who rules over the cemeteries.

Figure 4.12 Espiritismo recognizes a number of spirit guides that appear in the form of Indian mystics, Native Americans, gypsies, and African slaves.

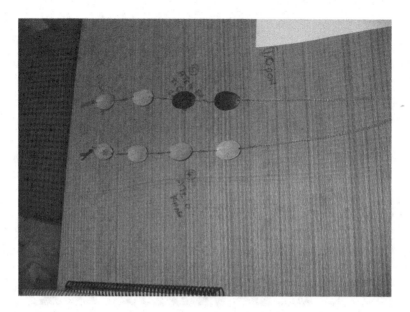

Figure 4.13 The *okuele* is a divination tool used by the *babalawó.*

is a special orisha to those who are dealing with sickness, as he owns the cure to sickness. He may also cause sickness. While he is historically associated with leprosy and smallpox, his contemporary association has also taken on AIDS as a sickness that he heals and causes. The shrines to Babalu-aye may contain a pair of crutches as well as sackcloth. His shrine may also carry a beaded fly whisk known as the aja. His color is purple. He may be received without being crowned. (*See* Asiento, Page 114)

Olokun

The orisha Olokun is commonly called "Yemaya at the bottom of the ocean." The orisha is a hermaphrodite being represented by an iron figure holding a sea snake and a mask. The artifacts of the orisha Olokun are placed on the floor to mirror the bottom of the ocean.

Orula

Orula is syncretized with Saint Francis of Assisi, and is the divine diviner. This orisha is also known in Yoruba as Orunmila and in Spanish as Orunla. He owns the tools of divination that are used by the high priest known as the babalawo. He is represented by the divination tools called the table of Ifa and the okuele. His colors are green and yellow.

Figure 4.14 All work with herbs in Santería must be performed through the power of Osain. Osain has one eye, one ear, and one foot. He is also represented by a hanging gourd.

Osain

Osain is syncretized with Saint Raphael, Saint Sylvester, Saint Joseph, and Saint John the Baptist. Osain governs the forest and is the spirit that rules over herbs. He is called upon to provide medicine for healing. Osain may be found in the form of a male figure with one arm, one leg, and one ear. Osain is also depicted as a beaded gourd that may be decorated with feathers. The gourd of Osain may contain herbs, animal bone, and various materials related to the orisha. His colors are the colors of all the orishas.

Osain can also be used for defensive spiritual work. The following is a portion of a prayer that was placed into an Osain talisman:

> Osain I ask you in the name of God you give me health,
> luck and peace spiritually. That you free me from the
> police, witchcraft curses and bad works and every-
> thing bad that can be done to me or against me.

In one particular case, a talisman of Osain was found hanging in the trunk of a car transporting narcotics. The talisman was believed to protect the driver from police.

Figure 4.15 Yemaya is the orisha who rules over the ocean waters. The name *Yemaya* is a contraction of "yeye omo eja," or "mother whose children are like fish."

The ibejis

The Ibejis are the sacred twin orishas. The are known in Yoruba as Ibejo or Meji and in Spanish as Jimugas. They are syncretized with Saint Cosmas as and Saint Damian. The Yoruba used these figures to represent the spirits of dead twins. In Santería, the Ibejis are the sons of Chango. They will be found in the form of twin dolls or statues. Their colors are red and white and blue and white. The Ibeji appear like innocent child dolls, but devotees speak of them as very powerful spirits.

Aganyu

Aganyu is syncretized with Saint Christopher. He represents earth forces, such as volcanoes and earthquakes. Aganyu is depicted in some myths as the father of Chango. His color is red.

Figure 4.16 Obi. The orishas are believed to speak to devotees through coconut shells and the patterns in which they land when thrown ritualistically.

Inle

Inle is syncretized with the archangel Raphael. Inle is the healer of the orishas and is the patron of doctors and fishermen. Inle lost his tongue to Yemaya, so he must speak through the shells of Yemaya. A silver cross ornament is kept in his shrine to represent his presence. The cross has two snakes and two small fish hanging from its arms. The post of the cross has two snakes wrapped around it. Objects connected to fishing, such as a net and fishing line, may be found in his shrine. Inle is the owner of medicine and provides healing. His colors are blue, yellow, and white. He is married to the spirit Abata.

Oko

Oko is the owner the earth and agriculture. He is represented by a miniature wagon and oxen. Oko is also represented by a Spanish roof tile as his shrine.

Oba

Syncretized with Saint Rita, Oba was the first wife of Shango. The mythology teaches that Oba was tricked by another one of Shango's wives into cutting off her ear and feeding it to Shango. Oba was turned into the Obba

Figures 4.17 and 4.18 Addimu and ebbo. Offerings like fruits and vegetables are given as minor offerings or *addimu*. Large offerings known as *ebbo* are given to the orishas in the form of animal sacrifices.

Figure 4.19 These artifacts representing orishas were discovered during a traffic stop of a recreational vehicle. The driver and his companions were transporting a large amount of marijuana when they were stopped by drug interdiction officers. The officers were concerned, as they discovered blood on many of the items in the vehicle. A local forensic examiner was able to conclude that the blood was from animals.

River in Nigeria. Her colors are pink and burgundy. Firecrackers are used to call Oba in ceremonies. Her numbers are nine or eight, depending on the house she is worshipped in. She represents marriage and fidelity.

The term *camino* is used to describe the various roads or avatars of an orisha. These are various aspects of an orisha's identity. Some orishas, like Elegua, are believed to have thousands of different manifestations or caminos. The camino may be distinguished by a particular characteristic of the deity; for example, the goddess over the ocean known as Yemaya has one particular camino, known as Yemayá Awoyó, that is motherly in nature, while she also has a camino known as Yemaya Asesu that is like a violent storm. Some caminos have specific relationships with other orishas, while some are enemies among the other deities.

One camino of the orisha Chango, known as Chango Sanfancon, is symbolized by various Chinese figures. In the myth (pataki) surrounding this version of Chango, the story tells of the deity traveling to a land where people are described as Asian in origin. Chango is believed to have transformed into a Chinese man. Shrines depicting this camino of Chango may have images such as Asian statues and Buddha figures within his sacred space.

Figure 4.20 The artifact representing Osun is placed in a high place in order for the orisha to be able to keep watch for the devotee. If the artifact tips over, this is a sign that something bad may be approaching.

There are literally hundreds of orishas as well as many other significant characters of great importance to those who follow them. These spiritual "personalities" are popular among practitioners of espiritismo (Spanish for "spiritism"). One is El Negro Jose. Jose is a statue of an elderly African man sitting in a chair. Sometimes he may be found leaning on a crooked staff. It is believed that spirits speak through his statue. He also may be used for spiritual protection.

Another spiritual figure that may be seen in statue form is known as La Madama. La Madama is depicted as an African woman wearing a dress, hoop earrings, and a scarf on her head. Madama is a spiritual protector.

The ancestors

In Santería, ancestors who are deceased are called egun. The egun are recognized in the lives of devotees as being the spirits of the family members or members of the religious community who have died. The egun are recognized in rituals and in altars, and some Santería practitioners will create a sacred space for the ancestors. The space is usually created in a dark place, such as a basement or bathroom. Shrines are placed near areas where

Table 4.1 Santeria Deities

Orisha	Saint	Color	Number
Aganyu	Christopher	Green, red and yellow	9
Babaluaye	Lazarus	Black, light blue	17
Eleggua	Anthony	Red and black	3
Ibeji	Cosmus and Damien	Red, white and yellow	2
Inle	Rafael	Green	7
Obatala	Our Lady of Mercy Resurrected Christ	White	8
Ochosi	Norbert	Violet	7
Ogun	Peter	Green and black	7
Olokun	Our Lady of Regla	Blue and white	7
Orula	Francis	Green and yellow	16
Osain	Joseph	Green	3
Oshun	Our Lady of Cardid	Yellow and white	5
Oya	Our Lady of Candelaria	Maroon, red or brown	9
Shango	Barbara	Red and white	4 or 6
Yemaya	Our Lady of Regla	Blue and white	7

there is running water. It is believed that water allows the dead to come to the land of the living. The space is marked off with chalk called efun.

A circle will typically be drawn with the chalk with a portion of the circle on the wall and a portion of the circle on the floor. This symbolizes the land of the living and the land of the dead. Nine x's are drawn on the circle representing the orisha Oya, who is the orisha over the dead.

A staff called opa egun is usually located near the shrine. The wooden staff is decorated with nine colored ribbons with bells attached to them. The concept of these bells is taken from the Yoruba use of bells on the costumes of masked dancers known as egungun, who represent the dead. Offerings of coffee, flowers, a glass of water, and fruit are placed in this space. Food and drinks eaten in the house where the shrine is located may be offered to the ancestors at this shrine. The egun may also be seen represented by a doll that is dressed in the colors of the ancestor's orisha.

Many Santería practitioners will have a shrine in their residence known as the boveda. The boveda is usually a table covered in a white cloth. The cloth symbolizes purity. Typically there will be nine glasses of water on the table surrounding a larger glass of water containing a crucifix. The glasses of water represent spirit guides and ancestors.

The main glass of water represents God, who is the head of the spirits. The boveda is also decorated with flowers, statues, photographs of the deceased, and items related to the deceased. Statues of Africans, gypsies, and Indians may be seen on a boveda. These are artifacts that represent spirit guides.

Devotees may pray and speak to their ancestors and spirit guides at these shrines. Prayers for the recently deceased may be offered to these shrines in order that the spirits may be elevated to heaven.

In one particular case, a detective shared with me that a suspect in a shooting was reported by informants of having photographs of a shooting victim on his boveda before the actual shooting took place. Further investigation revealed that the suspect was trying to prepare a place to pray for the spirit of the man he was about to murder.

Espiritismo

The use of the boveda shrine is taken from a practice known as spiritism, known in the Latin American communities as espiritismo. Spiritism is a set of practices and beliefs that many Santería practitioners embrace alongside Santería. Spiritismo was introduced into Cuba as a group of practices that came from Europe.

Spiritism is based on the works of a 19th-century French educator named Hippolyte Rivail, who is more popularly known by his pseudonym, Allan Kardec.

Kardec organized a number of metaphysical practices that involved techniques to communicate with the dead. He popularized practices such as spirit channeling and table tipping. Kardec's book, *The Spirit's Book*, features a number of questions regarding the work of spirits. Spirits of dead personas such as Benjamin Franklin, Augustine, Plato, and John the Baptist are believed to have helped write the book which is believed to have organized various doctrines and teachings regarding spirits. The book is usually sold in botanicas (retail stores that sell folk medicine, religious candles and statuary, amulets, and other products regarded as magical) and supply stores for the Santería faith. Practitioners may leave Kardec's books on their boveda. Spiritism became an additional practice of Santería when it caught on in areas such as Cuba and Puerto Rico. Prayers taken from Kardec's book are commonly recited in spiritualist rituals.

Kardec's teachings migrated to Puerto Rico from students who encountered Kardecian teachings in Europe. Initial Kardec spiritism groups were thought to be revolutionaries by members of the Puerto Rican government. The movement begin to spread into many Latin American communities.

Today, espiritismo uses doctrines and teachings of Christian and spiritualist texts and combines elements of African and Latin indigenous teachings. Spiritualist teachings indicate that the human soul survives after death, and that there is a spirit world that can interact with the material world. There are souls attached to the material world that can cause problems in the lives of the living and are known as enviaciones. Devotees are taught that negative spirits can control individuals on earth. Benevolent souls that have been perfected are known as espiritus de luz, or "spirits of light."

Mediums can perform consultations, or consultas. These spiritual sessions include forms of healing using oils, candles, and prayers to protect clients. Practitioners hold séances in which the spirits of the dead may appear. The séance is held at a table covered in a white tablecloth known as the mesa blanca. White candles, white flowers, and a bowl of water are placed on the table. The bowl of water is used to capture negative energies, which may manifest as bubbles in the bowl.

Spiritual masses known as misa espirituales are conducted in order to bring both the living and the dead to a higher spiritual level. A practitioner may fall into a trance and become possessed by the spirit of the dead. Practitioners known as mediums act as channels for the spirits. There are a number of types of mediums, including those who can see spirits, hear spirits, and see the future. Spirits of different cultures may also manifest themselves. Spirits known as madamas, who are West African women; gitanas, who are gypsies; indios, who are Indians; piratas, who are pirates; and Congos, who are Africans, can appear.

Spirits may be offered rum, coffee, cigars, and water by devotees. The spirit may possess someone at the service and is believed to be able to speak through the possessed.

Spiritual perfumes such as Florida Water may be sprayed or poured on to devotees as an act of cleansing by the spirits.

Puerto Rican-based spiritism, known as sanse, combines elements of Cuban Santería, Haitian and Dominican voodoo, and European spiritism to form a complex spiritual system that is practiced throughout Puerto Rico and in select areas of the United States. Devotees of the religion known as sansistas recognize 21 divisions of spirits known as misterios. These spirits are broken into three ethnic groups known as Division Blanca, Division India, and Division Negra. Rituals include ceremonies from the Santería religion and additional focus on elevated spirits. Encounters with altars and shrines of sanse will look similar to those of Santería; however, there are a number of spiritual personalities in the form of statues and images that are not seen in traditional Cuban Santería. For example, Candelo is a spirit that is depicted in statue form as a male African elder sitting cross-legged and smoking a tobacco pipe.

Group structure

There are several branches of the Santería religion known as ramas. Ramas are the lineages of priests into which an initiate has been initiated. Ramas can be traced back to one common ancestor. Some of the many names of ramas include La Pimienta, Culo Verde, San Jose Ochenta, Coral, Aina Yobo, and Efunche. Lineage is used many times as a verifier by the Santería community.

Suspects in criminal investigations who are initiated into Santería can be traced many times through their lineage. Investigators may find additional associates by mapping out the social networks of lineage.

The group structure in Santería uses the traditional family as a model. Initiates become the children of the parental clergy. A new member who has not undergone any sort of initiation in Santería is known in the community as an aleyo or an aborisha, which means "outsider." An initiate in his or her first year of initiation is known as an iyawo or "bride" of the orisha. Once a person has undergone initiation into the religion, he or she will be recognized first as a santero (priest) or santera (priestess). At this level the initiate is able to conduct rituals and access secret knowledge of formulas and spells used in the religion. An initiate will also be referred to as a spiritual godchild, known as ahijado, to the initiating priest or priestess. The godparent is then known as the padrino (godfather) or madrina (godmother) of the initiate. Godparents can "birth" new initiates into the religion. Some godparents have been known to have hundreds of godchildren in the religion.

Once the initiate has received the orisha, he or she is recognized in the community as being a babalocha or iyalocha. This title designates that the initiate is a priest or priestess of a specific orisha.

The high priest in Santería is known as babalawo, which means "father of the secrets." According to Santería theology, only males can be babalawos. The babalawo can call upon the orisha Orun and perform divination. Orun is believed to have been around since the creation of the world. It is believed that he can tell diviners about what has happened and what will happen in the future. The Yoruba use a divination system known as Ifa, a very complex system of divination that takes years to learn. The babalawo is considered a master of this type of divination.

Santeria proverbs contain advice on specific situations, and based on the proverb, the babalawo may suggest an offering or rituals for a remedy.

Babalawos are expected to memorize a complex system of wisdom known as the Odu. The Odu is a collection of 256 patterns of figures that have corresponding parables. The Odu is a mass collection of spiritual knowledge complete with hundreds of combinations of stories and prayers.

The babalawo uses a necklace called the okuele. This chain is made of eight shells, palm nuts, bone, and other materials. The chain is thrown onto a table or onto a mat on the floor, and the orishas speak through the pattern that the chain displays. The Odu are produced by the patterns in which the okuele instrument lands when thrown by the babalawo. The patterns are then marked in dust on a wooden table known as the table of Ifa. The Odu may instruct a believer to offer a particular offering or sacrifice to a particular orisha.

Rituals and ceremonies

To understand the mechanics of the Santería faith, it is important to know the various stages of initiation that members may attain.

Receiving the necklaces

The first initiation ceremony is a Catholic baptism. However, the first rite of the Santería faith is performed strictly by a Santería clergyman and known as receiving the necklaces.

Called elekes (*collares* in Spanish), the necklaces are sacred pieces of jewelry that put the initiate under the protection of the orishas. The necklaces appear in different colors with varying numbers of beads on each strand. The color and number of beads refer to one of the many orishas in the Santería pantheon. Typically 2-millimeter plastic beads are strung on cotton cloth. The santero, who performs a ritual over the necklaces, prepares the beads. The ritual gives the necklaces ashe, which transforms the beads from ordinary pieces of plastic into sacred symbols of power. The necklaces are washed in the sacred liquid known as omiero (made from herbs, water (rainwater, river water, ocean water, holy water), and steeped with a hot coal).

The believer receives the necklaces as a means of spiritual protection. The wearing of these beads publicly identifies the initiate as being dedicated to the orishas. The believer will initially receive the necklaces of Obatala, Chango, Oshun, Yemaya, and Elegua.

The most common versions of the orishas' elekes follow:

Elegua: His necklace is made of black and red beads, usually in combinations of three. They can alternate as one red, then one black.
Yemaya: Her colors are white or clear and blue and are usually in combinations of seven.
Ogun: His colors are green and black. Many times a translucent green bead is used to indicate the initiate has "received the knife" of Ogun. The pattern is usually in sevens or threes.

Shango: His colors are red and white and are found in combinations of six.

Orula: His colors are green and yellow and most often arranged in patterns of one green, then one yellow bead. Orula's number is 16.

Oshun: Her colors are yellow and white and are found in combinations of five. Amber-colored beads may be used in place of yellow beads.

Babalu-aye: His colors are purple and white. Some necklaces may contain all blue beads with white stripes.

Obatala: The necklace of Obatala is all white beads.

Oya: The necklace of Oya contains all brown with black stripes. Some variations include 9 black beads, 9 white beads, 9 black and white, until there are 18. Nine is the number of Oya.

There is a necklace that is worn to represent the seven powers that contains one clear bead, one blue bead, one yellow bead, one red bead, one green bead, one brown bead, and one white bead. Beads may be separated with small tools representing Oya and Ogun.

The ritual that is performed to receive the necklaces is conducted by an initiated priest or priestess. The man or woman who is receiving the necklaces will be taken with a member of the same sex to an area where he or she will remove and have their clothing torn away. The person is then washed with soap and the sacred omiero water. The devotee then puts on white clothing. The priest or priestess will clean the devotee's head with powdered eggshell (cascarilla), shredded coconut, cocoa butter, and cotton and honey. The necklaces are presented to the head holding the bell of Obatala and placed on the neck of the devotee who is then instructed to lie down on his or her stomach with arms at sides. The devotee is then lifted by assistants in the ritual and becomes part of an established house or body of believers.

The necklaces are treated with respect and are not to be worn while drinking alcohol or taking drugs, during sexual relations, or during menstruation. If the necklace breaks apart, this is a sign that the orisha has blocked something negative from happening to the initiate.

Practitioners may also receive a special beaded bracelet during a ceremony known as mano de Orula, or "hand of Orula." This green and yellow bracelet is given by a babalawo and is said to protect the owner from untimely death (iku). It is worn on the left hand.

On one occasion, members of a narcotics unit working undercover wore the bracelet, or Orula, while dealing with members of a Cuban drug ring. The appearance of the bracelet sent a subtle message to members of the drug ring that they were spiritually protected from death.

Warriors

After an initiate has received the necklaces, the next step of initiation is to gain the protection of the warriors, also known as los guerreros. This is a group of orishas (Elegua, Ochosi, Ogun, and Osun) that defend the initiate.

In Santería myths known as patakis, these gods travel together and the artifacts representing the orishas are presented to the initiate in a ceremony. Elegua is presented in the form of a cement head with cowrie shells for facial features.

Ogun is the orisha governing iron. He is given to the initiate in the form of an iron cauldron filled with iron or metal tools. Ogun also typically contains three black stones.

Ochosi is presented in the form of a metal crossbow. And finally, Osun is given to the new initiate in the form of a metal chalice adorned with bells and a small metal rooster on its lid. You will often see Osun placed near the doorway of a home, and preferably at a high location. This allows Osun to watch out for danger. If the tool of Osun falls over, this is a bad omen and means danger is coming. The chalice of Osun contains a hidden compartment that can be accessed by twisting the top of the chalice. The compartment contains powdered eggshell, cascarilla, stones, hair of the initiate, and various herbs. These are known as the secrets of Osun.

Receiving the warriors gives the initiate the spiritual protection of these orishas. The warriors are kept inside the initiate's house and are to be "fed" offerings and sacrifices on a regular basis. Elegua is the first to be fed because he is the orisha that opens the doorway to the spiritual realm. If Elegua is not fed first, the other orishas may not be able to receive their offerings. Cold water is dripped onto his image to call his spirit. A pigeon may be sacrificed to Ochosi. The priest who has presented the warriors to the initiate will perform a ritual in which a rooster is sacrificed in front of the warriors, and then the deities are invited into the house in which they will reside. This ceremony is known as ebbo de entrada.

Plante

Santería mythology teaches that man is guarded by a particular orisha. This is similar to the concept of having a guardian angel. The orisha is determined by a ceremony known as plante. The orisha ceremony is known as "owning the head." A divination is performed through Elegua or Orun to determine who owns the initiate's head. It is only after this determination is made that the orisha can be crowned onto the individual in the ceremony known as ocha.

Presentation to Oshun

The initiate then is taken to a river to be introduced and bathed by Oshun, the goddess of the river. The initiate removes his or her clothes and is bathed with the river water. Offerings are placed in the river, such as flowers, food, and honey. Oshun takes the items to heaven to announce the birth of a new initiate. The initiate reaches into the river and retrieves a stone. (This sacred stone is seen as a home to the spirits. The myths of the Yoruba say that the orishas descended to earth in raindrops that fell into the river and landed on stones. These stones are considered receptacles of spiritual power.) The stone is placed into a pot where it will act as a bridge between the orishas and the initiate.

Kariocha

The major ceremony in which the initiate receives the personal protection of an orisha is called kariocha, which is a Lucumi word that means "put the ocha on the head." This ceremony is also known as "making the saint." The ritual consists of the guardian orisha being crowned onto the head of the initiate.

Kariocha leads the initiate through a spiritual rebirth. Various materials that represent the orishas are placed inside ceramic vessels (soperas).

During the ceremony (which can be very tedious), the initiate's head is cut open to receive the orishas. The orishas are placed above the head of the initiate inside the sopera while songs are sung in the Lucumi tongue. (Trance possession can occur during this section of the rite.) The initiate's head is painted with symbols of the orishas, and an animal is rubbed over the body of the initiate and then sacrificed. The animal sacrificed differs according to the orisha; for example, a rooster may be given for a child of Elegua.

Other children of the orisha are there to sing and call the orisha down.

The ritual is a very complex ceremony that ends in a rite called the asiento. The asiento is the actual seating of the orisha into the initiate. During this ritual the head of the initiate is cut with a small blade. The cut has several herbs applied to it to crown the essence of the orisha into the head of the initiate. The initiate's head (ori) is fed the blood of an animal as well as other ingredients, such as cocoa butter and coconut. The orisha is then seated in the initiate's head. Babalawos and aleyos are not allowed in the room according to tradition. The oba, the godmother or godfather, and the ayubona (assistant) and several other priests must be present. Ashe has to be summoned to birth the orisha. The room of the initiate is blocked off from nonparticipants.

The following day is known as the middle day. The initiate sits and eats lunch at a table prepared for him. After the lunch, the initiate is dressed in an outfit that contains the colors of the orisha that he has received. A drumming ceremony follows in which the initiate is presented to the Santería community. The orishas are fed that day and are considered hot after receiving the blood. The middle day is a day of rest before the diviner can perform a reading.

The day after middle day is known as the day of Ita. Ita is a reading performed by a gifted diviner. The diviner gives the initiate a list of taboos, advice, and a reading regarding the spiritual mother or father of the initiate. The details of this ceremony are recorded in a book known as the libreta, which means "little book." This book is later given to the initiate after the completed initiation.

Decoding the libreta

Officers investigating subjects or victims who are initiated into the religion may discover a book known as the libreta. While typically kept from outsiders, it may be necessary for an officer to examine the book for intelligence regarding additional accomplices or insight into a victim's activities. To an officer who is not familiar with the culture, many names, terms, and symbols in the book may appear cryptic.

The following is an example of what officers may see in a libreta:

> March 5, 2012. My day at the river.
> Coconut for Oshun—Alafia
> Coconut for Aggayu—Eyeife

Translated: On March 5, 2012, the initiate was taken to the river as one of the first stages of initiation into the religion. The four shells of the coconut were thrown to determine whether Oshun accepted the initiate. The answer *Alafia* means that all four coconut shells fell with the white side face up. This is a definite yes. The four shells of the coconut were thrown so that Aggayu could communicate acceptance or refusal of the initiate to the river. The answer *Eyeife* means that the coconut shells landed with two white sides up and two black sides up. This means a yes from the orisha.

The initiate is dressed in white and must wear this color for a year and seven days. His head must remain covered, and there are several restrictions placed on him. Restrictions involving sexual activity, diet, and interaction with outsiders are usually listed in these taboos.

After three months, a sacrifice known as ebbo meta (three-month ebbo) is performed. The initiate's hair is cut for the first time since the initiation.

The secrets of the orishas are placed in soperas, typically ceramic or wooden bowls in a specific color that designates an orisha. These bowls are kept in the homes of practitioners. The stone inside is routinely bathed in water and herbs. Animals may be sacrificed, and the blood of the animal poured upon the stones. Substances such as honey, palm oil, and cascarilla are given to the bowls according to the orisha inside the bowl. These are sacred objects and are treated as if the gods themselves were sitting in the bowls. The soperas may be kept in wooden cabinets called canastilleros.

At this point, the initiate becomes known as omo orisha, or "child of the orisha."

Divination

Obi

In order to communicate with the orishas, Santería practitioners use a tool known as an obi. Use of the obi is known as darle coco al santo, which means "give coconut to the saint." Four pieces of coconut are thrown, and the orishas speak through the pattern in which the pieces land. There are five possible combinations in which the shells may land:

All white sides up—alafia. This means a positive yes.
All brown sides up—oyekun. This means no and possibly death.
Three white sides and one brown side up—itagua. This is an uncertain answer and the rinds are thrown again.
Two white sides up and two brown sides up—ellife. This means a definite yes.
Three brown sides up and one white side up—okana sode. This means no, but may also mean death.

If the devotee receives oyekun or okana sode, then the shells are thrown out and new ones are used.

Diloggun

Another form of communication that is used to interact with the orishas is the diloggun, which is a system of divination that uses 16 cowrie shells as a means of hearing the gods. These shells are given to the initiate when he or she receives the otanes and soperas. The cowries, known as caracoles, are thrown and land in various patterns. (The open side of the shell is the mouth of the orisha.) The patterns are then interpreted by matching the particular pattern with the pattern known as the Odu. Initiates are traditionally trained by a divination specialist called the italero.

Patakis

Believers are also taught about the orishas and how to serve them through stories or parables called patakis. These are legends about the personalities and lives of the orishas. These stories instruct the believers on the specific powers orishas can exert.

Offerings and sacrifices

The practice of Santería requires adherents to utilize the concept of offerings and sacrifices in interacting with the orishas. The orishas require minor offerings that are known as addimu and sacrifices known as ebbo. The orishas may ask for sacrifices as a form of exchange in order to carry out requests.

Addimu

Addimus are small offerings to the orishas. These can be foods, candles, candy, and other materials. They are usually found on plates and in bowls in front of the objects that represent orishas.

Elegua is given cornmeal with palm oil known as manteca de corojo, okra, coconuts, smoked fish (known as eya), a bush rat (known as jutia), toasted corn, and candy.

Ogun is given green plantains and the gifts that Elegua requests. The sapodilla fruit is his favorite food.

Obatala is given egg whites beaten with sugar, as well as rice and vanilla puddings, milk, and other white foods.

Chango is given a dish of okra and cornmeal cooked together, along with red apples and green bananas in groups of six.

Yemaya is given sweet plantains and pork rinds. Shrimp, dried coconut, white pears, and okra are also found in her addimu.

Oshun is given pumpkin, shrimp, eggs, spices, and raw fish. Honey is usually poured over the addimu.

Oya is given eggplants and okra with cornmeal.

Babalu-aye is given cigars and the aguardiente drink. He also likes coconut butter, milk, and bread.

Inle is given sweet wine and cake.

Ebbo

Perhaps the most misunderstood aspect of Santería is the practice of animal sacrifice. This is known as ebbo. The ebbo is a sacrifice that gives the orisha the energy found in the animal in exchange for the energy of the orisha, known as ashe. The blood that is given is called eje.

There are particular stipulations that are followed in order to offer a sacrifice. The initiate who gives an ebbo must first receive the knife used in the sacrifice in a ceremony called the pinaldo. The knife is said to belong to the orisha Ogun. In fact, the ceremonial sacrifice is blamed on Ogun. The animal's blood is usually dripped onto the stones or tools that represent the orisha. A prayer known as the moyuba is spoken in the native Lucumi tongue.

The meat of the animals that are sacrificed is cleaned, cooked, and eaten by the participants of the ritual. There is a saying, "La sangre para el santo, la carne para el santero," which translates to "Blood for the saint, meat for the santero." However, animals that are used to remove sickness or curses may not be eaten.

Each orisha has particular animals to be sacrificed for him or her:

Elegua is fed rum, cigars, turtles, goats, roosters, and opossum.
Chango is offered goats, turtles, quail, roosters, and rams.
Babalu-Aye is fed goats, roosters, and pigeons.
Oshun prefers yellow hens and female goats.
Ogun is fed opossum, roosters, goats, pigeons, and sometimes dogs.
Yemaya is given ducks, turtles, rams, and roosters.
Oya is fed female goats, pigeons, hens, and any black animals.
Aggayu is fed castrated goats, guinea hens, and pigeons.
Obatala is fed female goats, hens, doves, and guinea fowl.

Trance possession

Officers who encounter certain Santería ceremonies may witness a cultural phenomenon known as trance possession. Trance possession is a practice observed by many world religions, and involves a practitioner opening himself or herself up to a spiritual presence, such as a god or a spirit. The consciousness of the practitioner is taken over by the spirit, allowing the spirit to use the practitioner as a conduit to communicate with the physical world. In this state, practitioners may espouse wisdom from the gods and, in some cases, are alleged to perform miracles. Scientific explanations of this activity say that this altered state of consciousness is a result of deep hypnosis from the drumming and singing that accompanies the ritual.

One medical explanation has alleged that repeated auditory stimuli, such as drumming, can affect the central nervous system and the right hemisphere of the brain. In Santería, the possession of humans by the orishas is described as *subirse el santo a su caballo*, translated as "the saint climbs upon his horse." The presence of the orisha at a ceremony is evidence that the orisha has been pleased with the ceremony.

Officers who encounter scenes involving possession should be advised that these situations should be carefully approached.

Signs that possession is occurring include:

- The presence of drumming, chanting, and singing.
- The presence of a crowd of practitioners surrounding a single practitioner.
- Practitioners dressed in colorful clothing and handling large artifacts of the orishas.
- During the possession by Ogun, the practitioner may swing a machete around to depict his character.
- Practitioners dancing or shaking in erratic manners. Possession may appear as a choreographed dance or violent rolling around on the floor. Possession by Elegua appears in the form of a dance in which the orisha causes the practitioner to stand on one foot and twirl around.
- Display of supernatural acts, including consumption and handling of hot foods and substances.
- Increase in intensity of drumming and singing. This is to "call down" the orisha.

Upon encountering a Santería ritual, officers should not touch a practitioner exhibiting signs of trance possession. To touch the practitioner during possession can be viewed by devotees as interfering with the gods and can result in reactive behavior. Most likely, the ritual would be stopped due to the presence of outsiders. However, if you discover that you need to interact with someone at the scene of this ritualistic activity, it is advised that you address the leadership of the group. There is a culturally acceptable technique for the leadership to stop the act of possession without violating a cultural taboo.

Cleansings

Spiritual cleansings provide a way to remove negative energies and emotions from devotees. A priest or priestess will rub the body of the devotee with a chicken, herbs, or may perform a head cleansings. Some priests fill their mouths with aguardiente, a type of cane alcohol, and spew the contents onto the devotee. Some devotees are prescribed cleansing baths that are taken in a bathtub filled with water, herbs, oils, flowers, and various ingredients.

Brujería

The term *brujería* refers to the malevolent use of traditional tools of Santería. This spell is known as a trabajo, which means work. Dolls may be used to represent the victims of harmful magic. The orishas may be called upon to perform horrendous acts on the enemies of practitioners. Dead animals may be left in front of the home of the intended victim.

One example of a brujería spell is to take a cow's tongue and write the name of the targeted victim that you want to harm on a piece of paper and place them inside a pot. Cook them covered in salt. Remove and place in front of Elegua for three days. After the three days, take the tongue and name to the river. Dig a hole and bury them. This will affect your enemy magically.

Some practitioners believe that witches known as aje are active and can create spiritual problems for practitioners. Some devotees will take offerings of food and even animals to a crossroads at midnight to "feed the witches" and keep them away.

Festivals and holidays

There are several different types of ceremonies performed in the Santería community. One of the most popular is a celebration called the bembe. Bembe means "party" in the Lucumi language. It is usually a drumming festival held in honor of orishas. The ceremony may also be called a tambor, which is a Spanish word denoting the fact that drumming may be used in ceremonies. The days of celebration coincide with Catholic saints' days.

The drums used in the bembe are sacred objects that are believed to contain spirits. The drums, known as the bata, are three double-headed hourglass drums, and are consecrated and given a spirit known as Ana. Animals and offerings are presented to the drums. Drummers play a specific "call" in order to invite the orishas to manifest by possessing a believer. A bembe ceremony, known as Wemilere, uses consecrated bata drums.

One room used during the bembe usually holds the throne of the orisha. This room is often decorated in colorful banners and cloths spread across the walls and ceilings. There is also a tureen that holds the orisha inside on the throne. If the celebration is an asiento for the initiate, the iyawo will be found sitting on the throne. There is a large offering of cakes and other items, usually in the color of the orisha. This is known as the plaza. There are also fruit and vegetable offerings to the orisha found on the floor. A basket filled with money, called the derecho, is usually amid the offering and is used to help pay for all the food, tools, and time put into the celebration. At the base of the basket is a straw mat that visitors must fall down upon and show respect to the orisha. A maraca or a bell is used to rattle or ring to call the orisha.

Songs called cantos are used to call the orishas. The following is an exmple of a canto to Eleggua:

> Ibarakou Mollumba Eleggua Ibaco Moyumba,
> Ibaco Moyumba Omote Conicu Ibacoo Omot Ako
> Mollumba Eleggua Kulona. Ibarakou Mollumba
> Omole Ko Ibarakou Mollumba Omole Ko. Ibarakou

Mollumba Ako Eleggua Kulona Ache Ibakou
Mollumba ache Eleggua Kulona Ibarajou Mollumba
Omole Ko Ako Ache. Arongo Laro Akongo Larolle
Eleggua Kulona A Larolle Coma. Komio Akonko Laro
Akonko. Larolle Eleggua Coma Komio Ache Akonko
Laro Akonko Laro Ako Ache Iba La Guana Eleggua
Larolle Akonko E Larolle E Larolle Akonko Akonko
Larolle Akonko Larolle Akonko La Guana E Larolle.

The birthday of the initiate is celebrated every year. A celebration is held to commemorate the day that the initiate received the orisha. Desserts, food, and drinks are given to the orisha, and shrines are built to display the objects and tureens of the orisha.

Itutu

When a santero dies, an elaborate ceremony called the itutu is performed. This ceremony, performed by the community santeros, takes one year to complete. The deceased is dressed in the clothing that belongs to his guardian orisha. The tools of the santero are broken apart and placed where the orishas dictate.

Incident and crime scenes

The ritualistic use of the chemical mercury in Santería and other Voudon religions is a common practice. Mercury, known as azogue, is used in a number of magical operations. The chemical is known to ward off spirits, speed up spirits, and attract money and love.

In 1999, the U.S. Environmental Protection Agency (EPA) formed a multiagency task force to study the ritualistic use of mercury in various folk traditions. The task force discovered that a number of botanicas sold the substance to customers in the Santería, Palo, Voodoo, and Espiritismo communities. Mercury was discovered to be placed in small capsules for amulets. Mercury was also used in baths and sprinkled around homes of practitioners.

Short-term exposure to mercury can affect the respiratory system and result in pneumonitis, severe bronchiolitis, pulmonary edema, or death. Long-term exposure to small doses of mercury results in neurological problems.

Officers responding to residences where Santería is practiced may encounter shrines and ritual artifacts. Any disrespect toward altars, artifacts, or shrines can create a breakdown in communication between law enforcement and devotees, but could also provoke potential hostile reactions. Unless an item is presenting a threat toward the officer, or plays a role in a criminal case, the tools should not be touched by officers. If an outsider touches ritual implements, the items are viewed as desecrated. If an investigating officer must touch tools or altars in a crime scene, it is suggested that the officer remove all persons from the immediate area and set up a perimeter to keep bystanders away.

Crime scene investigators should use caution when handling artifacts, such as amulets. Residue of mercury may be present among these objects. If mercury is present, stay upwind from the area of contamination. Use a mercury spill kit if needed and utilize self-contained breathing apparatus (SCBA) if possible.

Investigators handling artifacts or patients may discover animal blood from sacrificial rituals. Utilize gloves, masks, and eye protection as needed.

Investigators who may be removing ritual objects, such as drums, should be advised that animal skins can be used for drum heads. Diseases may be present in these skins. Use protective clothing to avoid contamination.

Herbs and plants play a very important part of Santería. Herbs are used in healing in the Santería community. And officers may find a number of powdered herbs and crushed plants at the homes of practitioners. Many of these may appear as contraband.

Appropriation by DTOs

Members of the drug trade may be brought into Santería and may take part in the religion outside of their criminal activities. However, some offenders have sought to use the rituals and artifacts that they are familiar with to promote criminal activity.

One of the first areas of misappropriation focuses on using spirits and deities that have attributes that can be applied to the needs of the offender. Elegua has been patronized by some traffickers because of his ability to control the crossroads and fate. The ability to magically manipulate roadways to keep law enforcement or rivals away gives offenders confidence in transporting contraband. Look for toy police cars placed in the shrine to Elegua as a means of sympathetic magic.

The Miami (Florida) Police Department once had a case in which Yemaya, the goddess of the ocean waters, was used to protect a drug shipment on the waterways. American flags and images of eagles representing law enforcement were placed in the shrine to gain control over the waters.

The orisha Ochosi is frequently used by those in the drug trade because of the deity's reputation as the god of the hunted. There have been reports of the crossbow of Ochosi being hung above doorways of homes where drug activity is taking place.

Narcotics officers have reported serving search warrants and finding some traffickers hiding drugs inside of statues of saints and inside the sacred soperas where the otanes are kept.

Cultural terms

Ache/ashe: Term used to describe the magic of the orishas in Santería. Ache is divine energy.

Addimu: A lesser offering in Santería. Usually consists of fruits and items that do not contain blood.

Alafia: A positive sign in the Dilogun divination system.

Aleyo: A noninitiate to Santería. Literally means "stranger" or "outsider."

Asiento: "Making the saint" in Santería. *Asiento* is the term used to describe placing or seating of the orisha into the head of the initiate.

Baba: Term meaning "father."

Babalawo: Father of the secrets. The term is used to denote the high priest in Santería that can use the table of Ifa divination system.

Babalocha: A male initiate in Santería.

Bata: Sacred drums used in Santería ceremonies.

Batea: One of the fundamental symbols of Chango. A wooden mortar and pestle and a wooden bowl that hold Chango's mysteries.

Bembe: Ritual party for the orishas of Santería.

Boveda: The altar used to honor the eggun (ancestors).

Camino: A specific avatar or manifestation of an orisha.

Cantos: Song used to praise the orishas.

Cascarilla: Powdered eggshell used in rituals. Sometimes formed into chalk.

Collar de mazo: Large beaded necklace worn during initiation and then draped over the sopera that houses the orisha's fundamentos.

Cuchillo: The knife used to make sacrifices in Santería.

Darle coco al santo: Divination system using the coconut.

Despojo: A cleansing ceremony in Santería.

Diloggun: Divination system using the cowrie shells.

Ebbo: A major sacrifice in Santería. The blood from animals is typically used to receive ache from the orishas.

Eggun: Term used to describe the dead or ancestors. The eggun are honored in rituals and through the altars known as boveda.

Ewe: The herbs and plants used in Santería.

Guerreros: The warrior orishas of Santería; they include Eleggua, Oggun, and Ochosi. Osun is also received with these orishas.

Hacer el santo: To have the orisha placed in the initiate's head.

Idé: The beaded bracelet that is owned by Orun. The bracelet is colored yellow and green and protects the owner from death.

Ifa: West African system of divination. It also means "fate." The term is also used by practitioners of Yoruba religion who do not recognize the syncretism of Catholic saints.

Iku: The spirit of death.

Ile: "House." The ile is the fellowship of practitioners.

Ile-Ife: The holy city in Nigeria where creation began.

Iya: Known as the "mother" of the sacred bata drums used in ceremonies.

Iyalocha: Female initiates in Santería.

Iyawo: The initiate in Santería. Iyawo means the "bride" of the orisha.

Kariocha: The ceremony in which the initiate becomes a priest/priestess.

Lucumi: The Yoruba people in Cuba.

Macuto: Amulet filled with herbs and ache.

Malferefun: Lucumi term for "praised be."

Moforobale: A ritual greeting to the orishas and iyaorishas. Translated, it means "I bow before you."

Moyuba: An invocational prayer in Santería.

Obi: The coconut oracle used in Santería.

Omo: A child of the orishas.

Ori: The head or soul of an initiate.

Oriate: The song leader in a ceremony.

Orishas: The deities of Santería.

Otan: The sacred stone that contains the essence of the orisha.

Padrino: The spiritual godfather who initiates a believer.

Regla: Rule or path. Used to refer to the Afro-Cuban religions in Cuba.

Tambor: A ceremony in which the sacred drums are played.

References

American religious identification survey, Graduate Center of the City University of New York, 2001, http://www.gc.cuny.edu/faculty/research_studies/aris.pdf

Barnet, Miguel, *Afro-Cuban religions*, Princeton, NJ: Marcus Weiner Publishers, 2001.

Bascom, William, *Sixteen cowries: Yoruba divination from Africa to the New World*, Indiana University Press, Bloomington, 1980.

Bolayiidowu, E., *Olodumare, God in Yoruba belief*, New York: A&B Book Publishers, 1994.

Brandon, George, *Santería from Africa to the New World: The dead sell memories*, Indiana University Press, Bloomington, 1993.

Brown, David, *Santería Enthroned*, University of Chicago Press, Chicago, 2003.

Ecun, Oba, *Ita: Mythology of the Yoruba Religion* Miami, FL: Obaecun Books, 1989.

Garoutte, Claire, and Anneke Wambaugh, *Crossing the water: A photographic path to the Afro-Cuban spirit world*, Duke University Press, Durham, NC, 2007.

Ibadan, *A Dictionary of the Yoruba Language*, ldaban Nigeria: University Press PLC, 1991.

Juarez-Huet, Nahayeilli, Relocalization processes of Santería in Mexico: Some ethnographic examples, October 31, 2013, http://www.ssrn.com/abstract=2347904

Lindsay, Arturo, *Santería aesthetics in contemporary Latin American art*, Smithsonian Institution Press, Washington, DC, 1996.

Lopez, Christian, *Lukumi: Santería's beliefs, principles and direction in the twenty-first century*, Bloomington, IN: iUniverse, 2004.

Martinez, Rafael, Santería: A magico-religious system of Afro-Cuban origin, *American Journal of Social Psychiatry*, Vol. 2, No 3, 32–38. 1982.

Mason, Michael Atwood, *Living Santería: Rituals and experiences in an Afro-Cuban religion*, Smithsonian Books, Washington, DC, 2001.

Miller, Michael E., Los Miami gang nabbed in huge drug bust, *Miami New Times*, August 11, 2011.

Moroccan Santería guiding the operations of a disjointed network of drug traffickers in Andalucia, May 17, 2012, http://www.teinsteresa.es

Murphy, Joseph M., *Santería: An African religion in America*, Boston Press, Boston, 1988.

O'Brien, David M., *Animal sacrifice and religious freedom: Church of the Lukumi Babalu-Aye v. City of Hialeah*, Lawrence, KS: University of Kansas Press, 2004.

Olmos, Margarite Fernandez, and Lizabeth Paravinsi-Gebert, *Sacred possessions: Vodou, Santería, Obeah and the Caribbean*, New Brunswick, NJ: Rutgers University Press, 1997.

Pena, Ysamur Flores, *Santería garments and altars: Speaking without a voice*, Jackson, Ms: University Press of Mississippi, 1994.

Routon, Kenneth, *"Open the roads!": Religious sensibilities of power and history in Havana, Cuba*, publisher unknown, 2006.

Task Force on Ritualistic Uses of Mercury report, OSWER 9285.4-07, EPA/540-R-01-005, U.S. Environmental Protection Agency, Office of Emergency and Remedial Response, Washington, DC, December 2002.

chapter five

Palo Mayombe and Bantu traditions (Las Reglas de Congo)

Among the Afro-Caribbean religions that are appropriated by drug traffickers, Palo Mayombe is considered to be an aggressive spiritual practice. Palo Mayombe is one of the many traditions found in the group of religions known as Reglas de Congo (Rule or Law of the Congo). Reglas de Congo is a term used to refer to the numerous religious traditions of the Bantu people of Central Africa. These traditions include a number of religious cultures that are seen in the United States. Outsiders to the religions of Reglas de Congo frequently refer to it as the dark side of Santería. This is an inaccurate description, as the religion is not the same as the Yoruba practice of Santería.

There is very little information available to the public in the United States about the Kongo religions. (The word *Kongo* is commonly used by religious historians to refer to the kingdom of the Bakongo people. The spelling is considered traditional, as opposed to Congo, which refers to the new political state in the region.) The majority of the literature available on the subject is written in Spanish and is from Cuba, where the religion is openly practiced. The religion is very secretive. Rites are practiced in secret to preserve their sacred customs and because of the controversial use of human remains in their practices.

Traffickers and the religion (case examples)

The religion of Palo Mayombe has been utilized by various organizations within the drug trade. As with most of the religions used by narcos, the majority of practitioners of these faiths are law-abiding citizens. Some of the cases where the religion has been used include:

> In Chapter 2 we discussed the appropriation of Palo practices by the infamous Matamoros drug smugglers.
> In October 2009, members of the Bureau of Alcohol, Tobacco and Firearms arrested 38-year-old Ruben Ambrosio Fonseca Jr. after he sold 183 grenades to an undercover federal agent posing as a cartel member. San Juan, Texas, police and SWAT raided Fonseca's

Figure 5.1 Cauldron containing tree branches and human skull.

property and discovered scores of bloody artifacts, including an iron cauldron filled with tree branches and a human skull used in the practice of Palo Mayombe.

Legends surrounding Los Zetas founding member "Pretty Boy" El Mamito say that Mamito was believed to put his enemies' names into a pot in the tradition of Palo Mayombe.

A number of cultural informants that I have encountered throughout the years in the Afro-Caribbean religions have shared stories about how drug traffickers have sought out Palo clergy for spiritual services. The inaccurate reputation of Palo and the Bantu traditions as the dark side of Santería has made Palo a religion to fear.

Historical background

The traditions or branches of the Bantu religion are known as ramas. Ramas are likened to the denominations found in some world religions. Each tradition has its own unique practices, music, language, symbols, and social structures. Some of the Bantu religious traditions include Brilumba, Kimbisa, Corta Lima, and Palo Mayombe, as well as several others. Some of the lineages found throughout the United States and Mexico include Palo Mayombe, Brillumba, and Kimbisa.

Brillumba is also known as Vriyumba, which means "to work the spirit of death." Kenneth Routon (2006) shares an interview with a Brillumba practitioner who speaks about the history of the Rama:

Figure 5.2 The nganga ritual scene is viewed as a powerful magical weapon in the hands of the proper ritual specialist. The knives and gun in the scene are believed to become spiritual weapons in the hands of the spirits.

The first fundamento (the sacred pot used in the religion) 'Luwanba' was mounted in Camaguey. A black Congo slave from the Carabali tribe, in a moment of rage killed the mayoral. He was tired of his abuse and so he took his machete from him and severed his head. There's a song that says 'mambele mayoral, mambele, mambele mayorial, mambele'. He killed the mayoral with his own machete and used his head to serve his own needs. How? Because he used the head of the mayoral in his fundamento. That's where Brillumba Congo was born. The only ones (fundamentos) that contained the skulls of mayorals were the Brillumba Congo fundamentos. In Brillumba Congo they never looked for the skulls of black folk. They got the skulls of mayorals, of the whites so it would be a representation of what it was like during those times.

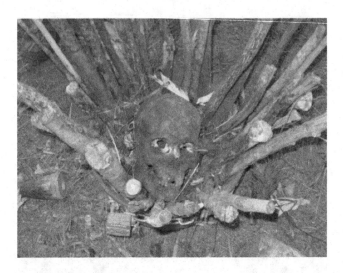

Figure 5.3 Nfumbe. Controlling the bones gives the operator the ability to control the spirit that is placed inside the nganga.

Kimbisa was started in 1843 in Havana, Cuba, by Andres Facundo de los Dolores Petit. Petit founded the branch known as Kimbisa or Santo Cristo Buen Viaje (SCBV) after he visited Monte Oscuro, an area where many African slaves lived in Cuba. Petit learned about the Kongo traditions from the slaves and brought the traditions back to his community. Petit's organization combined elements of Freemasonry, Catholicism, Yoruba Lucumi, Congo traditions, and Espiritismo to form the rama known as Kimbisa or Regla Kimbisa del Santo Cristo del Buen Viaje. Practitioners are known as Kimbiseros. One of the earmarks of Petit's tradition is the use of the crucifix intertwined with ritual artifacts.

Palo Mayombe is the Bantu religion that appears to be the most widely practiced throughout the United States. The core religion that gave birth to Palo comes from the hills of Mayombe in Cabinda and Calabari in the Kongo region. It was born as Palo Mayombe in Pinar del Rio Cuba.

Palo originated among the Bakongo people of Central Africa. The religion spread and was transformed as it was brought to Cuba and the Americas. The religion eventually spread through the island of Hispaniola, which is home to Haiti and the Dominican Republic. By the 19th century the religion began to spread into the United States and Mexico.

In order to understand the modern-day practice of Palo Mayombe, it is important to understand the basic elements of the Central African Bantu religion.

Bantu religions teach that the world is divided between that of the living and that of the dead. Spirits of the dead and spirits of nature are

Figure 5.4 Lucero is the spirit that guards doorways and is considered a messenger from the mpungo.

believed to interact with humanity, and in order to properly interact with these spirits, the Bantu enlist the help of the local herbalist and healer. The Bantu ritual specialist is known as the nganga. The Kikongo language describes the term *nganga* as referring to a "sorcerer" or "healer." Through the use of medicines, known as nkisi, the specialist could solve the problems of the local community. He or she would use elements found in nature, such as stones, bones, dirt, and water, to communicate with the world of the dead and with nature.

The Bantu religions and their ritual specialists were spread throughout the world when many of the Bantu were driven into slavery. A large concentration of Bantu people (properly known as Bakongo) were taken to Cuba, where their religions were suppressed by the colonialists. The religions started to take on different forms when the slaves began to incorporate European Christianity and the Yoruba traditions from Africa into their rites and practices.

The nganga of Africa was transformed from the name of a ritual specialist to the name for a ritual vessel. The contemporary version of the

Figures 5.5 and 5.6 River and justice. The top photo is of a prenda representing Mama Chola, the mpungo of rivers, while the bottom photo shows a pot dedicated to Siete Rayos, the mpungo of justice.

nganga is a clay or iron vessel that houses the spirits of nature and the dead. The Bantu religions were brought to the United States throughout the mid-20th century. While early members of these religions were predominantly Latinos, a number of Anglo Americans have become initiated throughout the years. Today the Bantu religions operate in the United States and Mexico, although somewhat secretly. The secrets of tradition and some of the practices of the religions make it difficult for them to be practiced in the same open manner practiced in Cuba.

Beliefs

The primary tradition we will examine will be Palo Mayombe, as it is the most evident of the Bantu religions in the United States.

The fundamental teaching of Palo Mayombe is that the creator of the world is known as Nzambi, a benevolent being that has been compared by some practitioners to the Judeo-Christian concept of a creator God. In Kongo past culture, Nzambi was a benevolent creator that gave man medicines to help the world. These medicines were known as minkisi.

According to Kongo mythology, Nzambi gave man the instruction on how to create sacred medicines from plants. These medicines had to be infused with a spiritual power in order to be functional. This spiritual power was attained by taking dirt from graveyards. The soil from these areas contained the spiritual energy from the dead who were buried there.

Bantu belief teaches that the spirits of the dead (known as the nfumbe) can interfere with the lives of the living. The dead can also be called upon to perform work for the living. The spirit of a dead human is placed inside the nganga. The spirit becomes a servant to the ritual specialists who own the nganga. Palo devotees may also refer to spirits known as nfuri. These beings are considered to be malevolent spirits of the dead that are agitated.

Alongside the dead, the spirits of nature (mpungo) are placed in the nganga. Mpungo also are found to be identified with Catholic saints. Practitioners may refer to the mpungo by one of its several different names. The Spanish, Yoruba, Bantu, or Catholic saint name may be used when speaking of the spirits.

Kadiempembe (lungombe) is the dark counterpart to the creator. Palo practitioners claim that magic can be performed with the power of the light (nzambi) or the powers of darkness (kadiempembe). Those who use magic for benevolent work are known as Palo Christianos, while those who use the adversarial powers are known as Palo Judios. Judios (Jewish Palo) merely refers to the absence of Christian images and references in the ritual vessel. The traditional indicator that a nganga may be used for Christian workings is the presence of a crucifix and holy water.

Figure 5.7 Offerings. Officers will discover a number of different types of animals offered to the nganga. This particular nganga has been fed a Florida condor.

Deities of Palo Mayombe

The myths and characteristics of the mpungo dictate what officers will find in the nganga. The nganga will be decorated and filled with implements, colors, and symbols that refer to the mpungo. Once inside the vessel, these items are known as the nkisi.

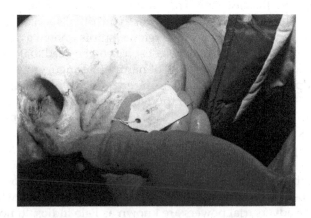

Figure 5.8 Kiyumba. Officers discovered a number of human skulls being sold by a Palo practitioner during a drug bust. (Courtesy of Michael Vincent, Orange County Sheriff's Department, Orlando, Florida.)

Figures 5.9 and 5.10 Firma. Examples of diagrams used in Palo Mayombe to summon the spirits and to give direction to spiritual forces during rituals.

Figures 5.11 and 5.12 This wooden statue representing the mpungo Zarbanda is clutching a photograph of a man who is being magically targeted by the palero who owns the spirits in this nganga. (Courtesy of Michael Vincent, Orange County Sheriff's Department, Orlando, Florida.)

Figure 5.13 The crucifix may be discovered in those ngangas that are considered Palo Christianos and have been baptized with holy water to perform positive deeds.

Table 5.1 Palo Mayombe Deities

Mpungu	Saint	Characteristics
Tiembla Tierra	Jesus Christ	Rules over the earth
Mama Sholan/Choya Wengue	Our Lady of Charity	Rules over rivers
Lucero	Anthony/Nino Atocha	Rules over crossroads
Zarabanda	Peter/Michael the Archangel	Rules over iron
Tata Fumbe/Kobayende Disease/Healing	Lazarus	Rules over
Siete Rayos/Nsasi	Barbara	Rules over storms
Madre de Agua/ Kalunga	Our Lady of Regla	Ocean/sea

Some Palo houses use syncretism (the fusing of different religious beliefs) much like that found in Santería. The saints of the Catholic Church and the orishas of Santería may be used to identify the mpungo.

The following are some of the most popular mpungo of Palo Mayombe:

Tiembla Tierra or Mama Kengue: Rules over the earth. Associated with the orisha Obatala and the Virgin de las Mercedes. The color white is used in the shrine to Tiembla Tierra. Represents wisdom and justice.

Mama Chola or Choya Wengue: Rules over the river. Associated with the orisha Oshun and the Virgin de la Caridad del Cobre. The color yellow is used in her shrines, alongside items associated with the river. Represents richness and pleasures. Her offerings may be left at river banks.

Siete Rayos or Mama Nsasi: Rules over thunder, lightning, and fire. Siete Rayos, or "Seven Rays," refers to seven bolts of lightning. Associated with the orisha Chango and Saint Barbara.

Kobayende or Tata Fumbe: Rules over disease and healing. Known as King of the Dead. Associated with the orisha Babalu-aye and Saint Lazarus.

Centella Ndoki or Mariwanga: Rules over the cemeteries and owns the gate between life and death. Associated with the orisha Oya and the Virgin de la Candelaria.

Vence Batallas or Watariamba: Rules over hunting and justice. His name means "conquers battle." Associated with the orisha Ochosi and Saint Norbert.

Gurufinda: Rules over the forest and herbal magic. Associated with the orisha Osain and Saint Norbert.

Lucero: Rules over the crossroads of fate and opens doorways. Colors associated with Lucero are red and black. Associated with the orisha Eleggua and the Catholic Saint Anthony and Niño Atocha.

Kalunga or Madre De Agua: Rules over the ocean waters and fertility. Associated with the orisha Yemaya and the Catholic saint Our Lady of Regla.

Zarabanda (aka Sarabanda and Rompe Monte): Colors associated with the spirit are green and black. Rules over strength, work, and iron. Associated with the orisha Ogun and Saint Peter.

There are a number of other spirits that can inhabit the nganga. The nfuri are wandering spirits, the bakalu are ancestral spirits, and the nkuyu are ancestors who are paying the debts for negative acts during their lives. They are ghostlike beings that can haunt people.

Figure 5.14 Foundation. The firma is drawn upon the base of the cauldron as the pot is prepared to be filled with the dead. Many ngangas have the firma drawn inside of the pot for consecration.

Figure 5.15 Kisengue, the Kikongo word for "dead cane" used in Palo Mayombe, refers to the use of a human tibia. The tibia is used to summon and control various spirits of the dead.

The nganga

As noted above, the spirits of the dead and of nature are kept together in a vessel known as the nganga. The nganga is viewed much like a small universe that is composed of trees, rivers, and mountains represented by dirt, water, and tree branches. Twenty-one tree branches known as palos are placed into the nganga cauldron, which is made of clay or iron. These are said to ground the pot. The branches come from specific trees that are believed to contain specific energies. Branches are numbered with specific numbers to identify their specific power.

Palos can be used to create magical spells. Palos may be wrapped in clothing in order to affect the owner of the clothes. Palos may be placed in bottles along with various ingredients to perform various works. Palos

(a)

Figure 5.16 Slave spirits. (a) Fransico and the Congo lady (b) are spiritual personalities that are considered spiritual helpers in some Palo houses. Officers may encounter large or typically small statues of these figures. *(continued)*

(b)

Figure 5.16 *(continued)* Slave spirits.

may also be ground and made into various oils that can be used in spell work. Every branch used in the nganga has a specific name and a specific power attributed to it. For example, palo amargo may be used to send away witchcraft, and palo tengue has the ability to heal wounds. Branches may be numbered, with numbers applied to the bottoms of the branches, typically with a marker or paint.

A special stone, known as a matari, is placed first in the pot, and elements of water, shell, herbs, and dirt are then added. The elements found in the nganga will reflect the mpungo to which the pot is dedicated. For example, a cauldron dedicated to a spirit of water may contain materials such as boat oars, fish, and fishnet. Cowrie shells may be found in the pot, as they can draw financial success to the owner of the pot. Cowries were used as a form of currency in some African communities. Other common elements include dirt from cemeteries, church grounds, and jails. Vulture

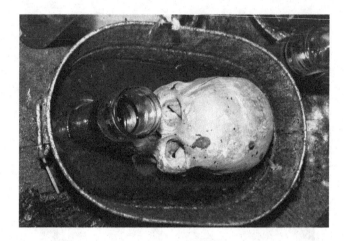

Figure 5.17 The nkuyu or "wandering spirit" may be found in the form of a skull placed into a vessel like a bucket or bowl. (Courtesy of Michael Vincent, Orange County Sheriff's Department, Orlando, Florida.)

feathers may be found in the nganga, as they are connected to a bird that lives among the dead. A piece of the ceiba tree is placed in the nganga for the nkuyo spirit to come. The nkuyo is considered the leader of the nfumbi and the nfuri and guides them through the tops of trees, where they come down to the earth.

Officers may discover a small piece of bamboo or cane that is sealed on both ends. This is the cana brava, and it is most likely filled with mercury.

Figure 5.18 This gourd represents the spirit of Ngurufinda, the owner of the forest and herbal magic. (Courtesy of Michael Vincent, Orange County Sheriff's Department, Orlando, Florida.)

The cana brava acts as a thermometer for the cauldron. The mercury can keep the spirits cool.

The cultural use of bones

Officers who encounter Palo Mayombe shrines may discover animal and human bones in the nganga. Bones play a special part in the building of the nganga, as they represent the ancestors and the spirits of the dead. The energy of these spirits resides in the bones. It is by using these energies that the practitioners of Palo Mayombe can interact with the spirits of the dead. Practitioners refer to human bones as the nfumbe.

The primary human bones used in the nganga are the skull, tibia, and femur. The skull, known as the kiyumba, acts as the intelligence of the dead and as a conductor between the world of the dead and the world of the living. The skull is placed in the center of the nganga's components.

(a)

Figure 5.19 Blood, known as menga in the Kikongo language, is necessary to appease the mpungo. Blood from animals is poured into the vessel in exchange for spiritual favors. *(continued)*

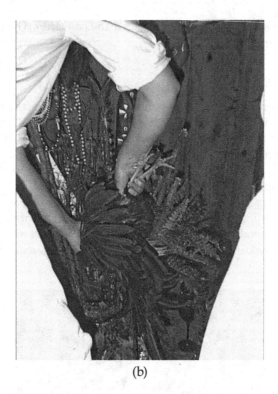

(b)

Figure 5.19 *(continued)* Additional view of menga ritual.

The tibia and femur may be found inside the nganga or near the vessel. These bones can be used as scepters when conducting rituals. These are the primary bones that are used; however, there are a number of case examples in which additional bones were found inside the nganga. In some cases, the skullcap was used as a bowl to hold various substances, such as herbs or water.

There are a number of sources that Palo practitioners use to obtain human bones, including medical specimen companies and scientific supply companies. In recent years bones from these sources have frequently been discovered to be the skeletal remains of Chinese males. There are currently a number of Internet websites that offer human bones. There also have been some Palo practitioners who have obtained bones by robbing graves.

The possession of human bones is a common practice for members of many African religious traditions. The bones are kept to show honor and respect for the dead. However, in the United States, state laws govern

Figures 5.21 and 5.22 The nso nganga is the place where the nganga is typically kept. In this particular case, members of a drug trafficking organization were using the mpungo to protect their operation. (Courtesy of: Winter Haven Police Department, Winter Haven, Florida).

Figure 5.20 This statue of Negro Jose was being used to magically guard a specific area being used for illegal activities. The statue is wearing a pair of handcuffs, a key, and a bell on a chain around his neck.

the sale, possession, and transport of human bones. Non-law enforcement officers who encounter bones should contact law enforcement for assistance. Physical anthropologists should be contacted to identify the bones. The skull (kiyumba) can be used to identify sex, race, and age of the bones.

Sacred spaces

The nganga is viewed by practitioners as a very powerful vessel. The belief regarding the legendary power of the cauldron is so great that early Cuban revolutionaries would carry the vessels into war with them to spiritually fight their enemies. The vessels of Palo Mayombe will traditionally be found in a shed or small house called nso nganga. The shed can be a garage or a small building used for storage. Some cases have revealed a nganga inside a bedroom closet.

Investigators may see a number of symbols and cryptic signs painted on the floors and walls near the nganga. These symbols are known as firma that represent religious concepts in Palo, such as rituals, deities, and prayers. The firma are painted in white, black, or red colors. The symbols most commonly used are crosses, X's, circles, skulls, and arrows. Each symbol represents a concept that is communicated to the spiritual world. Palo practitioners are taught the hidden meanings behind these symbols through oral teachings passed on by the priesthood.

The sacred vessels and artifacts of Palo Mayombe may be discovered by officers responding to calls. Below are a few of the most common vessels and artifacts that are used in the practice of Palo Mayombe.

Lucero

The vessel for Lucero is very similar in appearance to the artifact of Elegua in Santería. Lucero is usually found in the form of a cement head decorated with cowrie shells or painted facial features. Lucero can also be made in various forms according to which camino (road) he represents. Luceros may be made from bamboo or wooden statues. Lucero can be found placed inside of an iron cauldron or a terra-cotta pot. Lucero may be placed on a terra-cotta plate or in a cauldron. His vessel may contain toys, candy, or goats. There is a form known as Lucero Kini Kini that is placed into a wooden statue that is placed in the nganga.

Siete Rayos

The nganga to Siete Rayos may be painted red. The vessels associated with Siete Rayos may contain bones from birds, stones, and red roosters. The skull and horns of a large ram are favored items in his ngangas.

Zarabanda

The vessels for Zarabanda always contain elements made of iron and are always placed in an iron cauldron. The vessel can contain machetes, horseshoes, railroad spikes, knives, and tools. Snakes and snake eggs are offerings to the spirit.

Mama Sholan or Mama Chola

Mama Sholan is typically found in a ceramic or terra-cotta pot. The vessel may contain fishnet, boat oars, river water, and honey. The feathers from owls and vultures are placed in her shrine.

Centelle Ndoki

The vessel for Centelle Ndoki may contain cat bones and cemetery dirt because she rules the cemetery, the dead, and creatures of the night.

Figures 5.23 and 5.24 Forensic analysis. New Jersey state forensic anthropologist Donna Fontana examining a nganga and the contents of the vessel. (Courtesy of Dawn Perlmutter, Symbol and Ritual Intelligence.)

Figure 5.25 A rare offering of dogs is left in the ceremonial vessels of Palo.

Tiembla Tierra

The vessel for Tiembla Tierra may be colored white. The vessel is fed white animals and may contain snakes and bird remains. The palos (sticks) for Tiembla Tierra are from cotton trees, silk trees, and milk trees. Tiemble Tierra is fed pigeons.

Madre de aGua

The vessel for Madre de Agua may contain elements related to water and the ocean because she rules the sea and all the riches that dwell in it. The vessel can contain remains from a ram and turtle.

Ta Jose

There is a statue that is frequently used in the Palo culture of an elderly African man with a gray or white mustache and beard. The image is dressed in white and is seen wearing a white hat. The image known as Ta Jose is a spirit guide that may be used for spiritual protection by practitioners. One of the popular myths regarding the image teaches that Jose was born several hundred years ago. As a young boy, the spirit learned the ways of witchcraft from the Bantu people of the Congo. He was sold into slavery and separated from his family. He escaped into Cuba and was taught the ways of the Mayombe religion. Some statues have scars on his face to reflect his initiation into the religion. Jose is credited with bringing the Palo Mayombe spirit of Zarabanda to Cuba. While there is some controversy surrounding the historical accuracy of his life, Ta Jose is alleged to be buried in the Colon Cemetery in Havana, Cuba.

Investigators may discover statues of the spirit at scenes where practitioners are seeking spiritual protection.

Francisco and Francisca

These two figures are depicted in the form of an elderly African man and woman. They are used to symbolize strong deified ancestors in the religion. The hardships of slavery are depicted in the images of these two figures.

Seven Congos

This image is depicted as a female mother-type figure with seven children sitting around her. These images represent the seven tribes of the Congo that landed in Cuba.

The oldest nganga in Cuba is said to have dated back to the 17th century. It is called Vititi Congo Saca Empeno in Guanabacoa. Most ngangas are said to be able to trace their history back to this nganga.

Group structure

Organized Palo groups are known as munanso, a group of worshippers dedicated to a particular deity. The name of the munanso may reflect its affiliation. A group, such as munanso Siete Rayos, reflects dedication to the mpungo Siete Rayos. The initiated priest in Palo is known as the palero. Palo is traditionally handed down through family lineage.

Members of the munanso may hold a particular office in the temple. The culture observes a degree structure. The ngueyo is a practitioner who has made a pact with the mpungo of his godfather. The tata nkisi is one who has acquired knowledge of using herbs and magic, but has not attained the nganga. The tata nganga is a leader who has received the nganga and can lead a munanso. The tata ndibilinongo not only has a nganga, but has spiritual godchildren. The highest level of initiation is the tata luwongo, who is known as the godfather of the prenda. The bakonfula acts as an assistant to the tata of the munanso. Also known as the mayombero, the bakonfula assists with teaching new initiates about the symbols, rituals, and courtesies of the temple.

Rituals and ceremonies

There is a specific cultural etiquette that practitioners of Palo Mayombe must follow while interacting with the spirits of the nganga. The practitioner addresses the spirits with a salutation of "Sala maleko, maleko sala."

The practitioner treats the spirits with respect, but will always hold a dominant role over the spirits. Some houses use a leather bullwhip (kubula) to dominate the nganga and show authority over the spirits while "whipping" them into obedience. Practitioners may burn piles of gunpowder called fula to get the attention of the spirits. It is said among devotees that fula "shakes the dead." And traditional songs and prayers known as mambos may be uttered to call upon the spirits.

Divination

Practitioners may use objects to interact with the spirits in the nganga. The chamalongo are four pieces of coconut that are thrown to the ground in front of the nganga. The pattern in which the pieces land is interpreted by the practitioner as a response from the spiritual world. The dead are believed to speak through the chamalongo. Cowrie shells, known as encobo, are also used to interpret the will of the spirits. These are seven large cowrie shells plus two items called inkana. These are indicators that are usually a black stone and a shell.

An artifact, known as the vititi mensu, is an animal horn used in divination rites. The horn is filled with herbs and various materials and then capped off with a mirror and wax. The practitioner is trained to use the artifact to see messages from the spirits by looking into the mirror.

Sacrifices and offerings

Animal sacrifices in Palo Mayombe are performed using a knife called the mbele. The mbele must be received by an initiate from the mpungo Zarabanda. The blood of animals is used to feed the spirits that live in the nganga. Blood is known as menga and is an essential tool in interacting with the deities. Blood is taken from various animals offered to the nganga, including chickens, goats, rams, sheep, and dogs. Exotic animals may be used as well: snakes, spiders, and even horses.

The animal is presented to the spirit as prayers (mambos) are offered. The animal is killed and the blood of the animal is poured onto the objects inside the nganga. The carcass of the animal is placed inside the cauldron, where it will remain until the practitioner feels it is necessary to remove it.

The spirit inside the pot may instruct practitioners to offer specific items. Fruit, vegetables, and various animals may be added to the nganga according to the spirit's instruction. There are varying opinions on the issue of adding human blood to the nganga. Cultural informants inside the religion have advised that it is a risk to offer human blood to the spirit inside, as it would soon develop a taste for it and demand it on a regular basis.

Anthropologist and Afro-Cuban religious scholar Stephan Palmie (2002) tells the story of a drug dealer who began feeding his nganga narcotics:

> One story about a nganga named Avisa Me con Tiempo (Warn Me in Time) dealt with a drug dealer who began feeding his nganga lines of cocaine not only to enhance the spirit's vigilance but to bind him ever more closely into a relation of dependency. The stratagem backfired. The nganga began to demand more and more cocaine. Joining his owner in a vicious circle of economically fatal overconsumption until the latter was eventually done in, not by police, but by his suppliers and creditors.

Initiation

The Palo initiation begins with a pact between a god (nsambi), the living (munanso), and the dead (nfumbe). The initiate is given a ceremonial bath filled with sacred herbs and liquids.

The initiate may be taken to a cemetery to find the spirit that will work in the nganga. The priest will perform divination over various graves in order to find a willing spirit. Rum is poured onto a grave, and the priest listens for the sound of rumbling, which signifies that the spirit inside is willing to work in the nganga. If the spirits of the graveyard (Cobayende and Centella Ndoki) are not fed offerings in exchange for the bones, the restless dead of the nfuri may begin to cause problems for the priest. Offerings that are left at the grave site include tobacco, coffee, and candles. Bones may be taken from the grave and placed in the pot alongside bits of soil. Water, animal bones, peppers, and vegetables are added to create a new ritual vessel. Ingredients will also be taken from the priest's nganga and placed in the new pot in order to "give birth" to the nganga.

The initiate is blindfolded and a number of ritualistic cuts are made on his or her body. A razor or spur is used to cut the flesh in a number of locations. This cutting is known as the rayado; initiates may refer to this as being "scratched in." The neck, feet, hands, and chest area are cut, and the blood of the initiate is placed in the nganga to bind him or her to the spirit. Gunpowder, rum, and powdered bone can be placed in the cuts, and then the cuts are sealed with wax.

A symbol known as firma or patipemba of the spirit is carved into the flesh of the initiate. This symbol is used to call upon a specific spirit. The initiate also receives a secret symbol that is known only to members of the munanso. The tongue also may be cut. Drumming and chanting are performed to invoke the spirits, and fula is burned to obtain messages from the spirits. Initiates are given a set of firma signatures that are to be used only by the practitioners themselves. Paleros believe that anyone who has a personal firma can use it to control the owner's spirits. Fake firmas may be used for public display while using the real firma in private.

The initiate receives a large strand of beads called the collar de bandera. The beads are worn during certain Palo ceremonies. The bead's color reflects the mpungo that the initiate serves. The strand of beads is about 4 feet in length and is worn from the left side of the body over to the right side.

Trance possession can occur during this ceremony. The possession in Palo allows the initiate to see with the eyes of the spirits. This "mounting" of the initiate by the spirit is known as montado. The priest will blow cigar smoke behind the ears of the initiate to bring about possession.

Herbalism

Herbs play a very important role in Palo Mayombe practices. The herbs of the forest contain the energies necessary to heal and protect mankind. One of the most important herbal mixtures in Palo Mayombe is called chamba, which is a mixture of herbs, peppers, alcohol, bone, and other ingredients. Chamba is used to purify ritual objects and to invigorate the spirits.

There are a number of special powders created in Palo Mayombe known as mpolos. These powders are made from cemetery dirt, powdered bone, and snake and bat skins. The branches of the silk cotton tree, known as the ceiba, are used in various healing rites in Palo. A popular form of healing in the Palo religion is known as a limpieza. This is a type of cleaning that is performed by a priest or priestess and uses various herbs, rum, smoke, powdered eggshell, cascarilla, and sometimes a rooster. A similar type of cleansing may be done using cigar smoke blown over the body of a client and called a despojo. The nganga can also be used to cure illnesses according to some practitioners.

Some of the common herbs used in the Kongo traditions include:

Mecheiso: *Ocimum basilicum* (basil).
Dioke: *Ambrosia artemisiiflora.*
Carbonero naona: *Cassia biflora.*
Carbonero espanta muerto: *Petiveria alliacea* (anamu).

Yunkagua: *Guaiacum officinalis* (lignum vitae tree).
Cereke: *Ficus nitida* (Indian laurel, bay laurel).
Inkita: *Amyris balsamifera*.
Palo cuaba (West Indian rosewood).

Artifacts

Initiates may have received beaded necklaces known as collars de bandera (see "Initiation" section). These necklaces are nearly 4 feet long and contain beads, shells, and chain. They are worn over the left shoulder during ceremonies.

Charms known as makutos or resguardos are created by paleros. These charms may be found in the form of bones wrapped in cloth. The color of the cloth may reflect the mpungo to which the charm is dedicated.

The mpaka is an artifact that is made from an animal horn. The horn includes ingredients found in the nganga and is sealed with wax. The horn may be used to transport the fundamental materials used in the nganga.

Working the nganga

The following was a message sent between gang members online:

> My partner from Dena was facing a cool 15 fed, got involved and beat the shit. He rocking hard with it now. If you seen you would never know. He just the average joe blow but he has an nkisi at home that all he has to do is write someone's name down and place it on the spikes and that person will die. He say he tell clients his shit works within 21 days so it's fast.

Paleros are very secretive about their practices. While most exist to perform herbal healings and benevolent spell work, officers will probably find it difficult to gain access to intelligence about rituals and inner workings of the Palo religion.

Animal sacrifices to the nganga may be illegal in your state. Check state statutes regarding the use of animal sacrifices as it pertains to religious rites.

Appropriation of the religion

Because of Palo's reputation as being an aggressive form of occultism, it is sought out by some members of the drug trade. Some cases involving

Palo have been among traffickers seeking to use the religion as a means of protection and security from rivals.

One popular book on the subject advises readers how to use special firma (signatures) that can be used to make a person invisible to police. The signatures are to drawn on parchment or a brown paper bag. The paper is then placed on the nganga. The devotee is then instructed to offer two black pigeons, a red rooster, and two white quails. The blood of the animals should drip onto the paper. The paper is then folded and placed inside a small leather bag along with the heart of a hummingbird. It is then carried by the devotee as an amulet.

Incident and crime scenes

If a nganga is discovered in the course of an investigation, officers should look for human remains. The origins of these remains should be analyzed by a local medical examiner. Remains may have been attained from illegal means such as illegal trafficking or grave robbing. Although it is unlikely, the remains could be from a homicide. If the materials are found to be legal specimens, they should be returned to the proper owner. There are a number of Internet-based businesses that sell animal remains. Some animal bones can easily be mistaken as human bones. This determination becomes especially difficult when encountering fragmented bones. Agencies should contact a forensic anthropologist for determination of the origin of the bones.

Examining bones

When bones are discovered at a scene, the primary two tasks should be to:

1. Identify the types of bones at the scene: animal or human?
2. Identify whether they came from more than one animal or human.

There are a number of animal bones that appear very similar to human bones. Most mammal bones appear very similar to human bones. Fragmented deer, bear, and monkey bones appear very similar to human bones. When working scenes involving Palo Mayombe, the skull is going to be the most frequently discovered bone in the nganga because it contains the intelligence of the dead.

There are number of differences between animal and human skulls. The following are some of the differences presented by Dr. Tanya Peresduring the death investigation conference sponsored by the Southern Institute of Forensic Science.

Forenic anthropologist Donna Fontana has worked on cases involving Palo Mayombe artifacts. She advises that if bones are discovered in the nganga, then the nganga should be kept intact and placed inside a large bag for transport to the medical examiner's office. Bones that are removed should be handled carefully, as some may fracture. The human cranium may be located under several objects in the pot. The objects should be removed one by one, and then bones removed and examined separately. All items should be photographed *in situ* before removal.

Officers should use caution when handling artifacts, such as amulets. Residue of mercury may be present among these objects. If mercury is present, stay upwind from the area of contamination. Use a mercury spill kit if needed and utilize self-contained breathing apparatus (SCBA), if possible.

Officers handling artifacts or patients may discover animal blood from sacrificial rituals. Utilize gloves, masks, and eye protection as needed. When examining a nganga, use gloves to prevent possible contamination. Blood, feces, animal remains, and other hazardous contaminants have been found in the nganga. Some contain knives, guns, and even booby traps. Many paleros use gunpowder in rituals. Be cautious using anything that could ignite the powder.

Some medical examiners have utilized x-ray machines to inspect the inside of the nganga. Investigators may discover materials inside the nganga that may contain the names of rivals and associates. These can help provide narcotics officers with additional intelligence regarding affiliates in the drug trade. Toy dolls, dolls made from cloth and bundles of sticks, may contain pieces of paper with names written on them. Also, photographs of rivals may be found alongside items.

Exercise caution when opening packets and items such the cana brava, the piece of bamboo found in some pots. These can contain mercury and can present hazards to unprotected staff at the scene.

Table 5.2 Comparison of Animal and Human Bones

Human Skull	Animal Skull
Big head w/ small face	Small vault, big face
Vault is smooth	Vault is rough
Foramen Magnum is centered	Foramen Magnum is posterior
Chin is present	Chin is absent
Orbits at front	Orbits on side
Small nasal	Nasal projected
Jaw is 'U' shaped	Jaw is 'V' shaped

Table 5.3 Bones Used in Palo

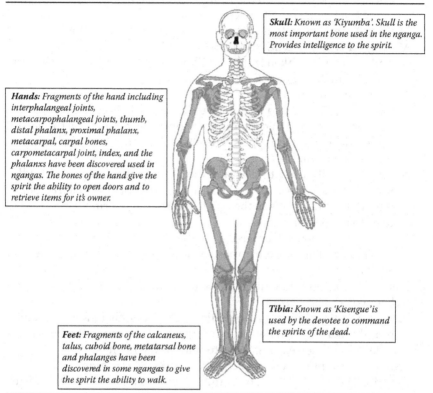

Skull: *Known as 'Kiyumba'. Skull is the most important bone used in the nganga. Provides intelligence to the spirit.*

Hands: *Fragments of the hand including interphalangeal joints, metacarpophalangeal joints, thumb, distal phalanx, proximal phalanx, metacarpal, carpal bones, carpometacarpal joint, index, and the phalanxs have been discovered used in ngangas. The bones of the hand give the spirit the ability to open doors and to retrieve items for its owner.*

Tibia: *Known as 'Kisengue'is used by the devotee to command the spirits of the dead.*

Feet: *Fragments of the calcaneus, talus, cuboid bone, metatarsal bone and phalanges have been discovered in some ngangas to give the spirit the ability to walk.*

Cultural terms

Bilongo: A spell or medicine, usually found in the form of a "bundle."

Chamalongo: Divination system using coconut shells to interact with the spirits.

Firma: The signatures of the spirits in Kongo religions. The firma are typically drawn to invoke the spiritual presence of a deity.

Fula: Gunpowder used in Congo-based rituals.

Kiyumba: The skull used in the nganga. Represents the intelligence of the dead.

Kuenda: Bones used in the nganga to control the dead.

Malongo: The original Bantu nkisi as a sacred medicine.

Mambo: A song used to invoke a spirit.

Matari: Stone used in the nganga.

Mbele: Knife or machete used in rituals.

Menga: Means "blood" in the Kikongo language. Animal blood is offered to the nganga in the Kongo religions, while songs that speak of menga being spilled are chanted.

Mpaka: Animal horn that contains the essence of the nganga.

Mpungo: The Bantu deities in Palo Mayombe.

Muinda: A candle. Taken from the Kikongo word *mwinda*, which refers to anything luminous.

Nfinda: Cemetary dirt.

Nganga: Originally used to describe the healer in West African Bantu religions. It is used in contemporary practices to describe the sacred vessel that houses the spirits. The nganga is usually an iron cauldron or a ceramic pot.

Nkisi: Originally used to describe the sacred medicines and bundles used by Bantu priests. The nkisi is used to denote the material object that houses the spirits of the dead. The Kikongo term *nkisi* is used to refer to a fetish or charm.

Nkobos: Divination system using seashells.

Palero/palera: The office of priest or priestess in Palo Mayombe and Kongo faiths.

Palo Christianos: Practitioners who dedicate their vessels to the benevolent deity Nzambi.

Palo Judias: Practitioners who dedicate their vessels to Kadiempembe or Lukankasi, which has been interpreted by some as the devil.

Prenda: Means "jewel." It is used to refer to the nganga.

Rama: The traditions or "branches" of the Kongo religions.

Rayado: The ritual in which an initiate makes a pact with the spirits. *Rayado* means "consecrated" and refers to the cutting ceremony. Also known as being "scratched in."

Resguardo: A charm used to protect.

Tata: Means "father." Used to describe a male office of initiation in Palo Mayombe.

Yaya: Means "mother." Used to describe female office of initiation in Palo Mayombe.

References

Arostegui, Natalia Bolivar, *Ta Makuende Yaya y las Reglas de Palo Monte: Mayombe Bbrillumba, Kimbisa, Shamalongo*, Cuba: Ediciones Unión, Unión deEscritores y Artistas de Cuba, 1993.

Bockie, Simon, *Death and the invisible powers: The world of Kongo belief*, Indiana University Press, Bloomington, In., 1993.

Cabrera, Lydia, *El Monte*, Miami, FL: Ediciones Universal, 1971.

Canizares, Baba Raul, *The book on Palo: Deities, initiatory rituals and ceremonies*, New York: Original Publications, 2002.

de Mattos Frisvold, Nicholaj, *Palo Mayombe: The garden of blood and bones*, Bibliothéque Rouge (Scarlet Imprint), 2011.

Fontana, Donna, author interview, Forensic Anthropology Services, LLC.

Guerra, Jesus Fuentes, and Armin Schwegler, *Lengua y ritos del Palo Mayombe: Dioses Cubanos y sus Fuentes Africanas*, Madrid: Vervuert-Iberoamericana, 2005.

Humes, Edward, *Buried secrets*, Humes, NY: Dutton Publishing, 1991.

Lage, Domingo B., *History has repeated*, Vol. 1, Pomona, CA: Botanica Tata Miguel, 2001.

Martinez, Rafael, Brujeria: Manifestations of Palo Mayombe in South Florida, *Journal of the Florida Medical Association*, August 70(8): 629–34. 634a 1983.

McGaffey, Wyatt, *Astonishment and power: The eyes of understanding Kongo minkisi*, Smithsonian Institution, Washington, DC, 1993.

Megenney, William W., Bantu survival in the Cuban "lengua de Mayombe," ISLAS 51.

Ortiz, Fernando, *Los negros brujos*, Miami, FL: Ediciones Universal, 1906.

Palmie, Stephan, *Wizards and scientists*, Duke University Press, Durham, NC, 2002.

Thompson, Robert Ferris, *Flash of the spirit: African and Afro-American art and philosophy*, Vintage, New York, 1984.

chapter six

Mexican folk religions and practices

Curanderismo

A number of artifacts, ceremonies, and icons associated with the practices of Mexican folk religion and curanderismo have been utilized by members of drug trafficking organizations for several years. Many members of Mexican-based drug trafficking organizations were brought up following the practices of this spiritual culture and still seek spiritual and physical guidance from the culture.

Curanderismo is not a specific religion, but is a combination of practices from Mexican and Spanish American communities. The word *curanderismo* is derived from the Spanish *curar*, meaning "to heal." The term refers to the healing practices that are the primary focus of this spiritual tradition.

The practices of curanderismo may be used by members of various faiths. It does not follow one specific dogma or ideology. Instead, there are several common shared beliefs that are passed along orally and through popular literature regarding this group of practices. Drug traffickers may be Catholic, Protestant, or not affiliated with any specific religion in order to subscribe to this culture.

Historical background

Curanderismo mixes cultural aspects of Aztec, African, Native American, and European witchcraft cultures. Early medicine in Spain was affected by the concept of Hippocratic medicine from the Greeks and Romans in the 16th century. This system of healing also acquired techniques and knowledge from the culture of the Moors. Spanish colonialism became familiar with the texts of European-based witchcraft during the witch hunts. Many of the writings and techniques of witchcraft were absorbed into the Mexican folk religions. The healing techniques and philosophies of Native Americans were also introduced into this folk system.

Beliefs

One of the main principles that curanderismo observes comes from the Greek philosophy of wellness known as humors. The philosophy teaches that the human body has a certain balance of hot and cold principles. These principles can be thrown off by various illnesses. Low metabolic rates resulting from colds and pneumonia may affect the cold concept. High metabolic rates from shock and diabetes may affect the hot concept.

The treatment philosophy is to approach the cold's imbalance with a hot remedy. Likewise, the hot imbalance is treated with a cold treatment. The goal is to restore harmony to these concepts. This may be resolved using teas, oils, herbs, and foods.

Group structure

There are no organized groups in curanderismo, such as those found in a traditional church; instead, the practices of this system of healing are used by members of various faiths. The typical organization in curanderismo consists of a healer and client.

The central figure who provides healing in curanderismo is the curandero (females are known as curanderas). These healers use special spiritual abilities to heal others. These abilities are called el don de Dios, or "gifts from God." The gift to heal may be something that the curandero or curandera is born with. Some children are recognized as potential healers from a very young age. Some curanderos do not realize their gift of healing until they receive a spiritual calling in their lives. Some healers are simply individuals who become apprentices to established healers in the community.

The curandero serves as a counselor, doctor, and even exorcist. Curanderos may operate spiritual supply stores known as botanicas or yerberas. Some curanderos are very discreet about their presence in the local community.

Drug traffickers may seek assistance from a curandero. Some have sought spiritual services to provide cleansings or to get magical assistance in escaping rivals and police.

Patron saints and folk saints

Saints are those spiritual personalities that are considered sacred to members of a religious faith. The saints as recognized in the Catholic Church were sufferers for their faith. Many of them were martyred for their faith.

Figure 6.1 Our Lady of Guadalupe. Statues used to honor the virgin at a grow operation in the mountains of California. (Courtesy of Butte County Sheriff's Office Special Enforcement Unit, Oroville, California.)

Many of them performed miracles during their lifetime. Now in the heavenly world, saints are mediators between humans and God.

There are a number of spirits that are honored in some Mexican communities and known as folk saints. Folk saints are considered sacred, and some are even worshipped, but they have not been officially canonized by the Catholic Church. They typically were people known for their ability to follow God through difficult circumstances and were recognized by local communities as saints.

They have become popular because families and communities have supported their existence. Frank Graziano, professor of Hispanic Studies at Connecticut College, says, "Saints emerge for the fulfillment of specific needs held in common by members of the community. The assignment of specialties which resemble indigenous (and also pagan Roman) belief in multiple deities with specific functions, provides a versatile, otherworldly alliance for remedy of the world's diverse problems" (Graziano, 2006).

An example of the development of folk saints can be seen in the origins and myths surrounding an obscure spirit known as Anima de Leyva or Difunto Leyva. The origin of this saint's story comes from an incident in Ojinaga, Chihuahua, where a Mexican man named Jose Maria Leyva

Figure 6.2 Juan Soldado. Images of this folk saint may be found among those crossing the border. It is believed that Juan Soldado will protect those who pray to him.

was killed by a member of the Mexican Army. Levya was accused of having an affair with a jealous soldier's wife. The soldier came to confront Leyva and set him on fire. Leyva burned while claiming his innocence. Leyva was later buried under the floor where he was murdered. Leyva's pointing finger soon appeared from the mound of dirt where his body lay. The local community soon began to gather and pray to this finger as a symbol of injustice. The finger was removed and placed in a local church. Church authorities condemned the practice as pagan and ordered the finger to be removed from the church. The icon was taken back to the scene of the crime, where a temple was established for the saint. This spirit is still worshipped today, by both criminal and noncriminal individuals, for matters dealing with injustice.

Some of the folk saints have been publicly opposed by the Catholic Church, and in some cases this has only increased their popularity. The

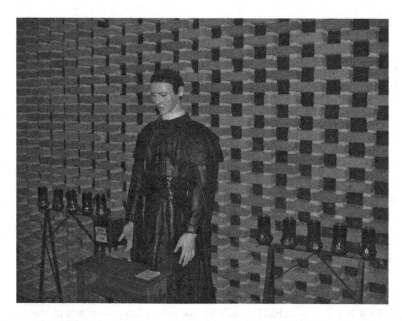

Figure 6.3 Father Toribio Romo. This shrine dedicated to Father Toribio is frequented by devotees who seek his assistance in bringing relatives into the United States from Mexico.

saints are considered intercessors with God and have the ability to perform miracles. Most miracles relate to health issues, love and romance, employment, and preservation of family. Each folk saint has its own personal history, prayers, rituals, images, shrines, and songs. Images of saints may be placed in various positions in order to compel the saint to act. A popular belief is that statues that represent saints can be placed upside down while they are being petitioned. The statue is viewed as being at work and will be returned to its normal position once prayers are answered. Devotees to the saints make promises or contracts with the saints known as mandas. This is a personal promise to do something in exchange for a favor by the saint.

Among narco traffickers, the saints may be called upon for benevolent purposes, or they may be called upon to perform supernatural work for criminal or deviant activities. .

Our Lady of Guadalupe

One of the most popular folk saints of curanderismo is Our Lady of Guadalupe. She is the patron saint of Mexico. The legends surrounding this saint say that on December 15, 1531, she appeared as the Virgin

Figure 6.4 Niño de Atocha. Legends surrounding this image tell of the saint's ability to access prisoners and, in some cases, provide release from confinement. (See Page 161.)

Mary to an Aztec farmer named Juan Diego on the hill of Tepeyac near Mexico City. Tepeyac was previously dedicated to the Aztec earth goddess Tonantzin. The virgin called herself Tleuauhtlaceupeuh, which was soon associated with the word *Guadalupe* in the Nahuatl language. The word means "she who came flying from the region of light like an eagle of fire."

The legend surrounding the virgin is that she told Juan Diego to build a temple to her and to tell others about her appearance. Diego shared his news with a local archbishop, who demanded that the appearance be backed up with proof of miracles. Miraculously, roses began to grow on a barren hill and Juan was told to pick them. An image of Mary also appeared on the cloak of Juan Diego. The virgin is honored every year with a pilgrimage to the spot where she appeared.

The virgin of Guadalupe became known as a symbol of national pride, as the image brought together the culture of the indigenous people of Mexico with the practice of Spanish Catholicism. The mother of God was believed to have brought peace between colonialists and the native people of Mexico.

Members of narco-cults may avoid Our Lady of Guadalupe, as she is seen as a very benevolent saint who loves the righteous. (Santa Muerte is sometimes referred to as the dark side of Our Lady of Guadalupe.) However,

Figure 6.5 Saint Raymond (second statue to the right) is petitioned to keep gossip away, but in the hands of the narco, the saint is used to keep informants and rivals quiet. (Courtesy of Orange County Sheriff's Department, Santa Ana, California.)

some officers have recalled crime scenes involving drug traffickers using the saint for protection and mercy after committing criminal acts.

Juan Soldado

Juan Soldado (Juan the Soldier) is considered the patron saint of illegal immigrants. He is also believed to have the ability to help in health and criminal matters. Twenty-four-year-old Juan Castillo Morales was a private in the Mexican army in the 1930s.

On Februrary 13, 1938, an eight-year-old Olga Camacho disappeared while walking to a local grocery store. The child's body was discovered raped and mutilated in an abandoned building. A woman claiming to have been guided by the Virgin Mary discovered the child's body the next day.

Figure 6.6 San Cipriano is the patron saint of magicians and can be prayed to to perform destructive magic known as brujería. (Courtesy of Michael Vincent, Orange County Sheriff's Department, Orlando, Florida.)

Tijuana residents began to riot. A local police station was burned down by rioters. Fire trucks that responded to the fire had their hoses cut by rioters with machetes. The day became known as Bloody Tuesday among the local community.

On February 17, 1938, police falsely arrested and executed Juan Castillo Morales, or Juan Soldado, for the crime. Morales was alleged to have been seen in the area of the victim. His common-law wife reportedly claimed that Morales came home covered in blood and confessed to the child's murder.

The crowd that turned him over to the police were said to have realized too late that the soldier was actually innocent. Stories began to circulate about strange voices that could be heard around his grave site, and that blood would pour from his grave. The spirit of Juan Soldado was believed to be seeking revenge. The crowd began to place piles of stones

Figure 6.7 Images of San Martin de Porres may be used by narcos to enable them to move throughout areas without being detected.

over his grave and telling stories of his miracles. He is known as the victim intercessor by many, as he was a victim of false accusations.

Juan Soldado is honored especially on June 24, which is the feast of John the Baptist. Devotees to the saint place offerings of crutches, locks of hair, and petitions written on pieces of paper in his shrines. Many cry out "Juan Soldado, ayudame a cruzar," or "Soldier John, help me across."

Santa Marta

Martha (Marta) was friend to Jesus and is the patron saint of cooks and servants. Santa Marta was known for taming a crocodile and, in some legends, a dragon. Marta is called upon to break women of infidelity and to command or compel a person to do his or her bidding. There are two forms of this image. The first is the image known as Saint Martha

Figure 6.8 Jesus Malverde shrine. There are a number of Malverde devotees who follow the folk saint as a symbol of hope to the impoverished. The growing trend in narcos appropriating Malverde as the patron saint of narcos appears to overshadow the minority of followers who are not involved in criminal activities. (See Page 172.)

of Bethany. This image of the saint depicts her as a white female holding a torch and standing on top of a dragon. The second image is Saint Martha Lubana, or San Marta Dominadora, which depicts Martha as an African woman clutching a snake around her neck. Both images can be used to dominate or control others. Dominadora is called upon to help return a wandering husband. The Lubana image is used frequently in Puerto Rican Espiritismo and Dominican Voodoo to represent an African spirit.

Dr. Jose Gregorio Hernandez

Dr. Jose Gregorio Hernandez is a folk saint who is honored for his healing powers. Hernandez, commonly known as Jose Gregorio, was a Venezuelan physician who provided healthcare to impoverished patients free of charge. After his death, Hernandez became elevated to the status of a saint by local communities.

Figure 6.9 This shrine in Culican, Mexico, is visited regularly by drug dealers seeking spiritual empowerment from Jesus Malverde. (Courtesy of Tomas Castelazo, www.tomascastelazo.com/WikimediaCommons/CC-BY-SA-3.0.)

San Toribio Romo

Father Toribio Romo was a Catholic priest who was known for his work among the poor and sick. Toribio was one of the 24 martyrs of the 1927–1929 Cristero Wars between the Mexican revolutionaries, the Catholic Church, and the Mexican government. Father Toribio was shot and killed by Mexican soldiers in 1928. In 2000, Father Toribio was officially canonized by Pope John Paul II.

Many pray to this folk saint for his ability to provide protection for those seeking to cross international borders. Devotees of this saint tell stories of how the saint has appeared in the desert to migrants who are hungry and tired. Some dioceses in the United States and Mexico are lobbying to have San Toribio Romo declared the patron saint of migrants.

Saint Niño de Atocha

One of the images appropriated by narco-cults is the icon of Saint Niño de Atocha. The image represents Jesus Christ as a child. The image was developed in the 16th century when Dominican friars placed a statue of a

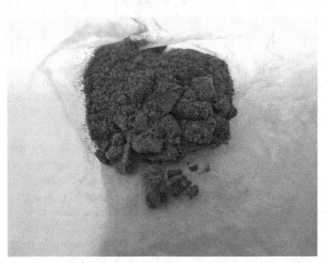

Figures 6.10 and 6.11 Heroin bust. Officers discovered a heroin dealer using various folk saints to magically protect his work. They also discovered black tar heroin in a homemade shrine. (Courtesy of Sgt. Phillip Edwards, St. Helens Police Department, St. Helens, Oregon.)

Figure 6.12 Cartel member. Jesus Malverede has become a frequent icon used in the photographs and websites of drug traffickers.

Christ child in the lap of a statue of the Virgin Mary in a sanctuary in the suburb Atocha in outer Madrid. Eventually the child was depicted alone and was recognized as a symbol of miracles.

The image of the child is believed to have appeared to imprisoned Spaniards who had been captured by the Moors. The child was said to bring food and water to those prisoners in need. The spirit of Niño de Atocha is called up by those in prison and those who are traveling. In some cases, human smugglers have been discovered using this saint for protection and aid.

San Ramon (aka Saint Raymond Nonatus and Nonato)

Saint Raymond is a Catholic saint who was born in Portella, Catalonia, Spain. Saint Raymond was believed to have been delivered by Caesarean section. Tragically, his mother died during his birth. He is known by his followers as Nonato, which is a Spanish adjective used to describe someone who was not born naturally.

Figures 6.13 and 6.14 Stash shrine. This image of Jesus Malverde (top) guards a stash of marijuana (bottom) discovered during a narcotics investigation. (Courtesy of Lt. Doug Gregg, Washington County Sheriff's Department, Johnson City, Tennessee.)

Figure 6.15 San Alejo. Saint Alexis is called upon by devotees to return enemies back to where they came from. See Page 169.

Raymond was a member of the Mercedarians, a fraternal order that helped the community and worked to rescue Christians who had been imprisoned by the Moors. Raymond became chief ransomer for prisoners and allowed himself to become imprisoned in exchange for freeing other Christians. While imprisoned, Raymond evangelized many of his Muslim captors. To stop his efforts, his captors sewed his mouth shut. After his death, he became known as the patron saint of childbirth, pregnant women, children, and priests who want to protect the secrecy of confession. Because of this, he is appropriated by those seeking to silence others. He is also believed to help those who have been accused falsely.

Padlocks may be kept on his altar to close the mouth of an enemy or to keep a secret. Several variations of spells are performed using the image of Saint Raymond. Many of these spells include the application of a dime to the image's mouth and a piece of gum or string to hold the dime in place. The spell is believed to close the mouth of an enemy.

Figure 6.16 Cartel saint. San Judas is frequently referenced among the cartels. This patron saint of impossible causes is called upon for his ability to aid anyone in society. (See Page 175.)

San Cipriano (aka Saint Cyprian)

There are two famous saints known by this name. The first, Saint Cyprian of Carthage, was believed to have been raised in the Greek religious culture, where he was reputed to have learned various forms of sorcery and witchcraft. He later became a Christian and put away his powers. The second, Saint Cyprian of Antioch, was said to have had a similar conversion, but kept his ability to perform occult practices. His legends teach that he kept his knowledge in a book. The book known as *The Great Book of Saint Cyprian*, or *El Libro del San Cipriano*, teaches readers how to perform spells, find treasures, make a pact with Satan, and other spells pertaining to black magic.

The book is used by some curanderos, but is more popular among brujas, or "witches," in Mexico.

San Cipriano is known as the patron saint of magicians. He is prayed to for spiritual protection from physical and spiritual harm. He is called upon to remove curses and perform brujería (witchcraft).

San Martin de Porres

Born in Lima, Peru, in 1579, San Martin de Porres is recognized as having the ability to relieve poverty. Porres was a Dominican friar who was

Figure 6.17 A statue of San Judas guards the stash of a member of Los Caballeros Templarios.

recognized for his acts of service to mankind. He was believed to have been given the ability to fly and the ability to be in more than one location at a time.

He established a hospital and an orphanage to aid underprivileged children. San Martin de Porres is believed to have the ability to move through locked doors and may be appropriated to open secure spaces.

Los Tres Grandes

Practitioners of curanderismo also recognize a special group of folk healers who were elevated to sainthood by locals who knew them. The three healers, known as Los Tres Grandes, or "Three Great Ones," are Don Pedrito Jaramillo, Niño Fidencio, and Teresita Urrea. These three figures were recognized as being gifted healers who served mankind with special spiritual gifts and can still be accessed by practitioners.

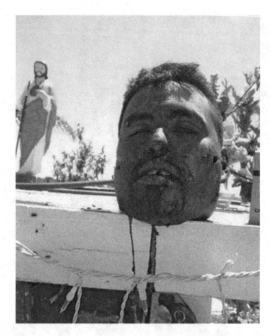

Figures 6.18 and 6.19 San Judas shrine. The remains of executed members of the Los Zetas cartel are left at a roadside shrine in Mexico. (Courtesy of Chivas at Borderland Beat.)

Don Pedrito Jaramillo was known as the saint of Falfarrias. He was born in 1829 in Mexico. He learned that he had the gift of healing when he fell from a horse and was able to heal himself. People from all over the country traveled to be healed by Don Pedrito until he died in 1907.

Niño Fidencio was born in Mexico in 1898. He worked with a German doctor for years, during which time he discovered his ability to heal. Followers, known as Fidencistas, travel to his shrine every year to be healed. Some spiritualists believe that they can channel the spirit of Niño to heal others.

Teresita Urrea was known as the saint of Cabora. Born in Mexico in 1873, Teresita was an apprentice to a curandera (female healer). She was attacked by a man and almost raped. She lapsed into a coma, and those around her thought she was dead and prepared for her funeral. She suddenly awoke from the coma and three days later her mentor died. Teresita took her place and became famous as a healer. She was involved in encouraging the Yaqui Indians to fight for their homeland. Many followers, known as Teresistas, wore images of her on their clothing during battles with the government. Teresista died in exile in the United States in 1906 at the age of 33, allegedly from overwork.

Saint Alexis (aka San Alejo)

The story behind Saint Alexis says that he was born into a rich Roman family. Alexis wanted to live a humble life helping the poor. His parents insisted that he marry a rich woman. Alexis married the girl but told her he wanted to leave and live among the poor serving God. She agreed, and he disguised himself and traveled to Syria, where he lived in poverty. One day an image of the Virgin Mary spoke and said that Alexis was "the man of God." Alexis began to become famous and fled Syria, as he was more concerned with living humbly and helping the poor. Alexis returned to Rome and came to his parents as a beggar. The parents did not recognize him and took him in. Alexis lived under his parents' stairs for 17 years and endured abuse from servants in the home. At the time of Alexis's death, his parents found a note on his body that revealed his identity and his life of penance. Known as San Alejo, which comes from the Spanish *alejar*, which means "return," his image is used to return enemies back to where they came from. Candles may be burned with his image to keep enemies away and turn evil away.

San Martin Caballero

The legend of San Martin Caballero tells that he was a centurion in the Roman army. One day, San Martin was riding his horse and came upon a beggar. The beggar had no clothes, so San Martin tore his cloak and gave half of it to the beggar. That evening San Martin had a dream

Figure 6.20 Drug shipments. More than $200,000 in marijuana was discovered by U.S. Customs inside these statues of a folk saint; 73 bundles of more than 233 pounds of marijuana were stuffed inside the statues. The driver of the vehicle was from Texas and was driving to the U.S. from Mexico. (Courtesy of U.S. Customs and Border Patrol.)

that the beggar turned into Jesus. San Martin left the army to dedicate his life to serving the church as a monk. It is believed that San Martin will help followers by bringing strangers to give aid to his followers. Some businesses display images of San Martin Caballero to bring in customers.

Juan Minero

Juan Minero (Juan the Miner) is a folk saint who is believed to have been a very violent person during his life. After his death, Juan was sent to mine coal to the fires of hell and purgatory. He is considered a tranquil spirit. He is also known as an anima sola, a soul suffering in purgatory. Juan Minero can be called upon in matters of love and can also be used to perform brujería (witchcraft). Juan Minero is frequently used in Venezuelan folk magic and may actually be of Venezuelan origins.

Don Juan Dinero

This Venezuelan folk saint shows up on some altars of curanderos and Mexican spiritual supply stores. Don Juan Dinero is known as Mr. Money, a

Figures 6.21 and 6.22 Saint Simon (aka Maximon) is a spirit that can bring devotees financial success. Traffickers have been using Saint Simon icons to insure financial success in drug operations.

spirit that can bring about financial success. Don Juan Dinero also appears in the form of the Peruvian spirit of Ekeko, who is the god of abundance.

Jesus Malverde

Jesus Malverde (also known as El Santo Bandito, or "The Bandit Saint") was a Mexican bandit who was hanged by governor's orders for being a public nuisance in 1909. His burial site is in his hometown of Culiacan. Some believe he was really a man who was named Jesus Juarez Mazo. The image of Malverde is frequently recognized as a narco saint by members of the drug trade. His tomb is in the capital state of Sinaloa, Mexico. His image depicts the mustached bandit sitting in a chair or standing. He is also known as the angel of the poor and a generous one.

One story says that Malverde had been wounded in the leg and had gotten gangrene. Malverde instructed his partner to cut off his head and carry it to the authorities to get a reward. He then instructed his partner to take the reward and give it to the poor.

Malverde's historical origins are contested. While there is no proof that Malverde existed, Malverde legends are very popular among the poor in Sinaloa. Some individuals from these socioeconomic groups have gotten into the illegal drug trade. Malverde's spiritual protection is sought by those in drug trafficking in order to protect the movements of drug shipments.

Many of Malverde's followers travel to Culiacan, Mexico, where a shrine is dedicated to him. In 1976, Eligio Gonzalez was working as a driver when he was stabbed and shot as he was robbed by an assailant. Gonzalez was left for dead. Gonzalez began to pray to Jesus Malverde, who was only represented at his shrine by a pile of stones. Gonzalez promised the folk saint that if he were allowed to live, he would build a shrine dedicated to Malverde. Gonzalez began work on a shrine and saw the need for an image of Jesus Malverde. Since there are no photographs or sketches of the saint, Gonzalez asked a local artist to create an image of Malverde using features from a local politician and a famous Mexican actor. The temple is located in Culican across from a government building. The temple is frequented by devotees who leave various offerings and gifts, ranging from firearms to narcotics, for the saint. It is rumored that the street to the shrine is closed off when drug dealers want to worship.

Artifacts including statues, amulets, prayer cards, and other items have been used by drug traffickers to petition Jesus Malverde. Many of these artifacts are carried by traffickers during drug runs and transactions. Malverde artifacts have been discovered by investigative agencies during the course of serving drug-related warrants. These same artifacts

Figure 6.23 Doctor Hernandez. Images of the Venezuelan folk saint of healing are used to improve health and get rid of sickness.

have been discovered in stash houses, drug courier vehicles, and clandestine laboratories.

Devotees to Malverde will give the saint offerings of money, marijuana, coca leaves, and music in exchange for his protection.

Pancho Villa

The famous Mexican folk hero who led the Division del Norte, or "Division of the North," in the Mexican Revolution is recognized for his courageous work on earth and as a folk saint. Pancho Villa is believed to give spiritual favors in areas of love, as he was known as a great lover. He is also called upon to aid in matters relating to work, health, and countering envy. As early as 1938, traditional healers began to channel the spirit of Pancho Villa. Recent media observations in Mexico document cases involving

Figures 6.24 and 6.25 The shrine of Santa Muerte at Tepito draws thousands of devotees from around the world. (Courtesy of Leigh Thelmadatter.)

Pancho Villa's image used by narcos in tattoos as a form of magical protection. Offerings given to Pancho Villa include cigarettes, cigars, and alcohol. Among narco groups, Pancho Villa is the name of a brand of marijuana from Sinaloa, Jalisco, and Michoacan.

Judas Tadeo

Judas Tadeo is the patron saint of impossible causes. Also known as Saint Jude, Judas Tadeo is said to be a relative of Jesus. His name means "praises given to God" and "brave to proclaim the faith." There are a tremendous number of positive examples of how Saint Jude is a symbol of hope for the majority of those who honor him. Folklore surrounding the saint states that once he has answered your prayers, you are expected to share the results publicly.

Unfortunately for the Catholic faith, Saint Jude has become very popular among drug traffickers. The power of Saint Jude to do the impossible is a highly sought after talent that those who are trafficking drugs may seek. Common forms of this narco saint have been discovered in prayer cards, statues, and various art forms during drug busts. In some cases contraband has been discovered inside the statues of Saint Jude.

San Simon

Saint Simon, a Guatemalan folk saint, is also known by the name Maximon (pronounced *mash-i-mon*), which is derived from the Mayan word *Ximon*, meaning "bundle" or "tie up." Mayan priests claim that Maximon originated at the beginning of time and is an integral part of Mayan mythology. Early figures representing Maximon were simple dolls made with cloth and wood. Offerings were made to this figure by the Mayans.

He appears as a well-dressed man wearing a hat and sitting in a chair. He is often identified with the spirit of a pre-Colombian deity. He is often given offerings of Coca-Cola, cigarettes, black beans and rice, and alcoholic beverages. He has the ability to bless those who pray to him with financial success. San Simon is known as the man in black to those in folk communities.

San Pascual

Also known as Rey Pascual, this Guatemalan folk saint appears very similar to Santa Muerte. The image is a combination of a human and a skeletal form. The image is depicted in some forms as wearing a crown, holding a scythe, and standing on top of a globe that represents the world. San

Figure 6.26 Statues of Santa Muerte decorate the shores of Catamaco, Mexico. (Courtesy of Dongringo.)

Figure 6.27 Cartel member. The relationship between narcos and Santa Muerte created hostility between the Mexican government and devotees of the death saint.

Figures 6.28 and 6.29 Death saint. Images of Santa Muerte are frequently found at drug-related homicide scenes. (Courtesy of Borderland Beat.)

Figure 6.30 Drug shrine. This shrine was discovered during Operation Hoodoo Voodoo, a multiagency operation that focused on a multistate methamphetamine ring that consulted a spiritual reader for insight into the best times to deliver contraband. (Courtesy of Polk County Sheriff's Department, Lakeland. Florida.)

Pascual is believed to be a reincarnated Mayan deity. The image is used in various forms of healing and to communicate with spirits of the dead.

Saint Michael

Michael is an archangel who is believed to have defeated Satan. The statue of this saint depicts him stepping on an image of Satan. It is believed that praying to Saint Michael will protect you from your enemies. He is also believed to help you repel evil.

The cult of Santa Muerte

Santa Muerte is perhaps the most prolific of the narco saints. The image has become a universal symbol for those in the Mexican drug trade. The

Figure 6.31 Santa Muerte statues used to protect members of a brothel. (Courtesy of Rosendo Perez, New Jersey Gang Investigator's Association.)

skeletal image has many different cultural interpretations, but has come to symbolize the spirit of death in the lifestyle and daily life of drug traffickers.

The historical origins of the image are debated among religious scholars, folklorists, and devotees. Research into the indigenous cultures of Mexico reveals a number of similar deities found among Aztec, Mayan, and syncretic cults throughout history. There are a number of examples of spirits that represent death throughout history.

It is important to note that the majority of Santa Muerte devotees are not involved in criminal activity. For many of her followers, Santa Muerte represents a saint that hears the prayers of the oppressed and the downtrodden. Santa Muerte has become popular among some Latin American law enforcement officers and correctional officers in the prison system. Many Mexican curanderos use Santa Muerte for healing and matters relating to love and prosperity, and have no ties to criminality.

There are several organized public bodies of worship that follow Santa Muerte. One of the most visible religious bodies for Santa Muerte is the Iglesia Tradicionalista México-USA, or "Traditional Catholic Church of Mexico-United States," founded in 2000. David Romo Guillén is the official bishop of the church. The church has locations in Mexico and

Figure 6.32 Chester County District Attorney Tom Hogan showing the 44 defendants in the drug trafficking organization that was responsible for more than $100 million worth of sales of cocaine throughout Pennsylvania. Images of various narco saints were used by the group as a form of protection from law enforcement authorities. (Courtesy of Chester County District Attorney's Office, West Chester, Pennsylvania.)

prayer groups throughout the United States. Although the church uses *Catholic* in its title, it also claims no affiliation with the Catholic Church of Rome. Guillén says, "We prefer to be near God and far from the Pope."

Cultural researchers believe that the first publicized public altar to Santa Muerte was established by Enqriqueta Romero Romero in the Tepito district of Mexico City. A Santa Muerte group known as Parroquia de la Misericordia, or "Mercy Parish," established a group in the Tepito. There is also a Chapel of the Most Holy Death located in the municipality of Pedro Escobedo. The chapel holds an annual Feast of Saint Death every year around All Saint's Day and All Soul's Day.

One of the most visible churches dedicated to Santa Muerte in Mexico is the Church of Santa Muerte International in Mexico City. The church erected a 20-foot statue of the saint in front of its chapel. Local religious organizations have complained to the media about the presence of the statue, saying that its ominous image scares children and attracts drug dealers to the area. The church, which attempted to register with the government as a religious organization under the name Traditional

Figure 6.33 Narcotics officers discover bags of cocaine at the base of a statue of Santa Muerte.

Figure 6.34 Santa Muerte sits as a guardian over a stash of narcotics discovered in a residential search. (Courtesy of Sgt. John Boese and Investigator Chris Lo, Metro Nashville Specialized Investigations Division, Gang Unit.)

Figures 6.35 and 6.36 Faces of death. Statues of Santa Muerte will be found in many different forms and colors. These scenes were discovered during residential searches for narcotics. (Courtesy of Webb County (Texas) Sheriff's Department.)

Figure 6.37 Muerte temple. This shrine had its own dedicated space for worship. (Courtesy of John Garza, Texas Narcotics Officers' Association.)

Mexico-USA Missionaries of the Sacred Heart and Saint Philip of Jesus, was denied on grounds that the church was promoting Santa Muerte and not the traditional liturgy of the mass. In the United States, the Templo Santa Muerte is serving the Santa Muerte followers in Los Angeles, California. The temple holds misas, or "masses," daily that are broadcast live over the Internet, as well as broadcasts a number of rituals related to Santa Muerte.

The Catholic Church in Mexico has been very outspoken against the Santa Muerte phenomenon. In November 2008, the Roman Catholic Archdiocese of Mexico City released a statement condemning Santa Muerte worship and stating that Santa Muerte is not a recognized saint. In 2010, over 500 Catholic devotees held an outdoor mass near a Santa Muerte shrine to demonstrate protest over the movement.

The momentum of protest against worship of the death saint spread throughout Mexico, and soon governmental officials found themselves

Figure 6.38 Images of Santa Muerte were discovered in a residence where narcotics were being sold. (Courtesy of John Garza, Texas Narcotic Officers Association.)

participating in a war against Santa Muerte. In 2009 members of the Mexican military began to destroy public shrines dedicated to Muerte. Bulldozers were used to demolish over 34 shrines along the highway between Nuevo Laredo and Monterrey Mexico. The Mexican government claims that the shrines were meeting places for drug traffickers, and that destroying them would create safer communities.

Santa Muerte researchers have discovered that these forms of public protest have actually done little to squelch worship of the death saint and have actually promoted the image's reputation as the saint who hears the prayers of those outside of mainstream society and church.

In some cases, Santa Muerte followers have become targets of violence. In March 2006, a man worshipping at a Santa Muerte shrine in Nuevo Laredo was shot and killed. Local journalists reported that when they went to the shrine to cover the story, they were turned away by individuals who threatened them if they covered the incident.

Figure 6.39 Statue form of Santa Muerte. Officers may discover statues of the folk saint with removable hands. These are removed until the spirit answers the prayers of the devotee.

Santa Muerte and traffickers

The image of Santa Muerte has gained popularity among many of the Mexican drug cartels. There is a common belief that the image will give spiritual protection to those who call upon her. Likewise, there is a belief among some of her devotees that if she is gives protection to someone and they do not show appreciation to her, she will punish them with death.

In 2003 two teenagers from the border town of Laredo, Texas, were recruited into the Los Zetas cartel to become Zetitas, or "little Zetas." The teens were ordered to become part of three-person sleeper cell of sicarios, or "hitmen," for the cartel. Teen recruits Gabriel Cardona-Ramirez and Rosalio Reta were taken to Mexico and trained in a Zetas tactical camp where they learned tactics and techniques of murder and dismemberment. Cardona-Ramirez and Reta became involved in a number of assassinations for the cartel and were eventually discovered by American law enforcement. Federal agents monitored the teens' activities using a wiretap. The teens bragged about killing a 14-year-old and a rival. An excerpt from the conversation demonstrates the cartel's macabre fascination with Santa Muerte:

> Juvenile #2 replies laughing "where did you cook them dude?" and Cardona-Ramirez laughingly

Figure 6.40 A number of street gangs have latched onto the icons of Santa Muerte as the folk saint's image grows in popularity.

replies "right there at the house. They died on their own thing from the beating, dude. They just died, they just died and shit, dude." Juvenile #2 states "Mother******, they couldn't handle it, dude?" Cardona-Ramirez replies "No dude. No, man you should've been there f******* Bart, it's just that, mother******, a little … a little earlier, man, if we would of waited a little bit longer to go over there with Mike dude. You would have been seeing Pancho, dude. He was crying and crying like a fag-got, 'Nio man, I'm your friend'. 'What friend, you son of a bitch, shut your mouth' and poom! I grabbed a f****** bottle and slash! I slit his whole f****** belly. And ppom! He was bleeding. I grabbed a little cup and poom! The little cup poom! Poom! I filled it with blood and poom! I dedicated it to Santisima Muerte. And then I went to the other faggot and slash! I slit him, and same thing."

In Tijuana, Mexico, a cartel member's associates turned on him because he had spent the cartel's money. The member was tied to a chair and

Figure 6.41 This healing shrine located in the back of a yerberia (spiritual supply store) is used by a curandero for his clients.

dismembered. The victim was then beheaded and the head was offered to Santa Muerte as an offering.

In Nuevo Laredo, members of the Gulf cartel captured members of the Sinaloa cartel and took them to public Santa Muerte shrines and executed them.

In Monterrey, Mexico, members of the Gulf cartel handcuffed and shot three men at a Santa Muerte altar. The assailants lit candles and placed candles with the bodies. The cartel left a banner for rivals that states, "This for everyone who messes with the Gulf cartel. Welcome to Nuevo Laredo, bunch of assholes."

The worship of Santa Muerte has been popular among many of the high-profile leaders of Mexican drug trafficking organizations. Juarez cartel founder Amada Carillo, known popularly as Lord of the Sky, helped financially to establish a temple for Santa Muerte in Mexico City. Gulf cartel cell leader Gilberto Garcia Mena (aka The June) was arrrested in 2001 by authorities who discovered an outdoor temple that Mena built outside of his residence.

In July 2014 members of a Peruvian drug cartel were arrested by police in Lima on charges of drug trafficking and murder. The cartel called itself La Santa Muerte, playing upon the nefarious image of the death saint.

Figure 6.42 Drugs may be placed in shrines dedicated to Santa Muerte as offerings and for her protection.

In addition to ties to established cartels, there have been a number of domestic cases in the United States that demonstrate ties between traffickers and Santa Muerte.

A $4.8 million cocaine trafficking ring was discovered in York County, Pennsylvania, during an investigation known as Operation Special Delivery. The investigation focused on a ring of traffickers who were sending and receiving cocaine through Fed Ex packages from Mexico to York County. Investigators discovered the head trafficker as having several shrines dedicated to Santa Muerte in his home. Many of the drugs were kept in these shrines, and lines of cocaine were discovered as offerings to the saint.

Members of a drug trafficking ring in Johnson City, Tennessee, who were responsible for the distribution of more than 13,000 kilograms of marijuana across the United States were discovered using statues of Santa Muerte to identify themselves and protect their operation. Amulets, statues, lithographs, and shrines were discovered in dealers' homes and vehicles during the investigation.

Police in Bisbee, Arizona, discovered 59 pounds of cocaine and 25 pounds of methamphetamine in the framework of a vehicle. The driver was carrying a number of Santa Muerte amulets and statues that were used to protect the shipment spiritually.

Figures 6.43 and 6.44 Muerte materials. Agents with the DEA discovered a drug trafficking ring that used the ritual services of a Santería priest to bless their shipments. The priest was a devotee of Saint Death and used her to provide the group protection. (Courtesy of U.S. Drug Enforcement Administration.)

Figures 6.45 and 6.46 More muerte materials.

Saint Death or Santa Muerte

Santa Muerte goes by many names. Devotees may call the spirit Holy Death, Saint Death, La Santisima Muerte, Most Holy Death, La Santisima, Saint of Saints, Hermana de Luz (Sister of Light), Sagrada Muerte (Sacred Death), Muerte Querida (Death Beloved), La Dama Poderosa (Powerful Lady), La Santa Niña Blanca (Holy White Girl), La Bonita (Pretty Girl),

Figure 6.47 Personal altar in bedroom belonging to a drug trafficker. (Courtesy of Washington County (Tennessee) Sheriff's Department.)

La Flaquita (Skinny Girl), La Madrina (Godmother), La Huesuda (Bony Lady), and many others.

Followers of Santa Muerte at the popular shrine in Tepito, Mexico, call the saint Santa Muerte de la Luz, or "Santa Muerte of the Light." Some of the popular prayer books dedicated to the folk saint call the spirit Death Mistress of My Heart, Abode of Life, and Lady Sovereign.

Icons

There are a number of icons or material representations of Santa Muerte. Many take the form of statues, paintings, amulets, and talismans. Icons, particularly statues representing the death saint, can be found in various colors. Each color represents a particular power.

Red statues of the saint are used to bring about love, passion, and emotional stability.

White statues of the saint are used to purify and bring protection. This statue can be used to remove negative energy between individuals.

Black statues of the saint are used for protection.

Figure 6.48 Many of the Latin America street gangs are showing an affinity for the Mexican saint of death.

Green statues are used to represent justice. They can be used for workings against the law and for favor in court cases.
Gold statues are used to attain financial wealth, jobs, and general
prosperity.
Blue statues are used to attain wisdom. These images can also be used
to increase spiritual harmony.
Bone-colored statues are used to bring about peace, harmony, and
success.
Copper-colored statues can be used to remove negative energies.
Purple statues are used to change negative situations into positive situ-
ations. Purple is also believed to give protection from disease.
Silver statues are believed to bring luck and success.
Seven colored statues contain all of the elements found in the gold, sil-
ver, copper, blue, purple, red, and green colors.

Some sources say that there are three colors of the image that represent three distinct forms of worship. The white or Santa Muerte Blanca is described as the skeletal remains of Jesus. White candles are used with this image to bring about health and wealth. The red or Santa Muerte Roja is used in blood rituals that include witchcraft and negative spell work. The black or Holy Black Death is used by a group of brujas for curses.

Figures 6.49 and 6.50 Scenes from a ranch in Veracruz, Mexico where the remains of 44 bodies were discovered. Victims' heads, hands, and feet were missing. The remnants of their bodies were found in various pits dug on the property. (Courtesy of Ignacio Carvajal García.)

Figure 6.51 A yearly brujería ceremony is performed in Catamaco, Mexico. Thousands of rujas and brujos throughout Mexico attend and participate. (Courtesy of Dongringo.)

The statues have a variety of different forms. The most common is the image of Santa Muerte standing upright holding the scythe. Mass retailers have produced a number of forms of the statue that depict the image sitting on a throne, riding a horse, and in the center of a cross. The popularity of the image has encouraged companies that do not necessarily specialize in religious artifacts to produce mass-marketed images of the folk saint.

Most images of the saint depict the spirit of death with various objects. The following are some of the common objects and their spiritual symbolism:

Scythe (guadaña): The curved blade of the agricultural tool represents the spirit's ability to cut away at the energy of enemies. It also represents a tool for bringing prosperity. Another interpretation is that the symbol represents nature, and nature brings about death.

Globe/world (mundo): The globe represents the power over the world. The globe is also symbolic of the presence of the spirit of Santa Muerte all over the world.

Scales/balance (balanza): The scales represent justice and balance and also the impartialness of death.

Figure 6.52 Some traditional healers pray to Santa Muerte as a protection from brujería. This healer in Veracruz, Mexico, says that Saint Death has protected him from death at least four times in his life and he prays to her to heal others. (Courtesy of Ignacio Carvajal.)

Hourglass (reloj de arena): The hourglass represents the time we have to live before we die. It also represents the motions that occur in the upper and lower worlds.

Owl (búho): The owl represents the ability to see into the darkness and also symbolizes wisdom.

Key (llave): The key represents the saint's ability to open doorways or opportunities for her followers.

Lamp (lámpara): The lamp represents the ability of Santa Muerte to walk through the darkness and allows her followers to see the path ahead of them.

Some forms of the statue will have removable hands. Informants have shared that these are removed from the statue as requests are made to the spirit. The hands will be replaced once the spirit has answered the request of the devotee. The bottoms of most statues will have clear undersides filled with various materials. These materials are known as mysteries and are used to give the image magical properties. The materials typically found include small horseshoes, grains of wheat, rice, coins, thread, and beans.

There are some spells or workings performed with the statue of Santa Muerte in which devotees add materials to the base of the statue.

Figure 6.53 Candles act as conductors of spiritual energy and prayers, serve as offerings to deities and spirits, and act as components in spells.

There appear to be some attempts to form standardized literature for use in Santa Muerte worship circles. The *La Biblia de la Santa Muerte* purports to be a bible for the movement. It lists a set of 10 commandments for followers:

1. Death is to be venerated with great respect.
2. Followers are not to take Santa Muerte's name in vain.
3. The days of the feasts are to be observed.
4. Honor all your brothers in the religion.
5. Harm no one.
6. Do not commit acts to harm the religion of Santa Muerte.
7. Do not abuse your spiritual knowledge.
8. Do not give false testimony concerning Santa Muerte.
9. Do not profit from false testimony concerning Santa Muerte.
10. Do not covet the wealth of others.

Figure 6.54 This horseshoe amulet is kept above the doorway to bring luck and provide protection for the devotee.

Altars and shrines

Shrines, known as altarcitos, are common in practitioners' homes. These small shrines are usually dedicated to a particular saint and will include offerings and photographs of loved ones. The shrine is recognized as a doorway to the spiritual realm, where adherents can pray and ask for requests from the saints. The shrine is considered a sacred space and gives devotees a visual place to focus on spiritual concepts.

Altars dedicated to Santa Muerte typically contain the statues used to represent the saint. Some statues may be dressed in clothing such as a bride's gown or nun's habit. Some statues have wigs placed upon their heads. Many feature the statue wearing jewelry and a feathered boa.

The altar may also contain materials that symbolize attributes of Santa Muerte.

Offerings that are commonly found on altars to Santa Muerte include tobacco in the form of cigarettes and cigars; alcoholic beverages such as beer, aguardiente, rum, mescal, tequila, champagne, and whisky; and food items including fruit, honey, candy, bread, sugar, dried beans, grain, and corn. Glasses of water are placed in the shrine to connect with the spiritual realm.

Flowers may be left in her shrine. The color of the flowers symbolizes the nature of the spiritual work that is being requested from Santa Muerte. Red roses represent passion and love. White flowers may be placed in the shrine for healing requests.

Figure 6.55 Saint shrine dedicated to Our Lady of Guadalupe and San Judas discovered in a location used for drug sales. (Courtesy of Texas Narcotic Officer's Association.)

Money is frequently placed in the shrine. Bowls of pennies and rolled up bills are placed in the crevices of statues of the saint.

Copal (botanical name: *Bursera oderata*) is a resin that is burned as incense for Santa Muerte. The use of copal as an incense can be found in early Mexican history, as it was burned in many religious rituals.

Some groups and individuals have used animal and human blood as offerings to the death saint. Artist Stephan Lugbaer, in his *Ramon and the Holy Goddess of Death*, shares an interview with a Santa Muerte devotee in Tepito, Mexico, who speaks candidly about blood offerings:

> I have participated in some sacrifices but they have been animals, black cats, black roosters which are very hard to find. If you are a devotee, this is how they baptize you. They draw a cross with blood on

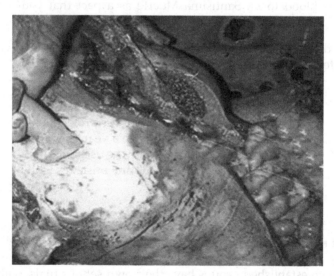

Figures 6.56 and 6.57 Flaying of victims. The ritualistic removal of skin performed by the Aztecs can be seen among the modern-day murders of Mexican drug cartels.

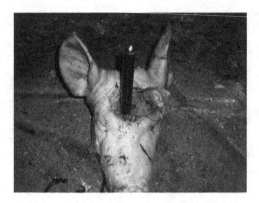

Figures 6.58 Practitioners of brujeria will use various animal bones, skins, and entrails in malevolent rituals.

> your forehead and you also offer some of your own blood to La Santisima Muerte as a pact that you signed with her. It means protect me and I will give.

The devotee goes on to tell about the use of human blood as offerings to Muerte:

> So there are extremes here in the neighborhood of Tepito. About six years ago they imprisoned a person who was stealing vehicle. For his protection he used to kill a virgin woman once a year. Since it is hard to tell if a woman is a virgin, he used to kill little babies to assure there wasn't any mistakes while offering them to La Santisima.

Rituals

Many of the rituals used in conjunction with Santa Muerte are self-styled, meaning practitioners may not follow a set format for worshipping the saint. Some established groups have their own set of rituals, with many of them passed down orally. Many of the rituals and practices, including rosary prayers, novenas, and crossing oneself, are taken from traditional Roman Catholic practices.

There are a number of guidebooks printed in Mexico and the United States that feature prayers known as oracions to the saint. The prayer books typically begin with a short prayer known in Spanish as a jaculatoria. Prayers, or oracions, are listed by days of the nine-day period. Prayers ask for various requests, such as protection, luck, happiness, money, and health. Many popular forms of prayer found in Santa Muerte worship combine prayers from traditional Catholicism, including the Apostle's Creed, Act of Contrition, and Mysteries of the Rosary, which are customized to include Santa Muerte.

Magical operations with Santa Muerte are commonly known as trabajos or workings. The three primary areas of magical assistance appear to focus on physical and spiritual protection, financial success, and issues relating to love.

The following are instructions on performing a ritual in order to resolve legal problems.

Materials Needed

A blue statue of the Santa Muerte
A white candle of the Santa Muerte
A scale
Grease from corojo (palm oil)
A piece of parchment paper (white)
Scotch tape
A new needle

Using the needle, write the number of the investigator or judge where your problem exists, light the candle, and place it next to the Santa Muerte. Pray the prayer below and ask for this problem to be resolved in your favor. On the parchment paper write the name or number of the investigator or judge where your case takes place, and place a little of the grease on the paper in the form of a cross. Fold it in three parts and using the Scotch tape, tape it on the middle of the scale and hang it on the Santa Muerte's hands. The candle should be lit for nine consecutive days. Pray daily and make your petition when you finish this novena. Do not remove the paper from the scale until your problem has resolved. The best day to do this ritual is on a Monday morning.

Prayer for this ritual

Blessed Santa Muerte, protector of the desperate and the weak. Mother of eternal justice and owner of wisdom, you who can see the bad and the good in our hearts, to you my lady do I come to implore

> justice to you Santa Muerte, I oblige your impartial-
> ity of your scale my lady, look into my heart, hear
> me imploring for my necessities, make your divine
> hand guide the decision of judges and jailers, great
> lady be implacable with the wicked who repeat
> offenses, justice with the innocent and be kind to
> those who repent with all their heart and soul oh
> white child, hear my petition and protect me from
> the wickedness and the indolence on this day, I
> oblige your favor so that my case may be subjected
> to your measures and obtain absolute pardon from
> the judges, in time you will judge me and take the
> words that I now pledge as my punishment or my
> acquittal. Amen. (http://www.santamuerte.org/
> english/3861-ritual-to-resolve-legal-problems.html)

Santa Muerte is frequently used with other Catholic saints and Latin folk saints. She has been identified as the wife of Jesus Malverde and the helper to healer folk saint Niño Fidencio.

Violence associated with Santa Muerte

There are a number of homicides associated with Santa Muerte wor-ship. These are ritualistic murders that appear to have been performed to provide offerings to the death saint. The majority of these murders have been performed by members of drug trafficking organizations.

In 2008 in Nuevo Laredo, Mexico, enforcers from the Gulf cartel cap-tured members of the Sinaloa cartel. The captured members were taken to shrines of Santa Muerte and executed. Later the same year, Mexican police found 11 charred heads at a shrine to Santa Muerte in the Yucatán. The shrine was tended by members of Los Zetas.

In 2010 in Ciudad Júarez, suspected members of the Hillside 13 gang burned a victim behind a house containing an altar and a small statue of Santa Muerte. Neighbors who were interviewed stated that the gang asked for "something big," and that there were multiple sacrifices made to Santa Muerte.

In 2012 Mexican officials in Sonora state arrested a family of eight accused of murdering two children and an elderly woman. The family confessed to cutting the bodies open while they were still alive and pour-ing their blood on an altar to Santa Muerte.

Robert Bunker notes in the report *Santa Muerte: Inspired and Ritualistic Killings* that there are incidents that have been alleged to have occurred, including victims with their skin and hearts removed. Cases include beheadings, castrations, butchering and quartering (Bunker, 2013).

Assorted spiritual personalities

There is a mythological figure in some Latin American countries known as the duende. The duende image is similar to an elf or a troll. Some myths speak about the figures luring children into the woods to capture them. Spiritual supply stores sell images of these figures that are believed to be able to carry out spiritual work for the owner.

Artifacts

Candles used as offerings to the saints are usually placed in front of statues of spiritual figures as offerings. Candles may be found in many different forms, including candles in glass jars and candles in various shapes according to their purposes.

There are a number of types of candles that officers may encounter at scenes. Colors of candles correspond with various spiritual purposes. Commonly used candle colors and their uses follow:

Black: To draw evil to you, to send evil away, protection, adversity.
Blue: Peace, tranquility, health.
Brown: Neutrality and balance.
Green: Money, luck, success, fertility.
Orange: Attraction, happiness.
Pink: Love, sex, romance.
Purple: Power, ambition.
Red: Strength, love, passion, sex.
White: Purity, spirituality, clairvoyance.
Yellow: Charm, confidence.

Candles can be purchased from spiritual supply stores, local ethnic markets. and over the Internet. The most common candle used is in a tall glass. The color of the candle can typically be seen through the glass. Candles may feature labels with names like "Law Stay Away" or "Chango Macho."

Candles are believed to slowly release magical energies. Among Mexican folk religious communities, candles are believed to be conduits for spirits. The manner in which a candle may burn, the appearance or lack of smoke, and the height of the flame can be interpreted as signs from the spiritual world.

Some of the lore surrounding candles and the spiritual messages that they are believed to send include:

If the top of the candle glass has burned black, the candle has blocked something negative from attacking its owner.

If the flame burns high, this is a positive sign from the spiritual world.

If the flame burns low, the owner may need to have a limpia performed to get rid of negativity.

If the candle burns down the side of the jar from the top to the bottom, the owner may be cursed and needs to take precautions.

If the candle or jar cracks, the owner may have broken his or her enemy's protection.

Many of these candles are "dressed," which simply means they have been anointed or prepared with ingredients considered to be magical. Oil is rubbed into a candle's glass by starting in the middle and rubbing upward to add power or increase energy in the candle.

Some of the candles may be prepared with various materials, like herbs and oils, along the tops and sides. The top of the candle may be covered in foil to keep the materials inside. *Warning*: Some candles are prepared with mercury. Use caution when exposed to unidentified materials.

Candles may come in various shapes. Candles in the shape of a man and woman can be used to represent couples. Candles in the shape of a penis or vagina are used to affect the genital region.

Candles made from seven balls of wax are commonly known as seven knots candles. These candles are burned once a day for a week. A larger candle to be burned for 14 days is also commonly used in spells.

Candles are found in the shape of crosses, Satan, skulls, and many other forms.

Officers finding pieces of jewelry inside candles are most likely looking at contagious magic. The owner of the jewelry is believed to be affected by the spell performed because of the law of contact.

Powders are used in the magical practices of curanderismo. Powders are usually comprised of dried herbs. Powders can be sprinkled on the ground to affect the person who walks across them. Powders may be sprinkled onto altars to give power to spells. Powders may be used in bags to enhance protective amulets.

Oils may be present at the scene. Oils are used for a number of purposes in spiritual workings. They may be used to anoint objects to give in object additional spiritual energy. They may be used to cleanse individuals and objects of negative energies. They may be used to enhance the power of a spell.

Incense may be burned to create a spiritual atmosphere. Incense is also burned as a means of cleansing an environment. The smoke from incense is believed by some to carry prayers to the spiritual world.

Offerings of fruits, flowers, and vegetables may be present. These items are believed to contain energy. They are offered and placed at the bases of statues. In some cases, they may be used in spells. For example, limes may be pierced with stickpins to place a spiritual working on someone.

Some of the tools used in the practice of curanderismo and folk magic are found in the form of protective amulets:

Horseshoe amulet: The horseshoe, also called herradura, is an object of luck. Patients may keep a horseshoe made of garlic above the door of a home or business. The garlic keeps away evil. Horseshoes may be found in a miniature form on necklaces, bracelets, and amulet bags. A popular form of this amulet depicts the folk Saint Martin de Caballero alongside a horseshoe. One popular amulet features a six-point star inside of a horseshoe. This image overlays an image of the folk saint. This amulet is known as herradura preparados, which means "prepared horseshoe." The four corners contain images of San Martin de Caballero. The amulet is nailed above doorways to bring success to businesses.

Lodestone: The lodestone, called piedra iman, is used as an amulet in a number of forms. The stone contains magnetic properties that are said to pull or attract positive desires. The stone may be placed in a small bag and "fed" magnetic particles to make it grow in size. Lodestones may be placed in a bag along with beads, coins, beans, and a horseshoe. These amulets provide protection of health, family, and success.

Scapulario: The scapular is a cloth worn by Catholics that displays an image of a saint. Followers of curanderismo may wear images of the folk saints such as Santa Muerte.

Milagro: The milagro (miracle) is a miniature body part that is used to represent the appendage that is in need of healing. The milagro may be placed on images of saints to bring about healing. The milagro may be left with an image of a saint when the devotee has made a promise (promesa) to a saint.

La manito de coral: This black image of a hand represents the "hand of God."

Ojo de venado: Also known as deer's eye. This is one of the more widely available amulets available at various Latin markets throughout the United States. The object provides protection from the mal de ojo (evil eye). The amulet is a velvet bean, also known as a buckeye, wrapped in red cord. The bean may have an image of a saint decorated on it. There are several variations of the ojo de venado. Some include the manito de coral, or "hand of God," in the amulet.

Cross of Caravaca: This amulet is a double-armed cross with angels appearing on both sides of the cross. The amulet is believed to bring financial success and ensure good health.

Other protective objects officers may discover include:

Garlic: Also known as ajo, bundles of garlic are hung to keep away negative energies.

Chiles: Chili peppers are hung in bundles to protect against envy.

Cat's eye: Stone used for spiritual protection.

Scissors: An open pair of scissors may be placed above a doorway to protect against envy.

Railroad spike: Also known as clavo de linea. When wrapped with seven colored ribbons of the seven African powers, may bring protection to the owner.

Rituals and ceremonies

Curanderismo provides a holistic approach to healing that incorporates the emotional, mental, and physical body. Healing may come from a ritual or from a prescription from a curandero, or even possibly a remedy that is taught by members of the community. The curandero may recommend a remedios casero, or "home remedy," that may be something as basic as a bowl of soup or an herbal treatment.

The curandero relies on a number of ritualistic practices in treatment of his clients. One of the most common rituals involves the use of an object to "sweep" away sickness. The baridda, or "sweeping," may involve herbs, lemons, eggs, or flowers.

These objects are swept over the body of the client to rid him or her of negative influences known as vibraciones malos that cause sickness. Prayers are spoken over the individual during the sweeping, which can include the Lord's Prayer and the Apostle's Creed. A ritual cleansing known as a limpia is usually performed by the curandero using an egg or an animal passed over the body of the client to clean him or her of a sickness. The animal may be killed, but the egg is traditionally placed in a glass under the client's bed. If by morning the egg has become cooked or bloody, it has been successful in taking away the illness. Limpias can be performed using an egg, flowers, alum, chiles, lemons, garlic, and fire from a flame.

The sahumerio is a ritual cleansing of an environment performed by waving the smoke from incense into a specified space. The ritual sortilegio involves the use of objects to "tie up" negative influences that may affect a client. Ribbons and cords may be used to tie up artifacts. The curandero may also use candles in the diagnosis of sickness. The pattern in which the flame moves or in which the wax burns may provide the healer with spiritual insight into the client's illness.

Objects may be used to transfer a sickness from a client. The treatment of folk illnesses sometimes involves a glass of water placed above the client's head. When the water boils, the sickness is believed to have been removed. Stomach problems may be treated with the application to the stomach of alcohol-soaked bread and herbs.

The use of medicinal herbs known as plantas medicinales is a primary healing technique used by the curandero. The specialized knowledge of herbs used by the healer recognizes not only the medicinal purposes of herbs, but also their magical properties. As in many religious cultures, herbs are recognized as living objects that contain energy and vibrations. These energies are believed to provide healing for the human body.

Curanderismo and folk saint practices do not typically involve organized worship, except in some of the new religious movements associated with Santa Muerte. Officers will most likely encounter individuals involved in these cultures on a solo basis. Most rituals center around health and healing, with the exception of some of the manifestations of folk saint worship involving narco saints.

Brujería

The power of the saints and spirits can be used in destructive spells known as brujería, or "witchcraft." Male practitioners are known as brujos, while females are known as brujas. Those who practice black magic in the Mexican folk religions have a reputation for being able to curse people to death, and regional superstition says that they can turn themselves into animals. There are brujas who are spoken of in Mexican folklore that are called luchuzas. These witches are believed to be able to transform into owls and fly. Some anthropologists believe that many of these beliefs are holdovers from the Aztecs. The Aztecs believed in a class of witches that could transform from a human into an animal.

Another contribution to the Mexican images of witches comes from early Spanish Catholic missionaries. As missionaries were trying to convert the indigenous people to Christianity, many of the native beliefs and practices were called witchcraft. As the indigenous people left many of their traditional beliefs, they began to attribute any phenomenon supernatural to witchcraft rather than religion.

While feared, the brujo has become a part of Mexico's national identity. The area of Veracruz has used a tourist ad that proclaims "land of the witches." Every year the Congreso Nacional de Brujos de Catemaco brings thousands of occult practitioners from all over Latin America to display ritual artifacts and perform a public "black mass" ceremony. Since 1977 the convention of witches has garnered a massive audience. Anthropologists have observed that the gathering of witches brings a number of con men and actual practitioners as well.

Narco brujería

The use of brujería by drug traffickers has been going on for several years in many Latin countries and focuses on the use of brujos and brujas as personal clergy for traffickers. Traffickers employ practitioners of destructive magic to bring about curses on enemies, including rival traffickers and law enforcement officers.

Traffickers may also casually visit brujería practitioners at botanicas and yerberias. Stories circulate among some of the communities where brujos/brujas act as spiritual "hired guns" for whoever will pay the price. Some brujos have gained quite a reputation for working for criminals. In the practitioner's worldview, the more effectively the magic of the brujo appears to work, the more sinister a reputation he will gain among the communities.

In the early 1990s Mexican witch Enrique Sanchez (aka El Bujo) worked as a ritual specialist for several drug traffickers. Sanchez boasted of having the power to affect the dogs belonging to U.S. Customs officials. Through the use of magic, he was believed to provide a covering for traffickers moving cocaine across the border at U.S. checkpoints. As his reputation as a powerful occultist grew, he was hired by members of the Gulf cartel. The cell offered him $240 million if he could free a cartel member from a La Loma Mexican prison. In order to gain the favor of spiritual entities, Sanchez provided animal and human blood to the spirits. Sanchez beheaded a female and used the blood in a ceremony that was believed to open the doors to the prison. Sanchez was arrested and imprisoned for the murder.

Servando Gómez Martínez (aka La Tuta), one of the top leaders in the La Familia Michoacana cartel, kept a personal brujo to perform services for the cartel. The brujo is alleged to have metaphysically chosen places for members to hide from the police, identified enemies, and consulted tarot cards for spiritual guidance.

Aztec religion

The Aztec culture not only is recalled and honored as a symbol of Mexican nationalism, but also permeates art, literature, and religious cultures throughout the country. The Aztecs are remembered as fierce warriors who served fierce deities throughout central and southern Mexico. This image of machismo is also used by many Mexican American street gangs. Organizations like SUR13, Barrio Azteca, and the Mexican Mafia use aspects of the Aztec culture, such as symbols, terms. and languages.

The Aztec war god Huitzilopochtli is a common icon found in gang tattoos. War against enemies is a theme found throughout the Aztec culture and street gang culture as well. The Aztec mindset focused on war so heavily that newborn babies were told by midwives that "they were only here for rest as they eventually were going to the battlefield." The battlefield and war were considered sacred by the Aztecs. The Mesoamerican deity of war has quite a reputation (Time-Life Books 1992), as his followers appeased him through bloody human sacrifices. It was estimated that Aztecs offered over 20,000 victims to their gods in ritual human sacrifice throughout their reign.

Huitzilopochtli represented the sun, which had to be frequently fed blood in order to return after the moon. Failure to return meant the Aztecs were doomed to everlasting darkness, which was considered the end of their civilization. Victims were carried up the steps of sacred temples, such as the Great Temple near Mexico City, and murdered to ensure the survival of the Aztecs.

Ironically, members of cartels such as Los Zetas have either intentionally or coincidentally recreated ritualistic murders using the practices and aesthetics of the Aztecs. A common practice among the Aztecs was to honor the war god with a ritualistic offering of a victim. The victim was given a potion that was prepared using the seeds of the morning glory flower. This victim's skin would be removed, and his heart would be removed while it was still beating. The flesh of the victim would be flayed, and the remains would be consumed in a ritual feast where human flesh would be consumed with corn to show appreciation for the earth's bounty.

Mexican journalist Jesus Lemus Burujas interviewed members of Los Zetas while serving time in Puente Grande prison in Jalisco, Mexico. One of the practices that Zetas revealed to the journalist involved the ritualistic murder of rivals and innocent victims. Victims were forced to undergo a shower that would cleanse the body. They were then shaved. The victim was then given a bottle of whiskey to destress. As the victim destressed, Zetas would kill him and take his body parts. The victim was killed quickly, as the group believed that adrenaline would spoil the flesh and make consumption bitter. Portions of the spine were taken and used as amulets that were worn by leaders of the cartel. The flesh would then be consumed by members of the group. The hamstrings would be prepared like steaks and eaten by leadership. Strangely enough, the Aztec leaders were offered the thighs of sacrifice victims. Like the Aztecs before them consuming corn with victims' flesh, Los Zetas have been discovered eating a victim's flesh with corn tortillas, in stews, and in tamales.

Los Zetas have a history of leadership that ritually consumed flesh. Infamous leaders Heriberto Lazcano Lazcano, known as Z3, and Miguel

Angel Trevino Morales, known as Z40, both were known for eating the hearts of their victims. Trevino told members of the cartel that he enjoyed consuming human hearts while they were still beating, as this gave him the ability to become invincible to the authorities and group rivals.

According to a report written by the Foreign Military Studies Officer, the act of consuming flesh by drug cartels serves three functions to the organization. The first function is that the act dehumanizes the victim. Cartel members are able to murder their victims easier, as they see them as objects, not humans. This practice could have come from the initiation exercises of the Kaibiles, the Guatemalan Special Forces. Many Los Zetas have been trained by these soldiers. The Kaibiles are instructed to raise a puppy, form a relationship with the animal, and then kill the animal. They then cook and eat the animal they raised. This is performed in order to lose emotional ties with victims that they have been commanded to kill.

Second, the act promotes group unity and gives a sense of togetherness among members of the cartel. The sharing of human flesh becomes an act of fellowship. Last, the ability to consume human flesh demonstrates that the cartel member is strong enough mentally to perform such a deviant act. This proves courage and builds mental strength.

The skinning of a victim as a ritualistic practice was observed among the Aztecs in their worship of a deity known as Xipe Totec, or "Lord of the Flayed." This violent deity was believed to have flayed his own skin in order to provide food for humanity. Ceremonial flayings of victims took place on the celebration of Tlacaxiphualtitzli, which translated is "the flaying of men in honor of Zipe." Victims' skins were removed while the victims were still alive. Cartel murders involving flaying of victims' skin have been documented throughout Mexico. In September 2012, two men were attacked by cartel sicarios in the colony of Guadalupe Los Lobos, north of Tepic in Nayarit. The men were skinned alive while the victims' hearts were removed. In the near region of Tepic in 2011, the heads of cartel members were discovered inside bowls of stew complete with tortillas, sodas, plates, and spoons.

Cultural terms

Billis: Illness caused by suppressed anger.
Brujería: Destructive witchcraft.
Curandera: The traditional title for a female healer.
Curandero: The traditional title for a male healer.
Don: A gift from God.
Empacho: Illness caused by food lodged in the digestive tract.

Los Tres Grandes: The Three Great Healers: El Niño Findenco, Don Pedrito Jaramillo, and Teresita.

Mal de Ojo: The illness known as the evil eye.

Partera: Healer who serves as a midwife.

Piedra iman: A lodestone used in magical workings to attract positive energies.

Recetas: The prescriptions given by the healer.

Sahumerio: A ritual in which incense is used to send away negative energies.

Sobador: A healer who uses massage techniques for healing.

Susto: Shock or loss of spirit due to trauma.

Yerbero: Title used by healers who use herbal treatments.

References

Arias, Patricia, and Durand, Jorge, Migration and cross-border devotions, *Migration and Development*, 2009, Vol. 12, pp. 5–26.

Aztecs: Reign of blood and splendor, Lost Civilizations Series, Time Life Books, 1992.

Bledsoe, B.E., Folk medicine and EMS: The Mexican American experience, *Texas EMS Magazine*, 2003, Vol. 24, No. 2, pp. 18–21.

Botsch, Robert, Jesus Malverde's significance to Mexican drug traffickers, *FBI* Law Enforcement Bulletin, August 2008, Vol. 77, No. 8, ProQuest Criminal Justice, p. 1.

Bunch, Jason, Zetas prominent in 50-page indictment, *Laredo Morning Times*, April 4, 2008.

Bunker, Robert, Santa Muerte: Inspired and ritualistic killings, *FBI Law Enforcement Bulletin*, February 2013.

Campos, Cinthia Marlene, Severed heads and excised human hearts, mimesis and the resurgence of pre-Colombian terror management in modern Mexican narco-violence, presented at the 112th Annual American Anthropological Association Conference, Chicago, November 2013.

Castro, Rafaela G., *Chicano folklore*, Oxford University Press, Oxford, 2000.

Chavez, Damien, Hundreds celebrate the white girl, Lanham, MD: *Diario de Queretaro*, November 2, 2008.

Chavez, Eduardo, *Our Lady of Guadalupe and Saint Juan Diego: The historical evidence*, Rowman and Littlefield Publishers, 2006.

Chestnut, Andrew R., *Devoted to death: Santa Muerte, the skeleton saint*, Oxford University Press, Oxford, 2011.

Clark, Jonathan, Judge allows Santa Muerte evidence in trial of accused drug smuggler, *The Herald*, October 26, 2006.

Coleccion de Ore La Santa Muerte Magazine, Mina Editores, Issue 2.

Creechan, James H., Jorge de la Herrán Garcia without God or law: Narcoculture and belief in Jesús Malverde, *Religious Studies and Theology*, 2005, Vol. 24, No. 2.

Drug gang kills rivals at Mexican death cult shrine, Reuters, May 11, 2007.

Drug trafficking: Religion and crime explosive mixture, *El Universal*, June 22, 2009.

El secreto de la Santisima Muerte, Cali Casa Editorial, Santa Ana, CA, 1996.

Freeman, Laurie, *State of siege: Drug-related violence and corruption in Mexico*, AWOLA Special Report, Washington Office on Latin America, June 2006.

Graziano, Frank, *Cultures of devotion: Folk saints of Spanish America*, Oxford University Press, Oxford, 2006.

Guillermoprieto, Alma, *The narcovirus*, Center for Latin American Studies, University of California, Berkeley, 2009.

Hagan, Jacqueline Maria, *Migration miracle: Faith, hope, and meaning on the undocumented journey*, Harvard University Press, Cambridge, MA, 2009.

Harris, Martin L., Curaderismo and the DSM-IV: Diagnostic and treatment implications for the Mexican American client, PhD dissertation, Julian Somra Research Institute Occasional Paper No. 45.

Huber, Brad, *Meso-American healers*, Austin, TX: University of Texas, 2001.

Ingham, John M., *Mary, Michael and Lucifer: Folk Catholicism in Central Mexico*, Austin, TX: University of Texas Press, 1986.

Jesus Malverde gets shrine in Mexico, *La Prensa Latina*, March 2007.

Jimenez, Alferedo, *Handbook of Hispanic Cultures in the United States*, Arte Public Press, 1993.

Los poderes magicos de la Santa Muerte, SM Ediciones, Mexico.

Lugbaer, Stephan, *Ramon and the holy goddess of death*, Lagunilla, Mexico DF, 2006.

Malbrough, Ray T., *The magical power of the saints*, Krakow, Poland: Jagiells University Llewelyn, 1998.

Marquez, Enrique Sanchez, Mujeres divinas, *Alarma*, December 16, 2004, No. 711.

Mauso, Pablo Villarrubia, La Santa Muerte, America Iberica, Ano Cero, No. 12.

Meets pact with Santa Muerte, Hidalgo, *El Sol de Hidalgo*, June 6, 2008.

Mexico's grim reaper gets makeover, *La Prensa Latina*, August 2007.

Mexico targets death saint popular with criminals, America's Intelligence Wire, April 19, 2009, General OneFile (accessed February 16, 2010).

Michalik, Piotr Grzegorz, *The meaning of death: Semiotic approach to analysis of syncretic processes in the cult of Santa Muerte*, Woodbury, MN: Institute of Religious Studies.

Moreno, Manuel Aguilar, *Handbook to Life in the Aztec world*, Oxford University Press, Oxford, 2007.

Mundo esoterico magia, *Ritos y astrologia*, Vol. 218, Mina Editores, 2010.

Narcotrafico: Religion y crimen, *Mezcla Explosiva*, June 23, 2009 (accessed January 1, 2010) http://iluniversal.complex/nacion/169196 html

Novena Santa Muerte, Cervantes Printing, Bell, CA.

Oliveira Jr., Pedro, The saints march in to drug wars, Gazette Xtra.com, November 15, 2009 (accessed January 1, 2010).

Olivo, Marisol Gonzalez, ed., *La Biblia de la Santa Muerte*, Ciudad Mexico Editores Mexicanos Unidos, 2009.

Pieper, Jim, *Guatemala's folk saints*, Pieper and Associates, 2002.

Prescott, William H., *Conquest of Mexico*, Vol. 1, Philadelphia, PA: .B. Lippincott Co., 1843.

Price, Patricia L., Of bandits and saints: Jesus Malverde and the struggle for place in Sinaloa, Mexico, *Cultural Geographies*, April 2005, Vol. 12, Issue 2, pp. 175–197.

Rulz, Victor, Do not end it, expose believers, *El Heraldo de Tabasco*, May 30, 2009.

Scheper-Hughes, Nancy, and David Stewart, Curanderismo in Taos County, New Mexico: A possible case of anthropological romanticism? *Western Journal of Medicine*, December 1983.

Thompson, John, Santo Niño de Atocha, *Journal of the Southwest*, Spring 1994, Vol. 36, No. 1, pp. 1–18.

Torres, Elisio Cheo, *Curandero: A life in Mexican folk healing*, University of Mexico Press, 2005.

Vanderwood, Paul, Juan Soldado: Field notes and reflections, *Journal of the Southwest*, Winter 2001, Vol. 34, No. 4, pp. 717–727.

Vanderwood, Paul, *Juan Soldado: Rapist, murderer, martyr, saint*, Duke University Press, Durham, NC.

chapter seven

Voodoo

The word *Voodoo* itself invokes images of zombies, black magic, and human sacrifice. The reality of Voodoo is something altogether different. The real world of Voodoo is a complex religion that focuses on the spirits of ancestors as well as spirits of nature. Because of the popular stereotypes and superstitions concerning Voodoo, it has become a culture that has been misappropriated by some in the drug trafficking scene.

Traffickers and the religion (case examples)

While there have been no direct examples of Mexican drug cartels appropriating direct practices of Haitian, Dominican, or West African Voodoo, there have certainly been elements taken from these religions and used in the mix of narco brujería spirituality. There have been a number of cases involving gangs and drug traffickers from the Caribbean and areas like Miami and New York who have appropriated the religion for protection and intimidation.

The Haitian street gang known as Zoe Pound, founded in Miami's Little Haiti by Haitian immigrants, has become well known among drug gangs for using Voodoo as a form of protection from and intimidation of rivals. Zoe Pound has been known to hire Voodoo priestesses (mambos) to bless members of the gang.

A European documentary about the gang shows its members having their firearms anointed with oil and blessed by a priestess in a Haitian botanica in Miami.

Historical background

The religion of Voodoo comes from Benin, formerly known as Dahomey, West Africa. The colonialists sought to destroy the African identity by forcing religious practices of Catholicism onto the Africans. To assimilate, the African people began to combine the Europeans' view of religion with the practices of African traditional religion. The practices of several African groups, such as the Yoruba, Congo, Fon, and Senegalese, evolved into Voodoo, which is a West African word that means "spirit."

The island of Hispaniola is composed of Haiti on the western third of the island and the Dominican Republic on the east. Voodoo was suppressed by colonialists in areas such as Haiti. However, today Voodoo is the major religion of that country, and a different manifestation of Voodoo appears in the Dominican Republic.

Beliefs

Voodoo practitioners follow a creator deity known as Gran Met Bondye. Gran Met means "Great Master" and Bondye comes from Bon Dieu, which means "good God."

The Voodoo belief system primarily focuses on the reverence of spirits known as loa. The loa are often referred to as mysteries or angels. Adherents believe that the loa come from a variety of African countries and ethnic groups. Because of this, the rituals and characteristics of these deities differ. Loa are typically organized into groups according to their location of origin and personality. These groups are known as nations among practitioners.

Some of the nations are the Petro, Rada, Congo, and Nago. The spirits live in a city beneath the sea known as Ginen. They must be summoned into this world in order to appear. The loa are also organized into families. Some of the families, such as the Ogou, Ezili, and Gede, have spirits that are known by the family name and the individual spirit name, such as Ezili Freda and Ezili Danto.

Deities

Rada

The loa that come from the holy city Arada of the Dahomey region of Africa are called Rada and are considered to be "cool" by followers and less aggressive as the Petro spirits. The following spirits are some of the most popular spirits among the Rada.

Legba

Legba is the owner of the crossroads and is called upon first in ceremonies to open the doorway to the spiritual world. Sometimes called Papa Legba, he is syncretized with Saint Peter, who guards the keys to heaven, and Saint Lazarus. His favorite color is red.

Marasa

These loa are sacred twin spirits that appear in Rada and Petro rituals. The twins may be invoked following Legba in rituals. They may have other spirit offspring known as Marasa Dosu, which means "boy." The Marasa are syncretized with Saint Cosmas and Saint Damien.

Loko

Loko is known as the first priest (houngan), and he guards the sanctuary (peristyle). Loko is the loa of healing with herbs and is associated with the images of Saint Joseph and the archangel Gabriel.

Ayizan

Ayizan is the wife of Legba and is depicted as an old woman with an apron that has deep pockets. She represents the marketplace and is sometimes referred to as the Mother of All Initiates. Ayizan is represented by mounds of dirt surrounded by fringes of palm fronds.

Sobo

Sobo is the loa of strength. He also rules over thunder and rain. Sobo acts as the judge of the temple and is depicted as a handsome soldier. He is symbolized by an emblem of lightning.

Agassou

The myth of Agassou tells of his birth from a princess and leopard. Agassou is referred to as the king of the Leopard Society of West Africa, a men's tribal society. He guards the traditions of Dahomey. Some Voodoo historians say that Agassou was the first human to develop into a loa.

La Sirene

La Sirene is a fishlike being that lives and rules over the oceans. Married to the loa Agwe, she is syncretized with La Diosa del Mar, and is represented by mirrors, combs, a small trumpet, pearls, perfume, and items from the ocean.

Azaka

Azaka is the spirit who is like a cousin from the country. He represents agriculture, and is depicted as wearing the clothes of a farmer, such as denim pants, and carrying a straw bag. Azaka is syncretized with Saint Isidore. His favorite colors are blue, red, and green. He is represented by his straw sack and a tobacco pipe.

Damballah Wedo

Damballah Wedo is the loa of goodness. In the Fon language, Damballah is called Dan; is the symbol of the origins of the kingdom of Dahomey, and is represented by a serpent. Damballah is syncretized with Saint Patrick.

Symbolized by a snake and a rainbow; his favorite color is white, and his offerings include eggs, milk, and champagne.

Ayida Wedo

Ayida Wedo is the loa of wealth and happiness. She is represented by a serpent and a rainbow. Ayida Wedo is syncretized with Our Lady of Immaculate Conception. She is the wife of Damballah and her favorite colors are blue and white.

Ezili Freda

Also known as Ezili Maitresse, Ezili Freda is the loa of love and luxury. She is represented by a heart and is syncretized with the Virgin Mary. Ezili is the wife of Legba, and her favorite colors are blue and pink. She is symbolized by a heart and a mirror and is given offerings of sweet desserts, perfumes, and flowers.

Ogou group

The Ogous are powerful warriors. Ogou (which means "justice") is the loa of blacksmiths and is symbolized by a sword stuck in the ground. An Ogou is also represented by an iron rod stuck in a fire. There are several manifestations of Ogous, and they are syncretized with Saint James the Greater. An Ogou's favorite color is red.

Agwe

Agwe is the loa of the ocean. He is the patron of sailors and fishermen and is represented by a boat. Agwe is syncretized with Saint Ulrich. His offerings are placed on small boats, and his favorite colors are white, green, and pink.

Petro

The loa that come from the colony of Saint Domingue are known as Petro loa. The Petros take their name from a man called Don Pedro who lived in the 1700s. Don Pedro promoted several distinct dances and ceremonies. The Petro loa are known as fiery and sometimes malevolent spirits. The Petro spirits may be used in sorcery and can be summoned with gunpowder and the cracking of bullwhips. Some of the more popular Petro spirits are discussed below.

Simbi

Simbi are a group of ancestral spirits. These spirits live in the water that separates the land of the living and the land of the dead. The loa of clairvoyance, Simbi are represented by a pond of water and are syncretized with the magi who visited Christ. Simbi's favorite colors are black and gray, and they are represented by a pond and slim snakes.

Kalfu (Carrefour)

Kalfu is the Petro loa of Legba. Kalfu allows bad luck and evil to enter the world through the crossroads. His symbol is the moon, and he may be used in malevolent magic.

Gran Bwa

Gran Bwa is Creole for Great Tree. Gran Bwa is the protector of wildlife. He is the lord over the forest and jungle and assists in healing and initiation. He is represented by a tree with a cloth wrapped around it. Gran Bwa presides over the ritual of the grinding of herbs known as pile fey.

Ezili Danto (Erzulie Dantor)

Also known as Ezili of the Red Eyes, Ezili Danto is the wife of Ti-Jean Petro and Simbi Makaya. She is syncretized with Mater Salvatoris, or Our Lady of Chestochowa and is sometimes known as the African Saint Barbara. She protects single mothers and children. Her images depict her holding her child named Anais. Scars on her face are from her rivalry with Ezili Freda. She is symbolized by a dagger and bowls of blood.

Marinette-Bwa-Chech

Marinette is the principal female loa of the Petro pantheon. She is a wife to Ti-Jean Petro and is represented by a screeching owl. She is a vicious spirit that is syncretized with Anima Sola and can free a person from or take him or her into bondage. Her colors are black and blood red. Marinette is believed to be the mambo who sacrificed the black pig that started the first Haitian revolution.

Ti-Jean Petro

Ti-Jean Petro is a spirit that roams through the bush. He is depicted as a dwarf with one foot and he protects sorcerers. He is the son of Erzulie Dantor (Ezili Danto) as well as her lover.

Gede

The Gede family of loa rule over the cemeteries. The Gede are symbolized by a cross that represents the crossroads. These loa have distinguishing characteristics in ritual, dance, and sacrifices. The Gede family of spirits include Gede Nibo, Gede Plumaj, Gede Ti Mails, and Gede Zaranye. The Gede are led by the baron spirits of the dead. Initiates who become possessed by the Gede are characterized by a nasal tone of voice and the appearance of a dead man. The Gede use black, purple, and white.

Baron Samedi

Baron Samedi is the master over the cemeteries and is depicted dressed in black clothes with a black hat and dark glasses. He has a skull for a face and is represented on altars by phallic symbols. The Haitian dictator Papa Doc (François) Duvalier dressed as Baron Samedi in most of his public appearances. Baron Samedi's other manifestations include Baron La Croix, Baron Cimitere, and Baron Criminel. His colors are black and purple.

Maman Brigette

Maman Brigette is the wife of Baron Samedi. Brigette is the mother of all spirits who enter this world. The graveyard is considered her womb. She is the female guardian of graves and is syncretized with Saint Bridget.

Spiritual bodies and guardians

Voodoo belief teaches that human beings have two distinct spiritual bodies. The first is known as the ti-bon-anj, which means the "little good angel." This is the consciousness. The ti-bon-anj leaves the body during sleep or in trance possession. The second spiritual body is known as the gros-bon-anj, which means the "big good angel." This body is the psyche of the individual and is part of the divine in man. The gros-bon-anj keeps humans alive.

Voodoo teaches that everyone has a loa that guards him or her. The met tet means "the master of the head." This is similar to a guardian angel. The loa may reveal themselves through dreams or through possessing the individual. The priest or priestess may identify the loa during the kanzo ritual.

Group structure

The hierarchy of practitioners in Voodoo ranges from an occasional associate to the full-time priest or priestess. There are practitioners who have not been initiated, but attend ceremonies and go to the priesthood for wisdom. These practitioners are known as vodouisant. An uninitiated practitioner who attends ceremonies and is preparing for initiation is known as the hounsi, which means "bride of the spirit."

The first stage of initiation is known as the hounsi kanzo. Initiates become "married" to a spirit. The second stage is known as as si pwen or sur point. This means the initiate is serving one particular loa. The initiate is permitted to use the asson, which is the sacred rattle used to invoke the loa. The initiate may lead prayers and songs in the temple and, at this level, may initiate others into this level of initiation. Also, initiates at this stage are taught how to care for the loa.

The third and final stage of initiation is called asogwe. Initiates at this point have become priests and priestesses of the Voodoo faith and can confirm initiations of all stages on other initiates. The priestess in Voodoo is known as the mambo and the priest is known as the houngan. Initiates may refer to clergy as mama or papa. The priest and priestess may oversee a group of believers known as a society that meets at various times for worship and ritual.

There are also a number of specialized offices in the Voodoo society, including choir director, animal keeper, and others. Some types of priests have a special title according to their specialty. The bokor is a priest who works with the spirits of the dead. Some practitioners use the term *left hand* to describe the malevolent work that a bokor can perform.

There are also a number of secret societies that exist in Haitian Voodoo. These societies may worship a particular deity or follow a particular religious tradition.

Artifacts

Asson

The asson is a rattle similar to a maraca and is usually carried by those who have been initiated into a priest or priestess position of leadership. This rattle is usually made from a large calabash. It is sometimes filled and covered with snake vertebrae or glass beads. The rattle may be used to strike the veve (symbol) signatures of the spirits.

Bottle

Bottles covered in sequins, beads, and fabric are used in many rituals. The bottles are decorated in colors representing the loa and also may be decorated with an image of a saint. Bottles are used to honor the loa. Some may hold offerings, while others that are decorated with doll heads may be used in divination rites.

Chromolithographs

Chromolithographs are images of the loa represented in Catholic saint form.

Flags

Multicolored flags known as drapo may be found during a search or observation of a residence in which Voodoo is practiced. Flags announce the spirits that will attend a ceremony. Voudon flags are usually made of fine cloth with sequined images of the spirits sewn into them. Flags may be kept on the pe (or central pole of the temple) to give them power.

Govi

A spirit can be called through a vessel of water using a white sheet of cloth that is placed inside a jar called a govi, which is used to call down the loa. These jars are found in the temple and may be decorated with symbols of the loa.

Packets

The packet comes from the Congo region. The packet is a bag that contains bones, herbs, stones, and other ingredients. The bag, usually decorated with satin cloth and sequins, may have one stem sticking out of it. This is a male packet. Female packets will have two rounded arms pointing down. The packet is found in the temple and is used to "heat up" the loa for ceremonies. The packet is also known as a wanga.

Swords

Swords are used in Voodoo rituals as symbols of the iron spirit Ogou. There is a ritual procession of the sword known as the sword of la place. The la place is the sword bearer who helps begin the rituals of Voodoo.

Ogan

The ogan is a cowbell-type instrument without a clapper. It is struck during ceremonies to summon the spirits.

Triangle

An iron triangle musical instrument is used in rituals as well. When it is struck, it opens spiritual doorways.

Conch shells

The conch shell is blown like a trumpet to call the loa of the ocean, Agwe.

Zins

Zins are three-legged pots. They are filled with oil and set on fire. The fire from the pots is used to warm the loa and increase their power.

Drums

Drums are core pieces of equipment in a voudon ceremony. The rhythms that are played on them call the spirits into the ceremony. The creation and preparation of the drums is a specific method and they are considered "alive." The drums fall into different categories, according to the type of spirit to be called. The three types of drums are Rada, Petro, and Congo. Each drum has its own particular style of play, and physical characteristics.

The three drums are described in detail below.

Rada drums are three in a set. Rada drums will typically have small pegs that stick out the sides of the tops.
Petro drums come in sets of two, with one drum larger than the other. The Petro do not contain pegs.
Congo drums usually come in sets of three.

Drums are treated as living beings and are given power and even fed sacrificed animals.

Ceremonies

Voodoo ceremonies are referred to as services. The service is performed to contact the loa. Practices and artifacts are used to heat things up (echofe) to summon the loa. Offerings of food, animals, and songs are presented in hopes that the loa will come to the ceremony. The traditional Voodoo ceremony has several components that must occur before the loa appear to the temple. The two main parts of the service are the procession and the invocation of loa.

Rituals

Entrance

The ceremony begins with the parade of the houmphors flags. These flags are decorated with the symbols of the loa. The houmphors drums are then greeted. The center of the temple is entered and the four points of north, south, east, and west are recognized. The loa are called upon as well as the Catholic saints. Drumming and dancing begin to call the loa. The veve (religious symbols for the loa) are drawn in cornmeal and powders on the ground to represent the loa that are manifesting. The rituals begin with a prayer to Legba to open the gates to the spiritual world.

Priye Ginen

The Priye Ginen, or "Prayer of Africa," is used to open Voodoo services. The prayer is sung in French, Creole, and African languages. The prayer creates sacred space for the ritual.

Manje loa: the sacrifice

The loa are believed to eat as human beings do. The second part of the service is known as manje loa; this is the ritual feeding of the animals. Plates of food and animals to be sacrificed are left at the poteau mitan. The animals are dressed in colors of the loa. The person in charge of the sacrifice (commanditaire) usually wears a red cloth on his or her head. He or she eats some of the food on the plates and feeds the animals some of the food. If the animals eat the food, this means that the animal has accepted the sacrifice. The animal is then rubbed with sacred herbs and killed. The person who kills it drinks some of the animal's blood, and then carries it to the four points of the ritual area. Devotees may rub the animal's blood on their foreheads in the shape of crosses. The animals are then taken outside to be cooked.

The loa have specific foods that they prefer. Some of the food offered to the loa include:

Legba: Cassavas, rice, green bananas, smoked foods, molted roosters.
Azaka: Corn, breads, unrefined sugar, brandy.
Gede family: Black goats and black roosters.
Baron Samdi: Black goats, black hens.
Dambala: Eggs, rice, white hens.
Ayida Wedo: White hens, rice, milk.
Ezili: Rice, chickens.
Ezili Danto: Fried pork.
Ogou Feray: Red roosters, bulls.
Agwe: White sheep, hens, and champagne.
Simbi: Black animals, turkeys, hens.

Rites of passage

There is a ceremony known as the *leve nom* in which the initiate receives the name of an ancestor for protection. The ritual of *garde* may be performed after the leve nom. The garde is a ritual of the cutting into the skin of the practitioner. The cut is a symbol that is used to identify members of the temple. Dried herbs may be rubbed into the cut to give protection to the initiate, and then he or she gives offerings in exchange for the protection of the deity.

A ritual called *lave tet* is a ritualistic washing of the head, which makes trance possession easier on the initiate. Later an initiate may receive a "refreshing" of the head called rafraichi tete to widen the path for the spirit to work inside his or her body.

To become an initiated priest or priestess, a ceremony is performed called haussement, or the "lifting" of the initiate. The ritual is a lifting of the devotee in a chair three times, and an oath is presented in which the initiate swears allegiance to the loa.

Initiation

The initiated is called the *ounsi*. The ritual to becoming *ounsi* takes one to two weeks. The initiate is dressed in white and is taught about the loa and how to function in the temple. He or she is then presented to the temple. If the initiate becomes possessed, it is a sign that he or she is connected to the loa.

Marriage

Initiates can be married to the loa in a ceremony. This is to give the initiate additional power from the loa. The initiate is married in a traditional-type marriage ceremony and signs a marriage certificate.

Trance possession

Possession is a normative practice that temples observe. The initiate is "mounted" as in Santería by the loa. The initiate actually becomes possessed by the loa and takes on the characteristics of the loa. For example, those possessed by the loa Dambala may act like a snake. Possession by Ogou will usually make the initiate wield a sword. Devotees who are possessed or "ridden" by the Gede loa will wear sunglasses and a hat, and will be given strong drinks like rum. The possession by the Gede spirits is usually marked by the initiate cursing and acting sexually promiscuous. The loa will often speak through the possessed.

Sacred days

The sacred days used by the Catholic Church are honored by the liturgical calendar of Voodoo practitioners.

> Bains de Chance: "Luck baths" on Christmas; from December 24 to January 6, herbs are crushed, and the creation of sacred baths using them takes place during the pile fey.
> January 6: Epiphany.
> July 16: Our Lady of Mount Carmel is celebrated in honor of Ezili.
> July 25: Saint James, Ogou.
> July 26: Saint Anne, mother of Ezili.
> November 2: Fet Ghede, "All Souls Day"; practitioners go to cemetery, give offerings.

Altar and shrines

Voodoo temples throughout the United States exist in two forms. The first is a traditional temple that is not only open to the public, but also very public in the eye of the media and the local community. The second type of temple is usually hidden from the public view and may exist in the basements and storage buildings of Voodoo practitioners. The Voodoo temple is called the *houmfort*. The main ritual area in which the majority of ceremonies occur is called the *peristyle*, which is usually decorated with drawings of the saints, hanging calabashes (hard-shelled gourds), and items representing the loa. There is usually an area that contains a fire pit, wherein resides an iron bar that represents the spirit of iron. In the center of the peristyle is a pole called the *poteau mitan*. This is a French word meaning "pole in the middle." It used by the loa to climb down from the heavens, and the pole represents the center of the universe. It is usually decorated with paintings of the serpents Dambala and Aida Wedo.

One of the most common items found in the Voodoo ceremony is the *veve*. This image originally came from the Congo region. The Congo religions utilize drawings and symbols in much of their ceremonies and rites. This is an image that is universally recognized as the symbol of a particular loa. The symbol is drawn on the ground with cornmeal, coffee, powdered brick, or chalk. His figure is usually placed where a spirit is to manifest with food, sometimes being left on the drawings for the spirit. The veve is a doorway for the loa to appear through.

There is also an altar called the *pe*. The pe is usually square shaped and holds several personal ritual objects that are considered sacred to the members of the temple. This may even include a snake representing Dambala, the serpent god.

The temple also contains chambers known as *kay miste*, or "huts of the mysteries," which are reserved for worship of a single loa. These chambers may contain images and tools used by the particular loa.

Officers may also encounter altars and shrines containing a number of items in the homes of practitioners. The personal altar is called a *rogatoire*, which usually contains a picture of the saint that corresponds with one's personal loa. Candles, crosses, and other voudon icons may be on this altar. Food may be left on the altar for the loa as well.

Many of the items frequently found on a traditional Voodoo altar include:

Lithographs or prints of Catholic saints
Ceramic or terra-cotta pots
Drinking glass or shot glass of rum or wine, bottles of rum or champagne
Statues

Objects representing the loa are also found on the altar. Each loa has several artifacts that reflect his or her personality.

Azaka is represented by a straw bag and tobacco pipe. The bag, known as the *alfo*, is worn much like a purse. The items of Azaka reflect his personality as a Haitian farmer.

Agwe is represented by a wooden boat that hangs from the ceiling.

The Ogou loa may be represented by a sword and objects of iron.

La Sirene may be represented by images of mermaids and seashells. She may also be represented by combs and mirrors.

Legba may be represented by a wooden crutch and tobacco pipes.

Ezili Danto is represented by a knife, which is frequently placed inside a bowl.

The Baron loa may be represented by a black top hat.

The Gede family of spirits is represented by a coffin, sunglasses, and a cross.

Images of skulls may also be used for Gede.

Ezili Freda may be represented by jewelry, perfume, and lace.

Dominican Voodoo (21 divisions)

The Dominican Republic shares the island of Hispaniola with Haiti. Voodoo from the Dominican Republic has a different flavor to its beliefs and practices. With many similar aspects, such as the use of the term *loa*, Dominican Voodoo practitioners refer to a creator named Papa Bon Dye and the loa as the 21 divisions. Dominican Voodoo includes some loa that are distinct from that geographical region, such as *Anaisa Pye* and *Candelo Cedife*.

West African Voodoo

West African Voodoo relied on the deities and practices of Voodoo before the religion traveled to areas such as Haiti. The rituals and practices are said by practitioners to be the oldest examples of the voudon religion in the world. The loa are referred to as spirits. Some levels of initiation in West African Voodoo can be attained only through birthright and inheritance. West African Voodoo has been appropriated by some human trafficking groups that use the religion's trappings to intimidate and keep victims psychologically bound to the organization.

Cultural terms

Asson: A rattle used in Voodoo by initiated clergy. Typically covered in beads or snake bones.

Baka: Dwarf-like spirit invoked by a Voodoo priest for protection.

Bosal: Means "wild" or "untamed." Refers to an initiate who has not learned to work with spirits.

Garde: A ritual scarring in which magical protection is placed on an individual.

Gros-bon-ange: The "big guardian angel" that is part of man. The term refers to the psyche of humanity.

La place: Master of ceremonies at a Voodoo ritual.

Lave-tet: Head washing ceremony.

Loa: The deities or spirits of Voodoo.

Mal dyok (maldjok): The evil eye in the Haitian community.

Mambo: An initiated priestess of the religion.

Poteau-mitan: The pole in the center of the temple used to call Voodoo spirits.

Ti-bon-ange (ti-bon-anj) : The "little guardian angel" that composes the soul. The angel is compared to consciousness.

Voudon: Original term used for "spirit" that later became Voodoo. Voudon is a term used many times to describe a Voodoo-type aspect and is used interchangeably with Voodoo.

Wanga: Charm used for malevolent workings.

References

Brown, Karen McCarthey, *Mama Lola: A voudou priestess in Brooklyn*, University of California, Berkeley, CA, 1991.

Consentino, Donald J., *Sacred Arts of Haitian Voudou*, University of Los Angeles Fowler Museum, Los Angeles, CA, 1995.

Davis, Wade, *The Serpent and The Rainbow*, Simon and Schuster, New York, 1986.

Deren, Maya, *Divine horsemen: Voodoo Gods of Haiti*, Mystic Fire Video, New York, 1953.

Hurbon, Laennec, *Voodoo: Search for the Spirit*, New York, Harry Abrams, 1995.

Metraux, Alfred, *Voodoo in Haiti*, New York, Schocken Books, 1972.

Rigaud, Milo, *Secrets of Voodoo*, City Lights Books, 1969.

Thompson, Robert Farris, *Face of the gods: Art and altars of Africa and the African Americas*, Museum for New York, African Art, 1993.

chapter eight

Christian-based groups

Two of Mexico's strongest drug trafficking organizations, La Familia Michoacana and the Caballeros Templarios, utilize elements of Christianity in their philosophies, rituals, and symbols. Approximately 83 percent of Mexico identifies itself as Catholic (U.S. Department of State). Various forms and denominations of Christianity are widely accepted and embraced among the Mexican population. Drug traffickers who appropriate Christian elements into their practices may find that potential recruits feel as if they can identify with the religious aspects of the group if they are predisposed to the culture. This chapter will look at the religious elements and how they serve drug trafficking organizations.

La Familia Michoacana

The drug trafficking organization La Familia Michoacana (LFM) utilizes a number of elements of religious culture in its practices. The group's goals of trafficking narcotics, murdering rivals, and producing methamphetamine are twisted with a spiritual philosophy in which members are taught to improve society and become ethical examples of masculinity.

The spiritual aspects of LFM are the brainchild of the group's now deceased leader, Nazario Moreno Gonzalez. Known as el mas loco, or "the craziest one," Gonzalez's nickname is believed to have come from famed Lebanese poet and thinker Khalil Gibran's book *El Loco*. The book speculates on the nature of man, God, and contains various inspirational sayings.

El Loco was one of Gonzalez's many nicknames, which also included The Pastor and El Chayo, or "The Rosary," which reflects his attempts to promote evangelistic zeal for his self-styled ideology. Gonzalez was born March 8, 1970, in Apatzingan, Mexico. There is little information available about his religious interests as a teenager, but in his later years Gonzalez began to embrace evangelical Christianity. As Gonzalez took control of LFM in 2004, after the organization's leader was captured, he began propagating his own form of Christianity into the cartel's practices.

La Familia initially formed as a result of the oppression of the Michoacán community by the Los Zetas cartel. This role of a "savior" began to give birth to a local mythology that the group was "heavenly sent." Members began to wear rosaries and crosses that identified themselves as members of this spiritual sect.

Gonzalez codified his personal teachings into a book that became required reading for members of LFM. *Pensamientos Del Mas Loco* (*The Sayings of the Craziest One*) is a 100-page booklet that shares the personal insights of Nazario, combining Christian terminology and regional sayings of inspiration. Gonzalez became obsessed with the writings of Christian writer John Eldridge, author of the popular *Wild at Heart* book series. Members of LFM were instructed to read the books and identify with the life of adventure that the books espoused.

Gonzalez formed study groups that used the concept of family to promote local confidence in the group. The organization began to hold spiritual retreats where new members would undergo hours of intense teachings and spiritual practices that included meditation and contemplative silence. Many of these practices are reflective of techniques used in destructive cults.

Coercive behaviors

Gonzalez's personality profile as a leader has several aspects that are commonly found in leaders of coercive groups. Much like Jim Jones and David Koresh, Gonzalez exhibited several behaviors that were used in building the LFM narco-cult.

- Claims a personal connection with a spiritual deity: Leaders will claim to have a personal revelation from a spirit or deity. The leader will overtly or covertly promote ideology that teaches that he or she has a relationship with a deity that cannot be attained by members of the group.
- Does not tolerate other's views: The leader does not allow anyone to question his or her authority.
- Builds a "kingdom": Leadership typically builds up the group's importance as a spiritual organization by increasing local support and confidence in the group as a helpful organization. Members may proselytize communities in order to gain new members and local support.
- Manipulation: Leadership is typically very charming and charismatic. These manipulative and abusive personalities have an uncanny ability to spot those who can easily be manipulated or those who have been victimized. Leadership has the ability to make others feel important and valuable to the group's cause.

Figure 8.1 La Familia Michoacana beheadings frequently feature messaging that references spiritual concepts and the group's ideology, along with threats, warnings, and challenges to rivals. (Courtesy of Borderland Beat.)

- Build paranoia: Leadership will build fear of the outside world and create an image of us versus them. Paranoia will also be instilled to increase fear of the leadership and suppress thoughts of becoming a traitor to the organization.
- Exploits: Leadership will frequently exploit members of the group for personal gain.
- Creation of a family role: Leadership will commonly refer to themselves as mother or father figures, while the group is depicted as a family. The role of blood family members is replaced by members of the group. This spiritual kinship brings a bonding mechanism to members of the organization.
- Demands possessions: Allegiance to the group is demonstrated in sharing or giving materials and money to the group's efforts.
- Harsh punishments: Leadership demands obedience to the group's cause at all cost. Punishments keep members of the organization in fear and create a dependence on the group for feelings of safety and security.

Members of the group were instructed to provide acts of service in which they would introduce drug addicts into the organization's rehabilitation centers. Sadly, many of the addicts were forced into becoming traffickers in exchange for rehabilitation.

Figure 8.2 Nazario Gonzalez created a messianic aura around himself that he used to manipulate and coerce members of the cartel to fight as spiritual warriors.

New members into La Familia were profiled for personality temperaments. Those who demonstrated a penchant for violent behavior were sent to a special training camp at a location known as Jesus del Monte. At the camp, members were tested on their ability to shoot, dismember, and cook rivals. New recruits were monitored for their sensitivity to being sickened while murdering victims and handling human remains.

Divine justice

La Familia Michoacana symbolically threw down the gauntlet and announced its presence in September 2006 when cartel members rolled five severed heads onto the dance floor of a Michoacán disco. A sign was left at the scene that read: "La Familia doesn't kill for money, it doesn't kill women, it doesn't kill innocent people—only those who deserve to die. Everyone should know this: this is divine justice."

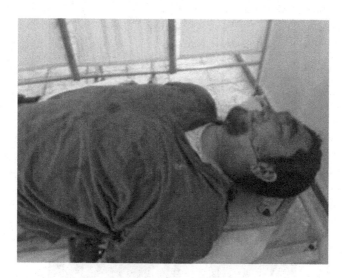

Figure 8.3 Death of Nazario. Gonzalez was originally thought to have been killed in a 2010 shootout, but he secretly survived and operated the LFM cartel until 2014, when he was shot and confirmed dead by the Mexican government. (Courtesy of Borderland Beat.)

This act was very important to the group's growth and reputation in that it communicated to the public a number of messages. The act produced an environment of fear and intimidation to the general public. The act also demonstrated the wrath and power of La Familia toward rivals, and last, the message left at the scene announced the narco-cult's connection to the spiritual. La Familia would promte themselves as soldiers of God who were carrying out divine appointments of violence.

La Familia would go on to take out ads in local newspapers telling of the "good deed" that the group performed in murdering the five victims. The newspaper ran ads that read: "Who are we? Workers from the Tierra Caliente region in the state of Michoacán, organized by the need to end the oppression, the humiliation to which we have constantly been subjected by people who have always had power."

La Familia would continue to send out spiritual messages and they would leave word on banners and on signs left on victims known as corpse messaging (Finnegan, 2010). In 2006, members of La Familia murdered Jesus Valenica Rodríguez, a member of the Milenio cartel that would later splinter into the La Resistencia and the Jalisco New Generation cartels. La Familia left a sign next to Valencia's body that read: "All that rises falls of its own weight, it would be like this, the family greets you." La Familia would use the color green in many of its messages as well as on the cartel's patches and symbols.

Figure 8.4 Nazario Gonzalez lives. The cartel leader was made into a folk saint by his followers and members of the local community. His image is dressed in the regalia of the Los Templarios Caballeros. (Courtesy of Borderland Beat.)

In 2010, President Calderon's administration claimed that Gonzales was dead after a shootout. Rumors persisted that he was still alive and no physical evidence of the cartel leader's death ever appeared. In 2014, Gonzales was shot and confirmed dead by the Mexican government. His ability to remain alive after his first reported death only increased his spiritual persona that had developed over the years.

After the death of the organization's leader, the group sent a message to Mexico's president that demonstrated the group's spiritual view of Nazario as a god:

> Beware Felipe Calderon, pray to your holy saint because we come with the blessing of our God. Our God Nazario, may God rest his soul. This will not stop until Familia Michoacana dies. And we will never die.

Figure 8.5 Los Caballeros Templarios (LCT) propaganda. is filled with rhetoric regarding religious zeal that the band of drug traffickers claims in their fight against rival cartels.

Caballeros Templarios

Following the death of La Familia's leader, cartel co-founders Enrique "El Kike" Plancarte Solis and Servando "La Tuta" Gómez Martinez formed the Caballeros Templarios after a split with the remaining members of La Familia Michoacana (LFM), now known as La Resistance. Martinez was a former schoolteacher. While living in the United States in the 1990s, Martinez converted to Christianity. Upon his return to Mexico, he discovered that religion could be used to structure his criminal organization.

The group uses cultural concepts borrowed from the Christian-based military order known as the Knights Templar founded during the Crusades. The original Templars were charged with protecting pilgrims on their way to Jerusalem.

Figure 8.6 A handmade code book belonging to the Los Caballeros Templarios.

The group uses terminology, symbols, and writings from the historical order. The focus of the organization, however, is on protecting the state of Michoacán, much like the original Templars protected the pilgrims. On March 10, 2011, the group posted 30 ads throughout the streets of Mexico. The ads read: "From today we will be laboring here the activities previously performed by La Familia Michoacana. We will be the order of society to meet any situation undermining the integrity of Michoacán."

The goals of the organization sounded very honorable, as the banners announced: "Our commitment is to safeguard order, avoid robberies, kidnapping, extortion, and to shield the state from rival organizations."

Figure 8.7 Templar automobile tag.

Figure 8.8 Members of the Knights Templar cartel mark their vehicles with various sacred symbols in order to identify membership.

Figures 8.9 Templar worship. A group of devotees show their allegiance to the teachings of Gonzalez at a local Templario temple. (Courtesy of Borderland Beat.)

Figures 8.10 Templar shrines. A group of devotees show their allegiance to the teachings of Gonzalez at a local Templario temple. (Courtesy of Borderland Beat.)

While the Caballeros sounded honorable, three months later the group would kidnap, torture, and murder 21 members of La Familia Michoacana. In 25 minutes, the bodies of victims were scattered at entrances of the city, mimicking the infamous 2006 disco shock-and-awe incident made famous by LFM. A banner was hung declaring, "Because society demands it, here are thieves of dwellings and assailants, rapists and there still are more."

The group also placed banners around communities in March 2012 during Pope Benedict XVI's visit to Mexico. The banners promised: "The Knights Templar Cartel will not partake in any warlike acts, we are not killers, welcome Pope."

One of the first public acts of violence by the group was a public hanging of two men flanked by a banner that read: "We killed robbers and kidnappers. Sincerely, Los Caballeros Templarios." The group became active in acts of savage violence, including the kidnapping and raping of young girls.

In May 2013, members of the LCT cartel ambushed and shot 10 farmers who had met with members of the Mexican government to protest the cartel's extortion practices.

Figure 8.11 A truck driven by members of the Templars is used in a shootout with a rival cartel.

Group structure

The Caballero narco-cult is structured into various divisions. Core members are known as apostles, while members known as preachers are responsible for various territories. Cartel members who are assigned as hitmen are known as celestial warriors.

New members into the group must be approved by a council. New members to the cult undergo a number of initiation rituals. There is an oath that is undertaken by initiates that reads:

> I swear before all to live and die with honor. I swear to fight all injustice and assist my neighbor. I swear in battle or in peace, which no gentleman will be considered by me as enemy. I swear fidelity to the temple and strive to perpetuate. I swear respect for others, reverence for the parents, protecting children or the elderly, assisted assistance to the sick and needy. I swear top respect the faith of others, and look over the viewing the glory, the honor honors. If unfortunately I betray my oath, I beg to be executed by the order as a traitor.

Figures 8.12 and 8.13 Templar jewelry. The cross of the Templarios is worn by members of the narco-cult to show affiliation with the organization.

Figure 8.14 Templar robes. Members of the Mexican army discovered a large cache of robes, swords, and helmets used by the Templarios in their rituals. (Courtesy of Borderland Beat.)

Group practices and mythology

The execution as a traitor is one of several punishments used by the group's leadership to ensure obedience to the group. Some of the other punishments used by the group include a continuum for those who disobey orders. The first punishment is to send the offender to rehabilitation. The second punishment is to put the member in isolation for 12 days blindfolded and tied up and placed into a crucifix position. The member is whipped 12 times as part

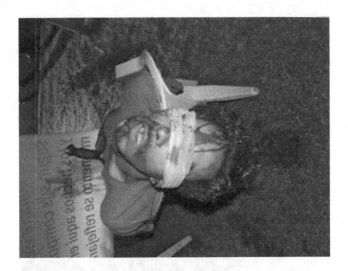

Figures 8.15 and 8.16 The Templars murdered three individuals in an act of justice, as their message decorated with the group's coat of arms reads: "Men live or die according to their behavior, and there is [sic] reflected in this moment."

of the punishment. The final punishment is a ritual execution by members. The group teaches that once a member of the order, you are a member for life.

The outside rules for the sect that are promoted to the media and public are concerned with protecting the innocent and prohibition of rapes, robberies, and kidnappings.

The group uses a lot of aesthetics that mimic the weaponry and dress of the original Knights Templar. Members of the cartel are equipped with armor, swords, and even custom-made jewel-encrusted firearms.

The group has created a coat of arms to identify members of the sect. The coat contains images of Nazario Gonzalez, Jesus Christ, a cross, and a medieval weapon. Gonzalez is considered a saint by members of the sect. The coat of arms was mentioned in a message left with 11 bodies that showed signs of torture and bullet wounds to the head. "So it is clear to you that we are never going to betray our coat of arms of the Caballeros Templarios. We are not fucking deserters like you, fucking asshole."

There are shrines dedicated to Gonzalez in the region of Apatzingán, Mexico. These shrines include statues of the now deceased cartel leader. There is a prayer that followers pray to the leader: "Oh Lord Almighty, free me from all sins, give me protection through Saint Nazario."

The group has become involved in human organ trafficking. In December 2012, in Tepalcatepec, Mexico, a refrigerated van was stopped and searched by authorities. The van was discovered to have seven children on board. The children were dressed in school uniforms and wrapped in blankets. The driver of the vehicle confessed that the children were taken to be used in organ trafficking.

In March 2014, a governmental officer from Mexico reported that new members into the sect were being forced to eat the heart of a child in a new initiation process. Local authorities believe that the human hearts came from local children who had been kidnapped for organ trafficking purposes. Even if this aspect of the LCT rituals is myth, the belief in this ritual is purposeful propaganda that builds the sinister reputation of the Caballeros.

Code of the Knights Templar

The doctrine of Los Caballeros Templarios can be found in their bible, called *Código de los Caballeros Templarios de Michoacán* (*Code of the Knights Templar of Michoacán*). This is a 25-page booklet that was seized by Mexican federal authorities during a raid on the cartel. The booklet has been discovered at a number of regions where the Templars are active and has been circulated among communities and the press. The book is written in

Spanish and is illustrated with several drawings of the original Knights Templars taken from an online website that sells swords and from a website promoting a Swedish film about the Templars.

The following is an English translation of the book.*

Cover:

> This struggle is for your people, my people, for ourselves and for our future generations.

Page 1:

> 1. Code of the Knights Templar of Michoacán: This code is obligatory for all those who form part of the Order of the Knights Templar of Michoacán.
>
> 2. The Knights Templar of Michoacán was created on 8 March 2011. Their principal mission is to protect the inhabitants and the sacred territory of the independent, sovereign and secular state of Michoacán.
>
> 3. To enter this order it is necessary to receive approval from the Council comprised by the brothers of greatest experience and good judgment.
>
> 4. Every individual who becomes a member of the Knights Templar of Michoacán does so for all his life and cannot abandon the order.
>
> A man with ideas is a strong man but a man with ideals is invincible.

Page 2:

> 5. All members of the Order of the Knights Templar of Michoacán should be under oath, which is administered via a ritual established by the Council, such oath shall comply at the cost of his own life.
>
> 6. Every knight is obligated to behave with honor, dignity, absolute discipline, loyalty and honesty as dictated by the sacred canons of the order.

---

* Partial translation taken from Mexico's Knights Templar and Code of Conduct Implications, Tribal Analysis Center, November 2013.

7. All knights should respect the CODE OF SILENCE, it is absolutely prohibited to divulge our activities and secrets.
8. Knights Templar should love and serve humanity in a disinterested manner.

A long journey begins with a first step.

Page 3:

Love, Loyalty, Equality and Justice.

Page 4:

9. A Knight Templar understands that there is a God, a life created by Him, an eternal truth and a divine purpose in the service of God and Mankind.
10. Members of the Order should struggle against materialism, injustice and tyranny in the world, beginning with their own home, community, city, state and country.
11. It is the duty of all the knights to prepare and equip themselves for battle and attain the objectives of the Order.
12. We Knights Templar will wage the ideological battle that confronts us in order to defend the values that sustain a society based on ethics that have been developed over the centuries.

Seeking the god of our fellow men.

Page 5:

13. Order will struggle against the disintegration of moral values and the destructive elements that prevail today in human society.
14. Order sustains natural justice and the fundamental rights of man, recognizing the right of all peoples and nations to govern themselves within their own natural economic environment.
15. Order supports freedom of expression, of conscience and of religion; collective self-defense and positive measures to eradicate the poverty and injustice that threaten world society.

16. Templars should not have a negative attitude against any man because of the way he addresses God, even if this should be different or strange. On the contrary, the Templar should try to understand how others seek God.

Destiny deals out the cards, we are the ones who play them.

Page 6:

I swear and promise to always fight to protect the oppressed, the widow and the orphan.

Page 7:

17. A soldier of the Templars should not be enslaved by sectarian beliefs or narrow opinions. God is truth and without God there is no truth. A Templar should always seek truth because in truth there is God.
18. Order foments patriotism, expressed in pride in one's own land and its achievements and the awareness of its place among nations and the duties toward all mankind.
19. Knights of the Order should conduct themselves with humility and be the most honorable, the most noble, the most polite, the most honest and the most gentlemanly, as a worthy Knight of the Templars.
20. A Templar should serve the Order and not expect to be served by it. What collaboration is given should be in the service of God and there should be no expectation of reward other than the knowledge that the Order is honored by his devotion.

There is a past that is gone forever, but there is a future that is ours.

Page 8:

21. Templars should not offend in any manner another person or other being. For all, the Templar should be a model of gentlemanliness.

22. No woman should fear a Templar, neither his actions nor his words. No child should fear a Templar either. No man should fear a Templar, but on the contrary should feel his protection.
23. Never should a Templar dishonor another Templar, because such conduct will dishonor himself and will discredit the Order.
24. In his conduct, a Templar will avoid the following: brutality, drunkenness in an offensive manner, immortality, cowardice, lying and having malicious intentions.

Never surrender, create your own path.

Page 9:

Life requires gentlemanliness and humility.

Page 10:

25. A knight should not seek positions of aggrandizement in the Order. He will be content with those positions which he has been given so that he can serve best.
26. A Templar should not judge anyone by his possessions or his social position. On the contrary, people should be judged by their character and their clarity towards others, or lack thereof.
27. Members of the Order must submit completely to the principles of the Templars and obey its officials in all things related to the Order.
28. For the Knights Templars of Michoacan, discipline is constant and obedience is always given, we come and go depending on the instructions by those in authority.

If you can dream it, you can make it happen.

Page 11:

29. Every member of the Order must remain firm and constant in the just causes of God.
30. All Knights Templar of the Order are under obligation to live a common life of sobriety and happiness, always maintaining a low profile so as not to attract notice.

31. All Knights must treat their companions and leaders with respect.
32. Work undertaken by all those in the Order must be for the benefit and progress of all the Knights Templar and not for the personal benefit of any individual.

For cowards, the future is uncertain, for the brave it is the great opportunity they are waiting for.

Page 12:

I swear and promise to spill my blood, if need be, to comply with all my oaths, and to assist my brothers.

33. The conduct of a knight should be unblemished, therefore abusing the innocence of virtuous women and minors, utilizing deception or power to seduce them, is prohibited.
34. For all members of the Order, the use of drugs or any mind altering substance is strictly prohibited.
35. A Knight Templar never gives the impression he is superior to others.
36. All members of the order of the Knights Templar of Michoacan should inform the Council regarding all matters of relevance that occur in their personal lives.

Man is a God when he dreams and pauper when he thinks.

Page 13:

Image of a knight.

Page 14:

37. Kidnapping for the purpose of making money is strictly prohibited for all members of the Order.
38. The leaders of the Order and their personnel must periodically submit to antidoping tests and inform the Council of the results of these tests.

39. No one can leave their assigned position without permission from his superior, in the case of the leadership there should exist good communication with the rest of that elite, the deputies of the leaders should coordinate effectively the functions of all personnel.

Thinking with your head is not the same as thinking with your heart.

Page 15:

No one has more pride than a Templar: He has the forest for his house and the sky as a window.

Page 16:

41. To use lethal force, authorization from the Council is required.
42. Knights of Templar of Michoacan should never be seen as lazy or getting involved in what is none of their business.
43. Knights Templar in leadership positions will behave in an exemplary manner; they will be intelligent, astute, humble, prudent, efficient, audacious and discreet: they are under obligation to improve themselves and learn.
44. Any knight who has a need outside his work zone, must inform immediately as soon as he enters the other zone, irrespective of his position in the hierarchy.

A man's strength emanates from his mind.

Page 17:

45. At the moment of the move, all necessary security precautions must be taken, including sending out an advance party and traveling with caution during the entire trajectory.
46. For security reasons, all knights must be on alert 24 hours a day.
47. If a knight commits a fault against a member of the Council and violates the code of silence of the Knights Templar of Michoacan, he shall be punished with death.

48. Knights Templar of Michoacan impose justice and because of that, no element should kill wantonly for money. When that decision is made, it should be first investigated thoroughly and if there are sufficient reasons then proceed.

A brave man does not turn away from life's battle.

Page 18:

Wine is strong, the king is stronger and women are very strong, but the truth vanquishes all of them.

Page 19:

49. The Knights Templar of Michoacan is a crusader at all times, committed to a dual struggle against flesh and blood temptations while at the same time confronting the spiritual forces of the heavens.
50. A knight should always be conscious that he is a soldier of the Templars and always see to it that his works are an example to others.
51. Every knight should advance without fear, but being careful what my happen to the right and left of him, with his chest uncovered and his soul fortified with faith.
52. The Knight that betrays the Templars shall be punished by death and his properties will be expropriated, and his relatives will suffer the same fate.

If you persevere, your dreams and desires will become reality.

Page 20:

53. When there is weakness, the Templar should bring his force. Where there is no voice, the Templar should raise his. Where poverty is greatest, there the Templar should distribute his generosity.

The richest is not one who has the most money but the one who needs the least.

Page 21:

> Because the manner in which we behave ourselves
> today, will be the example for our people on the day
> of tomorrow.

Page 22:

> Templar Oath
>
> I swear to live and die with honor.
> I swear to fight injustice and assist my neighbor.
> I swear in times of combat and in peace, that no
>   Knight be considered by me an enemy.
> I swear allegiance to the temple and to strive
>   to perpetrate.
> I swear respect to the ladies, worship mothers,
>   protect children and the elderly care for the
>   sick and needy.
> I swear to protect the faith of others and look
>   more to truth before glory. I will seek honor
>   before being honored.

Page 23:

> Unfortunately if I betray my oath, I beg to be exe-
> cuted by or order as a traitor.

Page 24:

> I agree if I miss my honor to be executed by the
> arms of the good fellow or be devoured by the wild
> beasts of the forests.

An analysis of the group's teachings taken from propaganda videos, booklets, and narco banners reveals the narco-cult's desire to become a state religion for Michoacán. The group continually speaks of being a friend to the citizens as well as a protector of citizens. Leaders of the group pass out money to citizens of communities they wish to take over. The group conducts marches and protests against the presence of federal authorities in the cult's territories. Current leader of the Templarios, Gomez Martinez (aka La Tuta) uses many references to Che Guevara and the philosophy of Marxism. The group portrays itself as a benevolent organization, as Martinez explained in a news release: "Our organization is not a cartel, and not an organized crime group, we are a brotherhood the Knights Templar."

Much like forms of radical Islam, the cult seeks to replace local government with not only manpower, but also the teachings of the cult.

References

Finnegan, William, Silver or lead? *New Yorker*, May 31, 2010.

Grayson, George W., *La Familia drug cartel: Implications for U.S.-Mexican security*, Strategic Studies Institute, December 2010.

Logan, Samuel, and John P. Sullivan, *Mexico's divine justice*, International Relations and Security Network, August 17, 2009.

Sullivan, John P., and Robert J. Bunker, *Mexico's criminal insurgency*, Small Wars Foundation, 2012.

U.S. Department of State. www.state.gov/documents/organization/193199.pdf

chapter nine

Investigations

Investigators who are working drug trafficking groups may discover a number of physical indicators that may link traffickers to a particular religious group or culture. These indicators alone do not denote criminal activity but can give an understanding into the behavior and affiliates of a trafficker.

Undercover operations

Undercover narcotics officers may encounter buyers and sellers involved in narco-cults. It is important that officers seeking to work undercover in these groups understand that religious cultures have many complexities. For example, members of these groups are familiar with spiritual lineage that exists in their religions. Working undercover among these groups and claiming to belong to any of these spiritual traditions will demand that the officer be well educated in the customs and norms of these traditions, and he or she may be faced with having to give evidence of belonging to a spiritual lineage.

For example, an undercover officer seeking to infiltrate a narco-cult that uses Santería may be asked questions regarding lineage such as:

What is your rama?
Who is padrino?
Where is your ile?
Have you been crowned?
When were you crowned?
Who owns your head?

An officer seeking to use a religious culture as a cover may need to affiliate with a noncriminal religious sect in order to gain credibility. In cases where traffickers are simply using self-styled saint worship, officers can simply learn about the history, myths, and practices associated with the culture. Narcotics officers working undercover can utilize amulets and jewelry that feature narco saints, such as Jesus Malverde and Santa Muerte.

Clergy who are not affiliated with the narco-cult but provide spiritual services to anyone in the public can make great sources of intelligence. There are a number of babalawos and santeros who have served as

Figures 9.1 and 9.2 Gulf cartel symbols.

informants to law enforcement. These members of clergy hear confessions and provide spiritual services to the public. Some clergy have been propositioned by drug traffickers to work for the group. Some have provided spiritual services, such as blessing drug shipments or performing consultations to find the best routes for traffickers. Most members of the Afro-Caribbean and Latin religions despise the use of their sacred traditions by drug traffickers.

Understanding cultural networks

The concept of social network analysis has been very helpful to law enforcement in mapping out networks of members when combating street gangs and terrorist organizations. Social network analysis involves mapping interactive patterns among people in order to understand their behavior. Social network maps can show leadership and how information is exchanged between individuals. The knowledge of social networks can help officers understand ties between groups and individuals and how they function within the criminal organization.

Figures 9.3 and 9.4 Sinaloa cartel symbols.

In addition to the networks that can be mapped out in looking at the drug trafficking organization (DTO), members with ties to narco-cults may have additional cultural ties that help in understanding the role of religious culture to the trafficker.

For example, John Doe is a member of a drug trafficking organization. The organization has ties to a Santería temple. Additional roles that may be examined and placed in a network map include:

Leadership of the temple
Members of the temple
Spiritual supply stores that provide artifacts for the group

Figures 9.5 and 9.6 Los Zetas symbols.

Animal suppliers for group sacrifices
Ritual specialists who assist with events
Drummers for temple ceremonies

Much like associates who provide services for street gangs, these associates supply services for the DTO. However, they may or may not be aware that they are affiliating with a criminal organization. Their place in the social world of the group may provide additional customers, associates, and intel to the group.

Figures 9.7 and 9.8 Jalisco New Generation cartel symbols.

There have a been some cases documented where law enforcement agencies have discovered conversations regarding the use of ritual specialists and drug trafficking operations. In the course of conducting wiretaps on drug traffickers, investigators have heard conversations between priests or priestesses and traffickers. In many of these cases, ritual

Figures 9.9 and 9.10 Los Caballeros Templarios shields.

Figure 9.11 Los Caballeros Templarios cross.

specialists were asked by traffickers when it would be safe to ship contraband, and if they would perform protective rituals for the traffickers. Investigators can benefit from being familiar with cultural terms that may be used during conversations between religious clergy and suspects, as they may reveal additional leads and activities.

Figure 9.12 Anthrax tattoo.

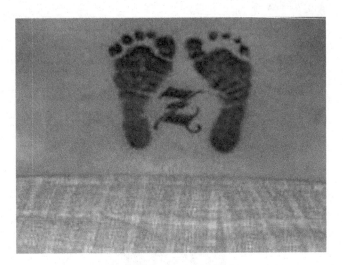

Figure 9.13 Los Zetas tattoos.

Interviewing subjects

Field interviews with members of narco-cults or suspects with ties to religious cultures may take place during car stops, at crime scenes, or when a suspect is in custody. In order to gain a better understanding into the functions of religion to the drug trafficker, it is helpful to have a basic understanding of the culture.

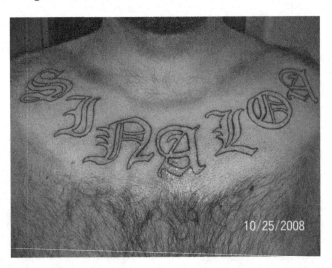

Figure 9.14 Sinaloa cartel tattoos.

Figure 9.15 Saint Judas Tadeo tattoos.

Because of the secrecy of some groups and an individual's belief that he is betraying the group and perhaps religious secrets, gaining information may be difficult. Understand that some members of narco-cults may fear not only physical retaliation for talking, but also spiritual retaliation. Some may even need to hold religious necklaces or medals while talking in order to feel safe. Some may refuse to speak on the grounds of religious freedom.

Tattoos

Traffickers may have tattoos for a number of reasons. Some may simply have an affinity for a specific image. Some may identify with a specific religion or deity. Some may have tattoos that identify him as a member of a specific group. Last, some tattoos may indicate a particular spiritual concept or degree of membership in a religious culture.

Scarification

Ritual scarring may indicate that a trafficker has been initiated into a specific religious tradition. Santería and Palo Mayombe both utilize ritual cutting as a part of an initiation process. The initiate in Santería may have cuts

Figure 9.16 Santa Muerte tattoo.

on his or her head, while the Palo initiate receives several cuts on his or her body on areas like the back, foot, and chest. Palo initiates may also have ritual scarrings from the firma (sacred symbols) carved into their bodies. Some of these scarrings identify the devotee with a particular spirit.

Haitian-based voodoo has a sacred act of protection known as a garde. This may appear as raised scar tissue on the skin. This scar provides spiritual protection for the individual.

Cultural reactions to law enforcement

Officers dealing with members of narco-cults may find themselves the targets of spiritual workings. Members of groups have been known to perform curses or have someone perform them on their behalf. Officers may receive mail or phone messages with spiritual threats. There have been several documented cases in which investigators have discovered physical evidence where their names or photographs have been placed in spiritual shrines in order to magically trigger attacks on investigators.

Some cultural specialists believe that the use of curses relieves inner tension as a form of psychological therapy. While in many cases the curse is strictly an attempt to manipulate officers through fear and intimidation, it is a good idea to document such threats in the event that an act of violence follows the curse.

Officers may encounter informants in narco-cults who believe they will be cursed if they turn against the group or give information to law

Figure 9.17 Santa Muerte tattoos.

enforcement. The psychological effects of a curse can be harmful if the informant has a magico-religious worldview and subscribes to a belief system that believes in the power of curses. The *Diagnostic and Statistical Manual of Mental Disorders* (DSM-IV) calls this phenomenon a culture-bound syndrome. These syndromes are described as "recurrent locality-specific patterns of aberrant behavior and troubling experience that may not be linked to a particular DSM-IV diagnostic category. They are indigenously considered to be illnesses or at least afflictions and have local names. They are localized, folk diagnostic categories that frame coherent meaning for certain repetitive, patterned and troubling sets of experiences and observations" (American Psychiatric Association, 2000).

Famed anthropologist Claude Levi Strauss (1974) said, "An individual who is aware that he is the object of sorcery is thoroughly convinced that he is doomed according to the most solemn traditions of his group." The psychological power of the threat of the curse can create despair and fear for those who believe in its power.

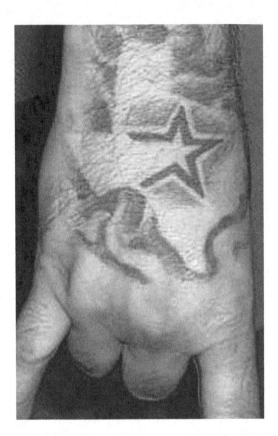

Figure 9.18 Tango Blast tattoo.

The concept of voodoo death was examined by psychologist Walter Cannon. Cannon's research showed that people who lived in cultures that believed in curses could become susceptible to death if they believed they had been cursed. The key to curses having a psychological and ultimately biological effect hinges on the victim of the curse having knowledge of the curse. The thought that he or she has become a victim of a curse will begin to take a toll on his or her mind. The victim also has to accept that destruction and death will be the results of curses. Last, the cursed individual's friends or associates will act as if the victim is going to die.

All of these factors combined will bring the victim into a state of hopelessness. The worry of death will bring a slow, self-fulfilling prophecy that will eat away at the victim's mental health. Physicians can attest to the power of dreadful news, as patients who are told that they are dying may succumb to the same type of mental breakdown (Barber, 2012).

Figure 9.19 Barrio Azteca tattoo.

Intelligence gathering

In order to gather intelligence on narco-cults, there are a number of avenues that officers can pursue. Groups that are very public and leave narco banners or videos online can be monitored to gain information regarding names, symbols, and locations. Original source materials such as group propaganda in the form of booklets, recruiting literature, prayer books, and sacred texts can provide good intel on the group's ideology.

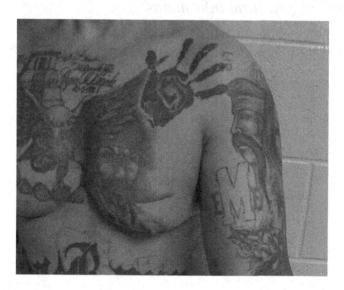

Figure 9.20 Mexican Mafia tattoo.

Figure 9.21 MS-13 tattoo.

Surveillance on cultural events can provide good intelligence regarding leadership, members, and social network ties. Funerals, weddings, religious ceremonies, and birthday celebrations for initiates and leaders can assist in revealing who the key players are in an organization.

Interviewing cultural informants

Officers who wish to gain an understanding into the religious cultures appropriated by drug traffickers might consult noncriminal devotees of

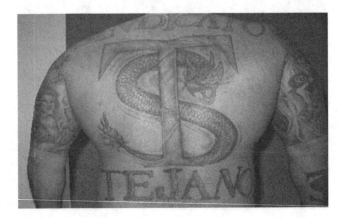

Figure 9.22 Texas syndicate tattoos.

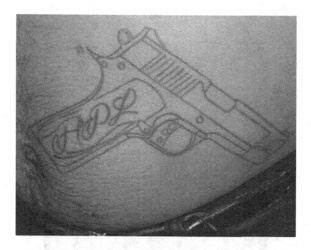

Figure 9.23 Hermandad de Pistoleros Latinos tattoos.

the same faith. Cultural informants can give valuable insight into their culture that cannot be gleamed from books or websites.

It is recommended that officers understand specific factors when interviewing cultural informants.

Remember that simply because an informant practices the same religion as a trafficker, it does not mean that he or she is involved in criminal activity. A culture that is unfamiliar to officers is not necessarily deviant or criminal.

Officers should remember that an interview with a cultural informant is not an interrogation. Officers should maintain a respectful attitude and an open mind when being educated about an informant's religion.

Officers should build a good rapport with cultural informants. Patience, courtesy, respect, and confidentiality will assist in building communication with informants. Officers should understand that many practitioners of these cultures may have experienced bad experiences with law enforcement or may have a biased view of the police based on experiences that members of their community have experienced.

Interviewing officers should listen and refrain from any gestures, comments, or behaviors that would appear judgmental or condescending. Officers need to understand that informants may be risking their reputation among their religious community by speaking with officers about their religion. Avoid using ethnocentric terms such as *Satanic, demonic,* and others that are personal adjectives that reflect a judgment or particular worldview. Officers do not have to agree with the culture of their informants in order to show respect to them.

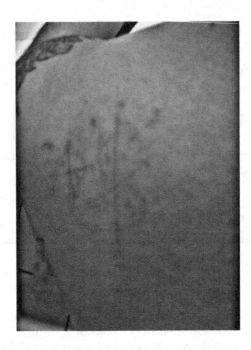

Figures 9.24 and 9.25 Firma. The signature of the spirits is cut into the body during a specific ritual. Some devotees will also tattoo the image on their bodies.

Figure 9.26 Worship. Remember that not everyone who follows a particular religion is the same. Many adherents abhor the thought of being considered criminals simply because of their religious affiliation.

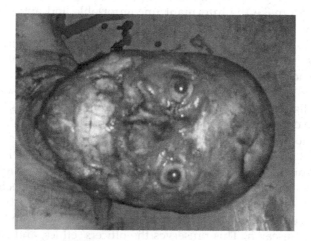

Figure 9.27 Skinned victim. Cartel-related homicides commonly include torture and gratuitous violence toward the victim before death.

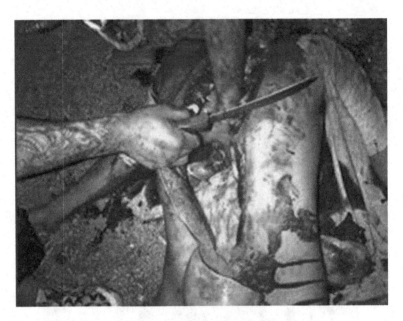

Figure 9.28 Organ removal. In an attempt to shock rivals and demonstrate desensitization to killing, many cartel enforcers will mutilate bodies and remove their organs. Many times these gruesome acts are filmed or photographed and sent to social media.

Officers may wish to interview informants while not in uniform, especially if they are in spiritual supply stores or at cultural events. A uniform can make the informant uncomfortable and apprehensive to share information.

Officers should take notes and document intelligence gained during the interview. Cultural terms, nuances, and specific cultural behaviors should be noted in order to gain insight.

Officers may discover that some informants may not share some details of their religion, as they may be considered religious "secrets." Religious secrets are details of ceremonies and rituals that are only available to the initiated. Some are not known to members of these cultures until they reach a certain level of initiation. The use of these secrets has been one of the mechanisms used to ensure the survival of many of these religions.

Officers should exercise discretion and avoid giving specific details about cases until they are confident that the informant is trustworthy.

As officers develop cultural informants, they should be up front about conducting research. This preserves the officers' ethics, and attempts at being dishonest may result in informants refusing to talk, as well as the officer being blacklisted among members of the religious community.

Figure 9.29 Santería victim. The sacred necklaces known as elekes can be seen on this gunshot victim. This could provide officers with additional leads and possible witnesses in the local Santería community. (Courtesy of Michael Vincent, Orange County (Florida) Police Department.)

Figure 9.30 Concealed weapon. Officers should exercise caution when stopping suspects where there is suspicion of drug-related offenses.

Figure 9.31 San Judas car statue. Officers who identify images of folk saints typically appropriated by drug traffickers should observe whether additional red flags may indicate possible contraband in the vehicle.

Thank your informant. Express appreciation for sharing his or her culture with you. Honesty, respect, and willingness to learn are invaluable skills in learning about cultures.

Deciphering communications

Investigators may discover various forms of communications, such as letters, rosters, and diaries, during narcotics investigations. Narcomantas that contain messages from cartels as well as signs left at "body messaging" scenes may contain the names of groups and individuals.

Some communications may contain cultural names and terms. For example, a member of the Almighty Latin King and Queen Nation (ALKQN) street gang of Arizona was discovered using social networking to communicate with other members of the gang who were dealing

Figure 9.32 De Valls Bluff (Arkansas) Police Chief Bradley Taylor performed a stop on a vehicle that contained over 103 pounds of marijuana. Chief Taylor spotted candles in the back seat of the vehicle decorated with images of narco saints on the glass jars that held the candles. A further inspection of the vehicle revealed that the contraband was hidden in the roof of the vehicle. Additional artifacts were discovered in the vehicle used to protect the occupants from detection. (Courtesy of Chief Bradley Taylor, De Valls Bluff (Arkansas) Police Department.)

narcotics. The member mentioned in her postings: "I am a daughter of Nsai for those in the know." In trying to identify this member's associates, it could be established that this member is also a member of the Palo Mayombe religious culture. Nsasi or Mama Nsasi is another name for the deity Siete Rayos in Palo Mayombe. Investigators could begin looking for additional associates in the local religious community.

Names written in documents may reflect the type of culture or group that a member may be involved in. Look at the following examples of names:

Omo Yemaya
Zarabanda Vento Malo Kimbisa
Houngan Bijean
Father Gideon Gonzalez

The names of these individuals reflect various details about their religious culture.

The first name, Omo Yemaya, tells us that the person is a member of the Santería religion. It also tells us that the person is initiated into the religion. Last, it tells us who the person's personal deity is. Yemaya is a

Figures 9.33 and 9.34 This marijuana grow operation was established by one of the Mexican cartels and was located in central California. (Courtesy of Butte County Sheriff's Office, Special Enforcement Unit, Oroville, California.)

deity in the religion of Santería who represents the spirit of the ocean waters. The term *omo* is used to denote that someone is an initiate or a "child of the orisha." Last, the person is a child of Yemaya. Yemaya is the person's personal deity.

The second name, Zarabanda Vento Malo Kimbisa, reveals that the person is a member of a Kongo-affiliated religion. It tells the name of the branch of the religion the person is associated with. It also reveals the camino, or "road," of his or her personal spirit, and last, the name of his or her personal spirit. Zarabanda is the name of a spirit or mpungu in the religion of Palo Mayombe. Kimbisa is the name of the tradition or rama of the Kongo religion that he or she practices. Vento Malo is the name of the road or camino of his or her spirit, and last, Zarabanda is the spirit of iron and justice.

The third name, Houngan Bijean, reflects the type of religion that the person practices as well as the position in the group's social structure. The term *houngan* is used in the practice of Haitian and Dominican voodoo. The term is also used to refer to an initiated priest in the religion.

The fourth name, Father Gideon Gonzalez, possibly reflects the type of religion that the person practices as well as the position in the group. The term *father* is typically used to denote priesthood in a Catholic-inspired religious culture. Gideon is a name taken from the Christian Bible.

There are a number of culture-bound expressions that may be found in communications that can give officers insight into the culture that suspects may be affiliated with. For example, letters signed with the salutation *alafia* would be from someone affiliated with the Yoruba religions, such as Ifa or Santería. Letters ending with expressions like *kiambote* would be from someone familiar with Kongo-based religions.

Homicides

Retired NYPD detective and homicide expert Vernon Geberth defines *drug-related homicides* as "murders which occur as a direct result of the use, sale and distribution of narcotics and other illegal drugs" (Geberth, 2006).

Geberth classifies drug-related homicides into four specific categories:

Drug hits: Premeditated murders intended to eliminate competition or to force control over members of a cartel or drug group. This includes crimes where an informant is murdered. Murders may also occur during a drug rip-off.

Interpersonal drug disputes: These types of homicides may occur spontaneously without any premeditation during disputes. The murder may occur while someone is under the influence of drugs or involved in illicit drug activities.

Figure 9.35 This grow operation was located in a mountainous region. A special enforcement unit had to utilize helicopters to remove the massive amount of marijuana grown in this covert location. (Courtesy of Butte County Sheriff's Office, Special Enforcement Unit, Oroville, California.)

Murder of innocent bystanders: Innocent victims may be killed during rival drug gang disputes.

Drug assassinations: Premeditated murders of law enforcement, government officials, and civilians are considered drug assassinations.

Cartel-related homicides appear to focus on rivals and traitors to the cartels. Cartel-related homicides appear to have a number of common earmarks of torture and violence. Victims may be beheaded or dismembered. U.S. military intelligence sources have traced the cartel-related beheadings to the Gulf cartel back in the 1990s. The Zetas at the time served as the armed faction of the Gulf cartel. The Zetas received training from the Kaibiles (Guatemalan Special Forces). The Kaibiles were known for

Figure 9.36 This icon representing Elegua, the orisha that guards doorways and open roads, was seized by U.S. Customs because of the presence of blood on the artifact. The owner of the object told officers that the icon was a "sleeping mask" that had been given to him by a curandero in Mexico. (Courtesy of U.S. Customs and Border Patrol.)

using beheading as a means to murder enemies. Beheadings have been documented throughout Mexico and Latin America. An array of weapons, including machetes, chainsaws, electric saws, kitchen knives, axes, farm tools, and a host of other bladed instruments, have been used in beheadings. One of the most popular tools used in cartel beheadings is the Gigli saw. The saw is commonly used by medical personnel to perform amputations. The saw is favored, as it makes clean cuts and is able to slice through bone.

The head may be displayed in a manner as to indicate shame or mockery. There have been a number of homicide cases in Mexico where the victim's head has been posed with dismembered parts of the body, including hands, feet, and sexual organs, placed in the victim's mouth or beside his or her head. Cases involving torture have been discovered; victims were electrocuted with car batteries and crude wiring systems.

Victims may be placed in barrels of acid, as some cartels use the term *guiso*, or "stew," to describe their method of displaying or getting rid of

Figure 9.37 Closed-mouth spell. The use of an animal's tongue using the magical law of similarity. The tongue is nailed shut to keep the target of the spell quiet. In narcotics-related cases, this may be performed to silence informants or prosecutors and officers working the case. (Courtesy of Animal Recovery Mission.)

the bodies of their victims. Some victims have had the skin removed from their bodies. While the condition of victims may appear very savage and performed in a chaotic manner, cartel sicarios are organized offenders and are often trained and seasoned in how to murder.

In some cases the torture or murder is documented using still photos, cell phone video, or digital video cameras. Suspects in these videos may appear wearing specific cartel symbols. Signs and banners indicating the name or symbols of the cartel may be present in the video. In many cases, cartel members will speak about why the victim is about to be killed, or the victim may be questioned on camera by his or her killers. Audio from these videos can sometimes provide insight into the killers' identity.

Crime scenes

Investigators may discover evidence of blood at crime or incident scenes. The presence of blood at scenes where religious artifacts are present may indicate ritualistic activities.

Collection of wet and dry blood samples is performed by removing either the entire object that is stained or a portion of the blood. Blood may appear on religious artifacts. Some rituals involve the spilling of animal blood directly onto artifacts.

Human blood is present in some religious rituals involving initiations. For example, some Palo houses use a bloodletting act in the initiation ritual that involves placing a piece of cotton with the initiate's blood inside the nganga. The presence of human blood in a shrine or altar may reflect the practice of sympathetic magic. Blood obtained from the target of a spell is believed to be able to affect the target.

Bodily fluids such as saliva may be present on some items at religious scenes. Cigars are puffed on to release the smoke around artifacts in many of the Afro-Caribbean religions. Possible DNA evidence can be taken from items that contain saliva and other fluids.

Decomposed bodies can pose a biological threat to officers at scenes where human remains may be present. During advanced stages of decomposition, fluids and gases escape from the body, and insect activity and airborne pathogen activity may increase. These elements may cross-contaminate a room or a building. Blood-borne pathogens may not die when a person dies. Hepatitis B and HIV can survive up to 16 days after death. Assume that all blood and biological materials contain potentially infectious blood-borne pathogens such as Hepatitis B or C or HIV.

Documenting the scene

Prior to collecting any evidence, investigators should document the scene. Photographs, video, and sketches can document the location and condition of evidence. It is important that artifacts are documented *in situ* in the location they are discovered. Likewise, it is important to keep objects found inside of artifacts with the artifact in which they were discovered. In one high-profile case involving a group using Palo Mayombe, a federal law enforcement agent poured out materials from several different vessels discovered at a crime scene. The contents of these vessels were scattered and mixed with objects of similar vessels. It is imperative that objects that may not appear to be of significance be kept with evidence they are discovered with.

If religious artifacts are taken from a scene, investigators should consider the following questions:

1. What is the connection between the artifacts and the crime?
2. Will these materials validate the crime or incident?
3. Can I substantiate the need for these materials?

Traffic stops

The discovery and identification of narco saints and elements of narco culture have been used by some officers as probable cause for searching vehicles for narcotics. The presence of these symbols commonly used by drug traffickers can make officers reasonably suspicious. Officers must be able to articulate why they searched a vehicle.

Drug traffickers known as mules may be paid to move small loads of drugs. They may travel alone or work with a team of traffickers.

Vehicles used in drug trafficking may be customized to transport drugs. Hidden compartments may be used. Limousine tint may be used to darken the windows of the vehicle. The vehicle trunk may appear to ride low to observing officers.

Officers may notice suspects being overly cautious or avoiding contact with officers altogether. Officers may observe indicators such as:

Only an ignition key on the keychain
Very little luggage but driver claims to be on long road trip
Drug paraphernalia
Visibly fatigued individual, bad body odor, scent of drugs
Air fresheners or coffee grounds
Car has a lived-in look
Multiple cell phones
Extra trunk release buttons
High mileage on a new vehicle

The behavior of traffickers can also create suspicion. Possible behaviors include:

Avoids conversation with officer or is very talkative
Does not make eye contact
Acts eager to leave
Sweating, veins can be seen pulsing
Body language such as arms folded, fidgeting, anxious movements

Narco saint images may be displayed on the outsides of vehicles as an attempt to provide protection to the vehicle.

A sticker of Santa Muerte helped aid a Travis County
deputy in making an arrest of a possible drug dealer.

According to an arrest affidavit, the deputy saw a vehicle speeding excessively down on Blake Manor Road and decided to make a traffic stop. The driver tried to make an evasive move to lose the deputy, but eventually pulled over. The deputy asked the driver, Ernezeto Martinez-Lara, 19, about a sticker on the back windshield of Santa Muerte.

According to police, Santa Muerte is a deity that drug dealers and traffickers use to help protect them from law enforcement.

The deputy then asked to search the vehicle and in the process found two plastic bags containing cocaine.

Martinez-Lara has been charged with possession of a controlled substance—a third degree felony. (KTBC Fox 7, Austin, Texas, http://www.myfoxaustin. com/story/18295837/santa-muerte-sticker-aids-deputy-in-arrests#ixzz2yFpmkKKZ)

Case law involving narco saints

United States v. Antonio Esquivel Rios, U.S. Court of Appeals 10th Circuit, August 2, 2013

The suspect in a car stop had a Holy Bible of Saint Death and a tattoo of Santa Muerte on the shoulder.

United States v. Victor Pena-Ponce

The case involved a car stop for excessive window tint and expired tags. Santa Muerte statues on the dash led to a drug search, which uncovered cocaine and multiple cell phones used in trafficking.

Digeo Mata Gonzalez v. City of Corneilas

A shooting suspect had drugs, notebooks of financial transactions, and a shrine to Santa Muerte.

U.S. v. Adrian Diaz-Fonseca

A car was stopped after state agents received intelligence regarding a car transporting methadone. A picture of Santa Muerte hanging from the rear view mirror was the basis for reasonable suspicion.

U.S. v. Joshua Israel Covarrabias Felix

A state trooper stopped a vehicle for speeding violations. The officer asked the driver where he was going. The driver reached down and grabbed a Santa Muerte pendant, kissing it.

U.S. v. Rafael Goxcon-Chagal

Officers stopped a vehicle and discovered a Santa Muerte statue and prayer.

U.S. v. Jose Alfredo Lopez-Gutiemez

A Jesus Malverde picture on a dashboard was used as probable cause to search a suspect vehicle.

U.S. v. Ricardo Cervantes Arez

The suspect was stopped for a speeding violation. A Santa Muerte prayer card visible in the vehicle was used as part of probable cause.

The issue of narco saints as probable cause has been challenged in some courts. On July 2, 2014, the 10th U.S. Circuit Court of Appeals ruled that expert testimony offered by U.S. Marshal Robert Almonte, an expert on Santa Muerte, be rejected on the basis that no direct correlation existed between a defendant's prayer to Santa Muerte and the discovery of drugs in a vehicle she was riding in. The U.S. Attorney's office claimed that the discovery of a prayer to Saint Death alongside several signs, including air fresheners and nervous behavior, could be used to demonstrate that the defendants knew that drugs were located in a secret compartment in the vehicle they were driving. The defense argued that the couple were unaware that contraband was in the vehicle. To demonstrate that the couple had knowledge of the drugs, the U.S. Attorney's office claimed that the female defendant was caught reading a prayer written to Santa Muerte during the traffic stop. The prayer is as follows:

> For protection during a trip Holy Spirit of Death,
> I invoke your Holy Name to ask you to help me
> in this venture. Make my way over the mountains
> valleys and paths an easy one, never stop bestow-
> ing upon me your good fortune weave the destiny
> so that bad instincts vanish before me because of
> your powerful protection. Prevent Santa Muerte,
> problems from growing and embracing my heart,

my Lady, keep any illness from embracing my wings. Glorious Santa Muerte be my protector and light my path. Be my advocate before the redeemer. Be my truth in times of darkness. Grant me the strength and faith to invoke your name and to thank you now and forever for all your favors. Amen.

Oh miraculous Santa Muerte, Niña Blanca of my heart and right arm of God our Lord. Today I come to you with infinite devotion to implore you for health, fortune and luck. Remove from my path [illegible] that hurts me, envy and misfortune; don't allow my enemy's slander reach and harm my spirit. May no one prevent me from receiving the prosperity that I am asking of you today, my powerful lady bless the money that will reach my hands and multiply it so that my family lacks for nothing and I can outreach my hand to the needy that crosses my path. Keep tragedy pain and shortage away from me. This votive candle I will light so that the radiance of your eyes forms an invisible wall around me. Grant me prudence and patience holy lady, Santa Reina de las Tinieblas (Holy Queen of Darkness) strength, power and wisdom tell the elements not to unleash their fury wherever they cross paths with me take care of my happy surroundings and that I want to adorn decorate. In my Santa Muerte, Amen.

The defendants were convicted of drug charges and sentenced to prison. The couple appealed the conviction on the grounds that they believed that the inclusion of the testimony regarding Santa Muerte tainted the court by concluding that the mere fact that the defendant had a Santa Muerte prayer indicated knowledge of criminal activity. Marshal Almonte pointed out to the court:

> The thing that is most glaring to me in this prayer is it says "may no one prevent me from receiving the prosperity that I am asking of you today my power-ful lady bless the money that will reach my hands and multiply it so that my family lacks for nothing and I can outreach my hand to the needy that crosses my path." So it is my opinion that this trip had something to do with gaining money.

Marshal Almonte also pointed out: "The theme mentioned in that prayer is common among traffickers who use Santa Muerte."

Investigators testifying in court regarding cases where artifacts are collected as evidence should prepare for potential questions regarding religious artifacts. There is a precedence of defense attorneys using issues related to religious freedoms and religious persecution in cases where artifacts have been used as evidence. In some cases, defendants have hired religious academics to testify as expert witnesses in their cases.

Investigators that choose to use religious items as evidence in criminal cases need to be prepared to answer questions regarding artifacts.

Grow operations

Signs of an indoor marijuana grow operation are listed below (*The Police Chief*, 2005).

Signs on a property include:
- Evidence of tampering with the electric meter, such as damages or broken seals or the disturbance of ground around the meter
- Houses that looked lived in, but there are very few people who enter and leave the house
- Water lines or electrical cords running to a basement or outbuilding
- An unusual number of roof vents in a house or exhaust fan noises coming from an outbuilding
- An outbuilding with air conditioners
- A house rooftop with no snow on it when other roofs in the area are covered in snow
- Excessive condensation around windows
- Little or no garbage put out
- Excessive security, such as guard dogs, "keep out" signs, high fences, heavy chains, and locks on gates
- A greenhouse or tin barn on property where these structures would normally not be used

Signs in behavior:
- People making late night or short visits
- People bringing excessive amounts of potting soil or other growth media inside of house
- People bringing items in and out in garbage bags
- People arriving at the house to carry out garbage, shovel snow, or cut the lawn and leaving immediately

- People coming and going from the house only once a week
- No deliveries of furniture or groceries into the house

Clandestine labs

Officers have discovered protective amulets and icons during investigations regarding clandestine laboratories. The cultural artifacts may be perceived by devotees as providing supernatural protection for these operations. A clandestine lab is "an illicit operation consisting of a sufficient combination of apparatus and chemicals that either has been or could be used in the manufacture or synthesis of controlled substances."

Clandestine labs are used in manufacturing drugs such as methamphetamine, other amphetamines, MDMA (ecstasy), methcathinone, PCP, LSD, fentanyl, and synthetic marjiuana.

Clandestine labs have been discovered operating from abandoned buildings, apartments, barns, automobiles, garages, hotels, private residences, travel trailers, and vans. Superlabs contain professional-grade equipment designed for legitimate scientific laboratories.

The Department of Homeland Security lists four distinct categories of threats to law enforcement that surround the discovery of clandestine laboratories:

1. Explosives
2. Fires
3. Firearms
4. Chemical exposure

Explosions are the most immediate threat. The lighting of a cigarette or the flip of a light switch can detonate an explosion. Fires are responsible for 20 percent of lab discoveries in the United States. Public safety agencies are called to the scene of these fires only to discover evidence of lab operations in manufacturing narcotics. The combination of heat from instruments and the presence of flammable chemicals creates a hazardous threat.

Clandestine labs may be monitored or guarded by armed security or individuals under the influence of drugs. Officers should avoid entering these structures alone. The U.S. Drug Enforcement Administration reports that 10 percent of clandestine drug labs are booby-trapped. Booby traps have been discovered in various forms. Some of those include:

- Shotguns and other firearms wired to shoot at various entry points when doors are opened

- Light switches wired to explosive devices
- Trip lines connected to explosive devices
- Attack dogs and poisonous snakes
- Pipe bombs

Officers should be aware that exposure to chemicals in clandestine labs can pose health problems them. Many chemicals are odorless and may be difficult to detect by smell. Personnel working these scenes should obtain breathing equipment and hazmat suits to avoid contamination.

Officers who encounter clandestine labs should avoid the following:

- Smoking in the area
- Opening or touching chemical containers
- Touching unknown substances with bare hands
- Smelling the contents of any container
- . Placing anything in the mouth while present at the scene
- Discharging firearms if possible
- Plugging in electronic devices
- Turning on lights
- Opening any refrigerators unless they are unplugged
- Using standard flash bulbs at the scene if taking photographs
- Staying in unventilated areas

Officers should be aware of any physical changes that may occur in the lab, including feelings of dizziness, shortness of breath, or a burning sensation in the lungs.

Customs protection

Customs inspectors may discover various artifacts related to magico-religious practices. Some may be used to protect illegal goods that are being transported. Some may simply be incidental to those passing through Customs. The discovery of these objects does not necessarily indicate criminal activity.

In some cases artifacts may contain contraband that is prohibited from being brought into the United States. Artifacts with various plants, seeds, animals remains, and blood may be encountered by Customs officials.

Spells involving the law

Court appearances

In his book *History Has Repeated*, Palero Domingo B. Lage shares an example of a Palo ritual for aiding in court-related matters:

> We take the judge's name, the lawyer, the district
> attorney and prosecutor. We get some soil from the
> courthouse, powder from the dead, powder from
> palos (sticks). We reward the nganga with a rooster
> and we take the rooster's tongue off. Then, we need
> to look for several types of palos (sticks) Vencedor,
> varia, yo puedo mas que tu and cambia rumbo.
> Following this we write with chalk the name of the
> judge, the district attorney and prosecutor with the
> sticks and seven types of threads including black.
> After this is done, we ask the nganga how many
> days it is going to remain on top of the fundamento.
> Finally, we give this work to the interested person.
> We prepare a powder for him/her to throw at the
> courthouse door. This person must take three baths
> and rub his/her head with fruits.

A common spiritual working to keep someone from testifying or informing against devotees is to place an object in a refrigerator freezer. This symbolically and magically is believed to "freeze" a subject. Photographs, written names, and objects that belong to the target of the spell are commonly used.

Honey is commonly used to "sweeten" someone or persuade him or her to do your bidding. Photographs, written names, and personal items may be placed in a jar of honey.

Objects that represent the tongue and speech are commonly bound to keep individuals from informing or testifying. In Miami, Florida, court-house workers discovered two lizards with their mouths wrapped with twine in a courtroom during a trial involving the prosecution of a cocaine dealer. In Orlando, Florida, a doll was discovered in a courtroom that when cut open exposed a paper with the judge's name written nines times on it. In Ohio, a toy doll along with a beef tongue were found bound with string and herbs outside of a courtroom.

There are a host of commercially made items that are promoted as helpful in legal matters. A small amulet consisting of a gold-colored nail refers to Jesus Christ as the just judge (*justo juez*). The nail is carried into the courtroom during court cases in order for the judge to issue a fair and just decision.

There a number of court case or caso de corte items, including baths, oils, powders, and incense. Items like powder are to be carried into the courtroom and blown onto the judge or jury's seats. These items are used to compel those in the legal system to favor the devotee in court. A similar mass-produced item is the "law stay away" line of items.

Officers as targets

Law enforcement may encounter magico-religious cultures during the course of work. Members of various faiths may be victims, complainants, or even suspects. An officer encountering members of unfamiliar cultures may find himself or herself in challenging situations.

Officer perception and personal beliefs

Perception affects operational decisions on a daily basis. Does this individual present a threat to society? Is there a crime present? Am I as an officer at risk? An officer's knowledge and ability to discern will affect how he or she will respond to situations. Likewise, when dealing with members of other cultures, an officer's personal belief system will affect how he or she will respond. In some cases, perception and truth may clash.

Some officers may not be able to separate personal beliefs and perception. This may affect an officer's ability to be nonbiased and professional. A recent case depicted on the true crime television show *The First 48* showed Miami Police detectives working a case involving a homicide victim who was a practitioner of Santería and Palo Mayombe. When detectives were asked to examine ritual artifacts found in the victim's closet, one of the detectives exclaims, "I can't do it. I believe in that stuff." The detective excused himself from the scene. This is a good example of how officers should maintain a check on personal bias and its potential to affect the handling of a case. If possible, officers who feel that personal beliefs may affect a case should seek another officer to assist in responding to situations and scenes.

Dealing with the media

Law enforcement and the media have traditionally had a love-hate relationship. The media have been very instrumental in spreading information that has developed leads in many cases for many agencies. However, the media can also complicate cases by presenting stories in a sensationalistic fashion. This can create local hysteria and tie up law enforcement with unnecessary calls and queries.

Cases involving magico-religious practices can become very fertile grounds for rumors of Satanism and devil worship to sprout when local media hear particular buzzwords. Headlines can become very sensationalistic when words like *Satanism, voodoo,* or *cults* are used. Agency spokespersons should avoid using terms that can be exploited by local media.

In some cases that I have seen, the release of information to the press that includes terms related to the occult has tainted public opinion and made it difficult to prosecute cases.

Likewise, the mere mention of the occult has made up the minds of many in the public eye, making it next to impossible for subjects to receive a fair trial. Many people perceive that any involvement in the occult means that someone is likely to be involved in criminal activity.

During investigations the local media should receive information from one designated department spokesperson. There have been cases where officers have made comments to the press that include ethnocenteric or biased statements regarding a case.

Statements regarding an officer's personal beliefs and religious practices can be used by defense attorneys as a sign of prejudice in a case. Avoid speculating or giving personal opinions on cases.

References

Appeal from the United States District Court for the District of New Mexico (D.C. Nos. 1:11-CR-2002-JB-2 and 1:11-CR-2002-001 JB) (Almonte Quote).

American Psychiatric Association. (2000) *Diagnostic and Statistical Manual of Mental Disorders* (4th ed., text rev.). Washington, DC.

Barber, Nigel, Voodoo Death I, The Human Beast, September 10, 2012 at http://www.psychologytoday.com/blog/the-human-beast/201209/voodoo-death-i

Cannon, Walter B., Voodoo Death. *American Anthropologist*, Volume 44, Issue 2, pages 169–181, April-June 1942.

Department of Homeland Security and Joint Regional Intelligence Center, *Identifying and differentiating among clandestine biological and chemical explosives and methamphetamine laboratories*, Joint Special Assessment, February 14, 2007.

Foreign Military Studies Office, Ritualism and Decapitations in Mexico, *Latin America Military and Security Watch*, October 3, 2011.

Geberth, Vernon, "Investigation of Drug-Related Homicides." *Law and Order*, November 1990, p. 76.

La Barge, A. and K. Noakes. Indoor marijuana growing operations. *The Police Chief*, March 2005.

Lage, Domingo. History has Repeated, 2001, Botanica Tata Miguel (No location listed).

Strauss, Claude Lévi, *Structural Anthropology*, Basis Books 1963, P.307: July, 2014.

Whitmarsh, Andrew, Understanding bloodborne pathogens: Risks, rights and responsibilities, *Evidence Technology Magazine*, May-June 2014.

chapter ten

A field guide for identifying artifacts

Investigators who are working drug trafficking organizations may discover artifacts and religious paraphernalia relating to narco-cult sects. There are literally thousands of artifacts found among Afro-Caribbean and Latin religious cultures. It must be stressed that these artifacts are traditionally used by noncriminal and non-drug-related devotees of these religions.

Possession of these items is legal unless they conflict with state regulations. Discovery of these items does not denote criminal activity. The images of these artifacts are being shared in this chapter to help investigators to understand the culture that they are traditionally used in and how traffickers may appropriate such articles to further criminal activities.

Artifact name: Macuto

Religion associated with: Santería/ Palo Mayombe

Cultural use: The macuto is an amulet that is empowered with spiritual energy. Provides access to spiritual energy for the carrier. May be used for protection, luck, and good health.

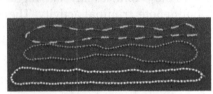

Artifact name: Axe of Shango

Religion associated with: Ifa/Santería

Cultural use: The axe of Shango is used to symbolize the energy or "ache" of Shango. This artifact is usually kept in shrines to Shango.

Artifact name: Elekes/collares

Religion associated with: Ifa/Santería

Cultural use: The elekes are necklaces worn by initiates to give them spiritual protection.

Artifact name: Chamalongos

Religion associated with: Palo Mayombe

Cultural use: The chamalongos are pieces of coconut shell that are used to communicate with the spiritual world.

Artifact name: Osun

Religion associated with: Ifa/Santería

Cultural use: Osun represents a guardian spirit that is placed above the floor in devotees' homes and businesses.

Artifact name: Ogun

Religion associated with: Ifa/Santería

Cultural use: The pot of Ogun represents the spirit of iron. Various iron tools and railroad spikes are typically placed inside the pot.

Artifact name: Herramientas de Ochosi

Religion associated with: Santería

Cultural use: The tools of Ochosi are used to represent various attributes of the god of hunting and justice.

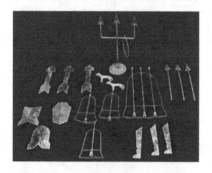

Artifact name: Herramientas de Shango

Religion associated with: Santería

Cultural use: The tools of Shango are used to represent attributes of the god of thunder and fire.

Artifact name: Guiro of Osain

Religion associated with: Ifa/Santería

Cultural use: The gourd of Osain is used to work with the orisha of plants and herbs.

Artifact name: Herramientas de Yemaya

Religion associated with: Ifa/Santería

Cultural use: The tools of Yemaya represent various aspects of the goddess of the ocean waters.

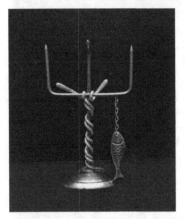

Artifact name: Herramientas de Inle

Religion associated with: Ifa/Santería

Cultural use: The tools of Inle are used to represent the spiritual attributes of the god of abundance and healing.

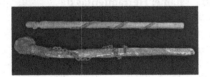

Artifact name: Baston de Muerto

Religion associated with: Palo Mayombe/Espiritismo

Cultural use: The wooden staff is used to call on the spirits of the dead. The owner strikes the ground with the tip of the staff a number of times to call forth a spirit.

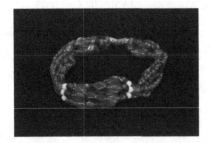

Artifact name: Ide

Religion associated with: Ifa/Santería

Cultural use: The ide is a bracelet that protects the wearer from death.

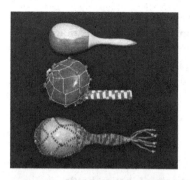

Artifact name: Maraka

Religion associated with: Ifa/Santería

Cultural use: Various types of marakas are used to call the orishas in their shrines.

Artifact name: Horse of Shango

Religion associated with: Santería

Cultural use: The horse references a myth or pataki regarding Shango and his horse.

Artifact name: Escalera de hierro de 7 peldanños

Religion associated with: Santería

Cultural use: The iron ladder of seven steps is used to represent the ladder that the orishas descended from heaven upon.

Artifact: Thunderstone

Religion associated with: Ifa/Santería

Cultural use: Found in shrines to Shango, the thunderstone is created when lightning strikes the earth.

Artifact name: Varies (cowrie shells)

Religion associated with: Various Afro-Caribbean religions

Cultural use: Cowries are typically used in performing divination.

Artifact name: Libation bottle

Religion associated with: Haitian voodoo

Cultural use: Bottles decorated with images of the loa are commonly used to hold libations that are offered to the loa.

Artifact name: Djakout

Religion associated with: Haitian voodoo and Dominican voodoo

Cultural use: Found in shrines, this straw bag represents Azaka, the loa of farming.

Artifact name: Boat of Agwe

Religion associated with: Haitian voodoo

Cultural use: The boat is hung from the ceiling in some temples and is found on an altar in others and represents Agwe, the loa of water.

Artifact name: Zin

Religion associated with: Haitian voodoo

Cultural use: The three-legged pot is used as a lamp that is filled with oil. Used in some initiation rituals.

Artifact name: Drapo

Religion associated with: Haitian voodoo

Cultural use: Sequined flags are used to represent the loa. They are found in shrines and are used in some rituals.

Artifact name: Ojo de venado

Religion associated with: Mexican folk practices

Cultural use: The amulet is carried or worn to keep away the evil eye.

Artifact name: Santa Muerte amulet

Religion associated with: Santa Muerte

Cultural use: Carried or worn for protection and empowerment from Santa Muerte.

Artifact name: Saint Toribio

Religion associated with: Catholicism/ Mexican folk practices

Cultural use: In some cases, images of Saint Toribio are carried to assist immigrants in crossing the border.

Artifact name: Ta Jose

Religion associated with: Palo Mayombe/Espiritismo

Cultural use: Ta Jose is used to represent a protective spirit.

Artifact name: Achibiriki

Religion associated with: Ifa/Santería

Cultural use: This contains objects representing the orisha Ogun and Ochosi. Usually found placed inside Ogun's pot.

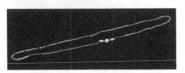

Artifact name: Collar de bandera

Religion associated with: Palo Mayombe

Cultural use: These beads are worn by initiates who have been "scratched" into the religion.

Artifact name: Iruke
Religion associated with: Ifa/Santería
Cultural use: The royal fly whisk is
made from horsetail and is found in
shrines dedicated to Obatala.

Artifact name: Yemaya
Religion associated with: Santería
Cultural use: Represents Yemaya,
goddess over the ocean waters.

Artifact name: Orisha crown
Religion associated with: Ifa/Santería
Cultural use: Various crowns are
placed in shrines to the orishas.

Artifact name: Jicara
Religion associated with: Ifa/Santería
Cultural use: The half gourd is used to
feed the orishas in some houses.

Artifact name: Pilon batea

Religion associated with: Ifa/Santería

Cultural use: Used to house the various tools of Shango.

Artifact name: Agogo

Religion associated with: Ifa/Santería

Cultural use: This metal bell is rung to call the orisha Obatala.

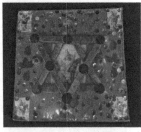

Artifact name: San Martin Caballero talisman

Religion associated: Mexican folk practices

Cultural use: This item is hung on the wall to bring luck and fortune.

Artifact name: Paquet

Religion associated with: Haitian voodoo

Cultural use: These items are placed in shrines to heat up the loa. Can be used in various spiritual workings.

Artifact name: Oyo y lengua

Religion associated with: Santería/
Espiritismo/Mexican folk practices

Cultural use: Hung on the wall to
protect from the evil eye.

Artifact name: Santa Muerte

Religion associated with: Cult of Santa
Muerte

Cultural use: Various forms of the
statue are used in shrines to represent
the spirit of death.

Artifact name: Prayer books

Religion associated with: Varies

Cultural use: These particular prayer
books contain suggested prayers to
Santa Muerte.

Artifact name: Elegua

Religion associated with: Ifa/Santería

Cultural use: This icon represents the
orisha Elegua and the avatars known
as Esu.

Artifact name: Ibeji

Religion associated with: Ifa/Santería

Cultural use: Represents twin spirits that are the children of Shango.

Artifact name: Candles

Religion associated with: Varies

Cultural use: These two specific candles are dedicated to Juan Soladado and San Simon. They are typically burned as offerings.

Artifact name: Saint Judas Tadeo amulets and talismans

Religion associated with: Catholicism/ Mexican folk practices

Cultural use: San Judas is known as the patron saint of impossible causes. Items may be worn, carried, or hung Belongs to aid in causes.

Artifact name: Jesus Malverde amulets and talismans

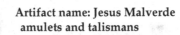

Artifact name: Niño de Atocha

Religion associated with Catholicism/ Mexican folk practices.

Cultural use: Scons of niño de atocha may be discovered among traffickers who pray to this saint while in prison.

Artifact name: Polvos

Religion associated with: Mexican folk practices

Cultural use: Worn or carried for protection from law or for help for the poor.

Artifact name: Mpaka

Religion associated with: Palo Mayombe

Cultural use: The animal horn can be used to transport the fundamental ingredients of a nganga to a new location.

Artifact name: Machete

Cultural use: The machete is used in a number of religions to represent the spirit of iron. In Santería, it represents the orisha Ogun. In Palo Mayombe, it is called mbele and is used in rituals and in the nganga of Zarabanda. In Haitian and West African voodoo, the machete represents Ogou, the loa of iron and war.

Artifact name: Mange-Marasa

Cultural use: This bowl is used in feeding the sacred twins spirits in Haitian voodoo known as Marasa.

Artifact name: Santo

Cultural use: Santos are pieces of religious art that depict saints, angels, or aspects of the Trinity. This particular piece depicts Our Lady of Guadalupe.

Jośe Gregorio Hernández
This Venezuelan folk saint is found in
   Mexican and Venezuelan folk practices.
   Many believe that prayers to this
   particular saint will bring about
   miracles of healing.

San Martin Caballero
San Martin Caballero is a Latin
   American folk saint that is honored
   among a number of spiritual
   traditions. Devotees believe that
   images of this saint will bring
   blessings from strangers.

Photographs by Lisa Barker, LB Photography.

Closing Comments

Just this month, July 2014, hundreds of children from Latin American countries were left to cross the border between Mexico and the United States, many of them claiming to be seeking protection from the violence and oppression brought on by the drug war. Immigration reform and the legalization of marijuana have become controversial topics that have brought drug trafficking and Mexican drug trafficking organizations into the public's eye. Millions of dollars have been spent on a virtual fence separating the United States and Mexico that did not come to fruition. And while it is easier to sleep thinking that cartels and cartel violence are "over there," the truth is that the drug war is in our own backyard. As you have read already, many of Mexico's and Latin America's most violent organizations have already stepped on American soil.

If we look at the cartels and the very core of their existence, we will discover that they only exist because there is a need for drugs because there is an addiction problem. In our efforts to stop cartels and the war on drugs, we must realize that they are but symptoms. The problem is addiction. Addiction in its largest manifestation fosters terrorist organizations. Addiction funds criminal street gangs and violent drug cartels. At its local level, addiction destroys families and it destroys lives. As we continue the war on drugs and its criminal elements, we have to address the gaping wound that drug addiction causes in our communities. Once we destroy the head of the snake, all that is left will wither away.

Tony M. Kail
July 2014

Glossary

Acculturation. Cultural change that occurs when one culture comes into contact with another culture.

Ancestor reverence. Rituals and beliefs that honor and connect with the kinship of ancestors even after death.

Ancestral spirits. A belief that the spiritual bodies of ancestors live on after death. Ancestral spirits may be the souls or ghosts of ancestors.

Animism. A belief that spirits animate people, places and objects. Animals and plants are believed to contain spirits as well.

Archetype. A universal symbol or concept that represents a pattern in human nature. A copy of an original symbol.

Artifact. An object manufactured by a particular culture.

Ceremony. A complex sequence of rituals.

Contagious magic. A belief that a type of magic can be effected on the principle that a part of something can control the whole. For example, a piece of a person's hair can be used to affect the owner of the hair.

Cosmology. A way of explaining the universe according to a particular culture.

Creation myth. A symbolic story that explains how the universe came to be according to a particular culture.

Cult. A system of religious devotion toward a particular person or object.

Culture. The patterns of learned and shared behavior and beliefs of a particular group of people.

Culture shock. A sense of disorientation resulting from being suddenly immersed into a culture different from one's own.

Curses. Incantations and spiritual workings that carry the intentions of causing harm to an individual.

Deities. The gods or goddesses of a people.

Deviant. Behavior that varies from the norm of a culture.

Divination. A ritual that uses secret knowledge to call on spirits to seek knowledge of the future or the past to determine a course of action.

Emic. The insider's perspective of a particular culture.

Ethnocentrism. The belief that one's own culture is superior to all others.

Etic. The outsider's perspective of a particular culture.

Evil eye. The belief that some individuals have the supernatural power to harm others intentionally or unintentionally because of their envy.

Fetish. An object believed to have magical powers.

Folklore. Traditional art, literature, knowledge, and practice disseminated largely through oral communication and behavioral examples.

God or goddess. Powerful supernatural being with an individual identity and recognizable attributes. Gods or goddesses are believed to have motivation and power to affect the course of human events.

Homeopathic magic. Rituals that compel or influence the supernatural by means of the law of similarity.

Icon. An image or emblem that is a representative symbol of an object and has religious significance.

Iconography. A pattern of imagery associated with a particular culture.

Ideology. A set of ideas that guide an individual's, social movement's, or institution's goals, expectations, and actions. The shared beliefs that define a social group.

Imitative magic. A type of magic built on the belief that like produces like. An example is the pop image of the voodoo doll. When the doll is affected, it is believed that the person that the doll represents will be affected.

Indigenous. Related to the original inhabitants of a place or to their culture.

Initiation. A ceremony, ritual, test, or period of instruction where a person is admitted to a particular cultural role or social position.

Liturgy. Ritual or ceremony that is performed publicly to show devotion or worship.

Magic. A system aimed at compelling or influencing supernatural beings to act.

Mana. An impersonal force that may be associated with people, places, or objects.

Mesoamerica. Southern Mexico and northern Central America.

Monotheism. Belief in only one god.

Myths. Symbolic stories about the nature of the universe and the role of the human beings in it.

Nativistic movement. A social movement that seeks to restore power to groups that may have been disempowered by colonialism and other social disruption.

Neo-paganism. Any of several spiritual movements that attempt to revive the ancient polytheistic religions of Europe and the Middle East. Some neo-pagans seek to revive the early Mesoamerican religions of the Aztecs. Some neo-pagans seek to incorporate practices and rituals of Afro-Caribbean religions into their religious culture.

Normative. Appropriate and expected behavior among a group or culture.

Pantheon. A catalog of the gods and goddesses of a religion.

Polytheism. A belief in more than one god.

Prayer. The use of language to influence or communicate with the supernatural.

Priest or priestess. A male or female religious leader who is part of an organized religion.

Prophet. An individual who receives divine revelation.

Protective rituals. Rituals performed to prevent harm to human beings.

Religion. A symbolic system involving beliefs and practices that focuses on connecting humans and the supernatural.

Religious ritual. Behavior that is performed to influence the supernatural to effect change or to show appreciation for change.

Revitalization movement. A religious movement that focuses on social change.

Rite of passage. Rituals that celebrate the changing of one social status to another.

Ritual. Symbolic behavior associated with religion and magic that is repetitive, sequential, nonordinary, and believed to be powerful.

Sacred. Dedicated to a religious purpose or holiness.

Sacrifice. An act of offering a living animal or human or surrendering a possession as an offering to a supernatural being.

Scarification. The process of decorating the body by inflicting wounds and allowing the wounds to heal into scars.

Shaman. A religious person who has the ability to control spirits or supernatural forces.

Sorcerer. Religious practitioners who coerce or manipulate the supernatural to cause harm to others.

Soul loss. The belief that one's spirit has left his or her body. This loss is believed to cause sickness and even death.

Souls. The animating spirits of human beings.

Spirit possession. The belief that a disembodied spirit can inhabit the body of a living person.

Symbol. An image, word, or behavior that expresses ideas too complex to explain directly.

Syncretism. The fusion of diverse religious beliefs and practices.

Taboo. A cultural rule or practice of avoidance.

Trance. An altered state of consciousness characterized by a degree of disassociation from ordinary experience and, in some cases, loss of consciousness.

Witchcraft. The attempt to coerce or manipulate the supernatural to control events, people, or animals.

Worldview. How a person sees the world around him or her. A system of beliefs and values shared by members of a culture.

Worship. Rituals performed to express adoration.

Index

Printed in the United States
by Baker & Taylor Publisher Services